JAN
24.95
JUL 2007

Truth, Lies, and Online Dating: Secrets to Finding Romance on the Internet

Terry Ulick

Alyssa Wodtke

THOMSON
™
COURSE TECHNOLOGY
Professional ■ Technical ■ Reference

Educational facilities, companies, and organizations interested in multiple copies or licensing of this book should contact the publisher for quantity discount information. Training manuals, CD-ROMs, and portions of this book are also available individually or can be tailored for specific needs.

ISBN: 1-59200-916-6

Library of Congress Catalog Card Number: 2005924930

Printed in Canada

05 06 07 08 09 WC 10 9 8 7 6 5 4 3 2 1

Publisher and General Manager, Thomson Course Technology PTR:
Stacy L. Hiquet

Associate Director of Marketing:
Sarah O'Donnell

Manager of Editorial Services:
Heather Talbot

Marketing Manager:
Heather Hurley

Associate Acquisitions Editor:
Megan Belanger

Senior Editor:
Mark Garvey

Marketing Coordinator:
Jordan Casey

Project Editor:
Jenny Davidson

Technical Reviewer:
Michael D. Sullivan

Thomson Course Technology PTR Editorial Services Coordinator:
Elizabeth Furbish

Copyeditor:
Kim Benbow

Interior Layout Tech:
Bill Hartman

Cover Designer:
Deborah VanRooyen

Indexer:
Sharon Shock

Proofreaders:
Elizabeth Furbish
Kelly Talbot

THOMSON

COURSE TECHNOLOGY

Professional ■ Technical ■ Reference

Thomson Course Technology PTR, a division of Thomson Course Technology
25 Thomson Place ■ Boston, MA 02210 ■ http://www.courseptr.com

To my love, Lisa, who I have loved throughout time
(but met online this time around!)
—*Terry*

To my sister Christina, without whom I never would have
done this book. And to both her and her husband, who
met online, giving me reason to believe it really works
—*Alyssa*

Acknowledgments

We would like to thank everyone at Course Technology for their efforts to make this a truly useful and helpful book, with heartfelt thanks to Megan Belanger and Jenny Davidson for all the winks. And for the icebreaker, we thank David Fugate. For their stunning profile photos, Alyssa would like to thank Angela Serna who was as giving with her image as she is with her friendship, Kelly Shepard who hates having his picture taken, and John Paul Watts who bared his knees.

About the Authors

*T*erry Ulick is a how-to book author, but along the way he worked as an art director and photographer at *Playboy*, owned a magazine publishing company, created the first online photo service for AOL, and later went on to start Good Time Networks—a broadband TV network. He lives in Northern California and loves to play guitar and take photographs of just about anything. He was an online dater until he met the love of his life on a popular dating site and they have since hung-up their online shingles for good.

Alyssa Wodtke is a writer, an editor, and an online dater. This is her second book about online dating. She does freelance writing about dating and fashion and has a successful personal Web site. She lives in San Francisco where she wanders the beach, goes to independent films and documentaries, and explores taquerias searching for the perfect margarita. She continues to online date, enjoying the process as much as looking for her geeky dream guy who loves Green Day and Ella Fitzgerald.

Contents

Part I
How Online Dating Services Really Work

4 Subscribing and Taking Advantage of Free Trial Subscription Offers 43

Part II
Presenting Yourself Online

5 Putting Your Best Face Forward 53

9 Writing Profiles and E-mails–Watch What You Say 111

Part III
Learning about Others You Meet Online

10 Edited Photos: Spotting the Phonies 129

14 Background Checks: Additional Peace of Mind 175

Part IV
Power Dating: Getting the Word Out

15 Creating Template E-mails Using Your Word Processor 189

16 Creating Custom Letters for Outstanding Results 199

19 Making Contact: Take It Safe 233

20 Dating Technology 101: Getting Tested for HIV and STDs 247

Introduction

Use Every Tool You Can in Your Search for Love Online

*W*e are all very savvy, grownup people who have embraced the online world as the best place to meet someone. But underneath our savvy exteriors, we're all little babies when we get hurt.

When it comes to love and relationships, we've learned the lesson of touching the hot stove. Burned once, or lots more than once, we are all understandably cautious. Nothing feels quite as bad as being dumped, falling for the wrong person, or making a fool of yourself over someone who doesn't care about you. It's human nature to be cautious with your heart and your emotions. At the same time, nothing is quite as exciting as the thought of meeting someone new. Finding the one you've always dreamed of. The first calls. The first dates. The realization that you really like each other. The first *time*. Yep, it's hard not to get all misty just thinking of it.

Unfortunately, the yin/yang of wanting to fall in love but not wanting to fall in love with the wrong person can really screw things up. The cautiousness of not wanting to be hurt—the not exposing yourself too quickly, can also make it hard to get to know each other. What can a poor online dater do?

In the world of online dating, quite a lot! One of the benefits of technology is that you can gain access to lots of potential dates—and learn all about them before you ever meet. The safety net of e-mails and IMs, and the ability to learn lots of little details first, can really help overcome the fears that plague most daters. Online dating can help you learn a lot about each other, but that's assuming that everything you say about yourself, or what your potential date says about him or herself, is true.

Truth, Lies, and Online Dating

This entire book is about truth and lies in the online dating process. It will take you through the process of finding online dating sites where you can hang up your shingle and say, "Here I am, give me a shot!" and of finding lots of potential partners who are saying that to you in return. You will also learn how to "market" yourself by creating a great profile and adding flattering pictures of yourself to attract someone wonderful.

Hey, we're all delicate flowers. We want to look as fresh as the morning—as youthful as spring. It's only natural to present ourselves in the most flattering light. But what light is flattering? Have you ever looked at a picture of yourself taken out in the midday sun? It shows every flaw and the shadows create bags and wrinkles that a Hollywood makeup artist could use in the next sequel to *The Mummy*. And it's not just the picture that can glaringly show your flaws. The script could use an overhaul, too. With all the baggage, the loves lost and won, the aliases, sketchy jobs, and a few car chases from irate lovers looking to run you down, the story can be just as shocking as the photo.

So, what do we do about that? We get selective in what we say, and show, about ourselves. We pick pictures from a few years and 20 pounds back. We somehow forget to mention that we've been married five times before. We kind of leave out the fact that we lost our job three years ago and haven't found a new one yet. We get creative in our writing. We paint a pretty picture of ourselves. But putting the best foot forward often means putting on a shoe that simply doesn't fit.

It's understandable. If you want someone to date you, you do need to put that best foot forward, even if the shoe is a Manolo slingback you could never afford worn by some slinky model in a Macy's ad. The goal is to get a response, and the more attractive you make yourself, the better the response will be. Right? Well…

Here are two important things to consider:

First, if you're embellishing yourself, what do you suppose the people you're interested in are doing? Are they retouching their photos and describing themselves as some ideal rather than who they really are? Nah, who would do such a thing?

Second, let's say that you do meet someone nice after you've painted an overly rosy picture of yourself. When you meet that potential love of your life, what will they think of you when you look and act differently than the person they were so enamored by in your profile?

Isn't there some biblical reference that the truth will set you free? Lie in your profile and yes, once you meet, the truth will set you free—and so will your date.

Unlike meeting in person, it's easy to stretch the truth in your profile. Everyone can. So, much of online dating is about spotting the people who are telling the truth, and spotting the liars. If you want to find a real relationship, you'd better learn that when it comes to online dating, the truth may hurt, but not nearly as much as lies can.

Tom Cruise and Nicole Kidman

One of the interesting comments we heard along the way from people looking for someone online was:

"She wants Tom Cruise, but she's no Nicole Kidman."

Everyone wants to date someone hot. It's human nature. But if you eliminate anyone who doesn't fall into the "hot" category, you're eliminating a lot of the people who are looking to date. How many Toms and Nicoles do you see in your daily life? The last Tom you saw, wasn't he already with a Nicole? Isn't it more important if someone's smart and interesting and has a great smile? Wouldn't you hate it if that smart, interesting, great smiling person eliminated you because of your non-Nicole-ness?

The fact is that a lot of online dating is about the photo. Once you're online and looking for someone, you'll learn very quickly how important a good photo is. All the online dating services strongly suggest adding a photo as the best thing you can do to increase your response rate. Take your photo down and you'll go long stretches without any responses. Put the photo up and you'll get lots of inquiries. So, it's tempting to put up a photo that you're sure will get responses… regardless of its authenticity.

Depending on how you look right now, you may be tempted to fall back on photos from times gone by when you were younger or thinner or simply happy. Here you are sitting all alone staring at your computer. Maybe you just went through a breakup. Maybe you've been comfort-eating with Ben and Jerry for weeks now. This may not be the best moment in your life to take a picture. But wait—here's one of you last summer, tan and happy! Or hey, that picture from a few years back in the bikini, before the stretch marks, is pretty good. Yeah. Use that one. You look just like Tom or Nicole in that one.

You are not alone. Others are having this same dilemma. So, how can you be sure that the photos you see online are any more current than yours? Truth, lies, and online dating. It can be a stumper. But we're here to help.

Honesty Really Is the Best Policy

When all is said and done, and all the winks and icebreakers, e-mails and IMs, are sent, you will learn that honesty really is the only way to go in the online dating world. Here is the best advice we can give, and we are giving it to you up-front and if you're reading this in the store, hey, you've gotten what you need and you can go read the next book. Pay attention:

If someone can't love you for exactly who you are, then you shouldn't be with him or her.

The worst thing you can do is make yourself into someone you're not. And the worst that can happen to you is meeting someone online who isn't telling the truth about themselves. This book is about how to tell the truth, and how to spot the lies. It shows you how to use all the tech tools your PC offers to contact people online and get a lot of responses. It also shows you how to take a good photo of yourself—as you look right now. Finally, it will show you how to find out if the person you met online is really the person they say they are.

The tools of successful online dating are: Your PC, knowing the dating sites that are right for you, a great profile that describes you perfectly, and an honest photo that you're proud of.

Online dating is simply a way of meeting the right person using the Internet as your matchmaker. Use all the right tools, and in time, you will find someone. Honestly!

GUY SAYS

Hi, my name is Terry, and along with Alyssa I'm writing this book and wishing you all the best in your search.

Like you, I took a chance and gambled on finding love online, and I am so happy to say that I found it. I met the love of my life on Match.com and you know what? I never thought it would happen. I was actually down to my last day of being on Match.com and was ready to give up when I got a response from the woman I've always hoped I would meet.

The really good news is that I practiced all the steps outlined in this book. I painted a realistic picture of myself, used a current photo, didn't hide the fact that I was a bit overweight, and didn't change my age. And I got a "wink" from a woman so beautiful and amazing that I thought she must have clicked on the wrong button thinking she was contacting someone else!

She liked the fact that I was comfortable with myself. I read her profile, and just like me she had told the truth in her profile. When we met, she was so much more than I had expected. More beautiful than her picture. So much nicer than her words could ever say. I can't describe how happy I was that I played every step honestly. It was the best way to start our romance, and I knew that she loved me… not some made-up version of myself.

In the chapters that come, I'll share my thoughts in this little box about the subjects covered. I've been where you are, and I want you to learn from my mistakes and from the things I did right. The things that led me to my true love.

-Terry

CHICK SAYS

Welcome daters! I'm Alyssa and I'm still knee-deep in the muck. Unlike Terry I haven't found that person, that guy who makes my toes twinkle. But I am looking and having a good time doing it. In fact, I buy into that old line about the chase being half the fun.

Sure, I'd like to find that perfect man who is macho but caring, fixes the car then fixes me a drink, brings me flowers for no reason, and does all my laundry and dishes… hmm, actually I may just be looking for a good mechanic and a maid service. Perfect man? Is there such a thing? Anyway, perfection is overrated.

The big, shiny, gold key to finding the person you want to spend your life with is, as Terry says, honesty. The equally important but slightly rusty key somewhere in the bottom of your purse is dropping your illusions of finding the perfect man. Your perfect man may be a 6'2" blue-eyed dreamboat who's independently wealthy and makes you laugh all the time. And I'm not going to tell you he's not out there. He is. His name is Brad Pitt. And if you find him on Match.com let me know. But you're far more likely to find Joe Pitt, 5'10", brown eyes, a few extra pounds, works in IT, and loves a good knock-knock joke. He's not Brad, but give him a chance. Maybe he'll make you laugh. Maybe he's got a great twinkle in his eyes. And he's being honest about himself. That's worth a lot.

Like Terry's boxes, you'll find mine in each chapter, giving my point of view. I'm the chick in the trenches, the roving reporter/dater, the one who's seen it all and then some. Welcome to the online dating world.

-Alyssa

Part I

How Online Dating

Services

Really Work

Chapter 1

First You Find the Site, Then You Find the Love

*Y*ou want love, you want sex, you want friendship… and you want to find it sitting at your computer. What luck! You can! Welcome to the world of online dating. Once upon a time, dating was a scary practice of looking around a bar, walking up to strangers you found attractive, and hoping to connect with them quickly enough to get a phone number. Now it's a far less scary practice of sitting at your computer, flipping through ads on various Web sites, and looking for clues into which stranger you might connect with well enough to want to date. Okay, so it may not sound that different, but online dating does have its advantages. You just need to understand how to navigate the sites, read the clues, and find that one truly wonderful person you were meant to be with. It can happen. It happens every day, to people we know—to people just like us.

As with any adventure, the search for love online has to start somewhere. What you'll find is that which online dating sites you pin your hopes to are every bit as important as which people you select to contact and how you present yourself to them. Maybe a friend suggested coolpeople.com or maybe your mom said you should try peopleyouwanttomarry.com. Take their suggestions and look around, but ultimately you should choose the site that will most likely find you the person and relationship you're looking for.

Online dating has become such a mainstream activity that there are now hundreds—if not thousands—of online dating sites. This is both good and bad news. The good news is that there are online dating sites tailored to your lifestyle and interests. The bad news is that with a large number of sites, no single site has all the people you may want to learn about or meet. There may be a dozen sites tailored to your lifestyle and interests—which do you choose? Your true love may be on bingosingles.com or redheads.com. She may be on a big site—a redheaded bingo player hidden in a sea of blond Monopoly-ists—or a small site you haven't discovered yet, like callmynumber.com. How can you know? Where should you look? As you begin your search, try different sites on for size.

This chapter is about how to find the online dating site that is right for you.

The Name Brands of Online Dating

There's a reason why Wal-Mart is the biggest retailer: one-stop shopping.

Oh, there may be cute little boutiques nearby. Yes, you can get sexier lacy items at Victoria's Secret. And you can get a mop at the local hardware store. But when you want it all, you tend to go to a place that has it all—like Wal-Mart. Clothing, hardware, gardening supplies, and milk—all under one gigantic roof.

When you begin your online search, a trip to the big-box retailer is probably the best starting point. Big online dating sites have price, selection, and variety going for them. You'll find potential dates from all walks of life, of all shapes and sizes, and from locations near and far. Your eyes will glaze over at all of the choices—all the exotic, previously unobtainable forms of dating possibilities you've only dreamed about.

Now, wake up and remember where you are! It's a big store with lots of product to be sure; but the parking lot's so full it's hard to find an open space, shoppers are pushing to get to the good deals first, and the lines are pretty long to check out. The high volume of potential dates on the big sites also means a high volume of people competing for your true love's attention. The big sites are crowded, so smart shoppers do best. Get in early, know what you're looking for, and don't stand there waiting to make your decision. The best deal may be snatched up while you're thinking things over.

So you're in the store and you're striding confidently down the aisles toward your goal. You know what you're looking for, you know what section it's in, and you know how much you're willing to spend. But stop for a second and look around you. See who else is shopping. The aisles are littered with people. They're picking up cans and reading the backs. They're holding up dresses to see if they'll fit. They're wandering down the aisles just having a good time. Some people just love to look. And they're in your way. They stop and talk and are on their cell phones and they're blocking you from that bag of chips you want. Wait a minute... they aren't here to shop; they're here to browse.

The well-known sites are full of browsers. People are there just "checking things out." They're there on a dare. They're just curious how it all works. They've posted a profile just to see what happens. And you get your hopes up and contact them, only to find out that they were just window-shopping.

Big-box stores. The stores we love to hate but shop there anyway. It's just too convenient.

But, let's be fair. If you're just starting your online dating experience, you're a browser too. You want to wander the aisles, see what's available, and squeeze the Charmin if you can. That's why the big-box online dating sites are so important. Despite the pedestrian mix, the browsers, the crowds, and the long lines, they probably have what you need—and at a pretty reasonable price.

The big-box stores of online dating are

▶ Match.com (www.match.com)
▶ Yahoo! Personals (personals.yahoo.com)

Figure 1.1 shows Match, one of the biggest sites in the online dating world.

Figure 1.1
Match is the big name in online dating. When finding lots of different types of people is the goal, it's a great place to start.

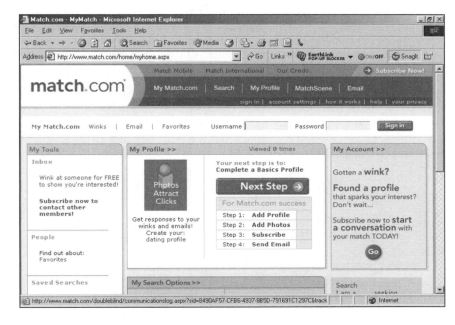

Figure 1.2 shows Yahoo!, one of the first sites to enter the online dating market.

Figure 1.2
Yahoo! is the most visited site on the Web, so their online dating area gets lots of members, which means lots of choices for you.

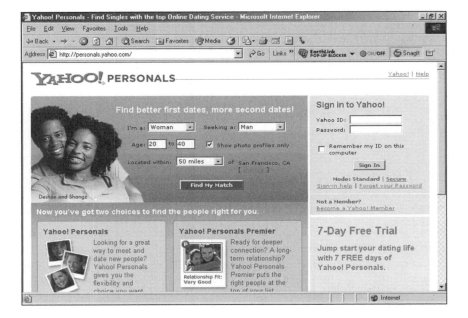

There are other big players, but Match and Yahoo! are the sites most daters try first. And it's good to find people when they're first starting. They're still optimistic and have a positive attitude.

Like the big-box stores, the good news about these two online dating giants is that they offer a good value. Match charges about $25 to subscribe for one month, and Yahoo! Personals charges about $20. In each case, you can send as many e-mails as you wish to any member who is listed.

If you want to browse the aisles and hold on to your dollars for awhile, each site allows you to search and browse the listings without having to pay. You can even post your own profile for free and "wink" at or send "icebreakers" to other members to let them know you're interested. However, when someone winks back and wants to communicate with you, hey, you'll have to pony up. It's possible that's kind of what the online dating sites had in mind when they offered the free browsing and winking… .

Here are some of the nice features that are offered by both of these sites:

▶ Post a profile with a photo for free.

▶ Browse for free.

▶ Send a Wink (Match) or Icebreaker (Yahoo!) for free.

▶ Customize searches to your specifications and save them.

▶ Once you find someone good, you can save him or her to a Favorites folder.

▶ Once you've paid, you can send unlimited e-mails.

▶ Yahoo! offers a special separate service for those looking for a serious relationship.

▶ Match offers a mobile dating service that allows you to search personal ads and chat from your phone.

The things that make us good sometimes make us bad. The same is true with big online dating sites. Since they are all about high volume and getting you to subscribe:

▶ They have a low cost of entry, meaning just about anyone can list himself or herself, even if they aren't serious candidates.

▶ If a paid member sends you an e-mail, and you're not a paid subscriber, you can't e-mail them back. You both have to be paid subscribers.

▶ The high volume of winks and icebreakers some members receive (meaning women getting lots of non-paid winks from every guy on the service) can overwhelm some people and make it hard for your message to be noticed.

▶ There's no real protection for you regarding the location or authenticity of people who are contacting you. The person who says he's the hottie from down the road may be located in Russia and operating out of a boiler room.

When you weigh the good and bad, ultimately you'll find that the big-box, name brand sites are a good place to shop. Their impressive selection and low low prices give them the advantage. And unlike in the dry goods world, you don't have to feel guilty about shopping there. The smaller sites will survive, offering their specialized product to a special population at a higher price for their designer goods. Meanwhile, the big sites take care of your most basic and mainstream shopping needs, and they do it well.

Affinity Dating Sites

If you're not a big fan of crowds and really know what you're looking for, affinity dating sites may be right for you.

If Match and Yahoo! Personals are like Wal-Mart or Kmart, then affinity sites are the fine jewelry shop, the little clothing store, or yes, even the dark little adult toys store… the boutiques of the online world. When it comes to narrowing your search to find someone with your interests, it's time to shop where the selection is, well, select. Just as you wouldn't go to Wal-Mart for Vera Wang, you wouldn't go to Match to find a Jewish doctor who likes nipple rings and leather parties.

One of the most challenging aspects of dating, live or virtual, is finding something (other than physical attraction) that you and a date have in common. Having a shared interest is a good way to get things started. When you go to an affinity site, you're sure to have at least one thing in common—the reason you're on the site.

Let's say you love wine. You could go on Match and search and search for someone who lists "wine" as one of his hobbies or interests—but it may not be his real passion. Or you could go to an online dating site like www.winesingles.com and find other wine lovers who are also single and would love to meet someone with whom they can share a glass of vintage Zinfandel.

And we all know how a little alcohol can grease the wheels of romance!

Figure 1.3 shows Winesingles, a site for wine lovers looking for wine lovers to love.

Figure 1.3
Finding people who share your interests and passions is easy with special interest dating sites like www.winesingles.com.

There are special-interest/affinity dating sites for an amazing number of interests and backgrounds. You'll be able to find sites that focus on:

▶ Shared interests, such as sports, arts, or hobbies.

▶ Similar backgrounds, such as professionals, parents, or newly singled.

▶ Shared ethnicity, such as Indian, African-American, or Irish.

▶ Looking for marriage.

▶ Even a shared love of certain TV shows or movies.

Affinity sites even go as far as sub-categorization within groups, such as dating sites for divorced Christian single parents. Although there is no guarantee that the person you see online is divorced, Christian, or a single parent, it probably is the case. Even if it's simply that the other person finds divorced Christian single parents very attractive, you're way ahead in the game of acceptance. The tips and techniques in this book will help you find the truth in profiles, so it may be even easier to spot a phony when visiting affinity sites.

If there is one drawback to such specialized sites, it's one of numbers. Chances are such sites will have a much smaller number of profiles in your geographic area than one of the big-box sites. So, quantity or quality? You decide!

Figure 1.4 shows how limitations may affect your ability to find someone in your area.

Figure 1.4
Affinity sites offer laser-guided precision in finding someone who shares your background or interests. But you may find that there are zero matches in your location and will need to expand your geographic horizons.

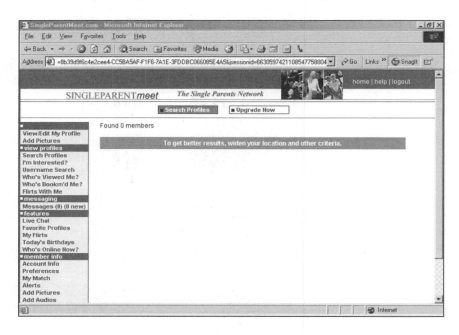

Lifestyle Sites to Match Your Lifestyle

Sometimes an affinity site might have too narrow a focus and too low of a membership, while the big sites could be too mainstream for you. You don't absolutely have to find someone who shares your love of model shipbuilding, but it would be nice if she was the same religion or sexual orientation as you are. Well, maybe more than nice. Whereas most mainstream online dating sites allow you to specify what religion your future date should belong to, you won't know if she's serious about her religion or merely accepting the classification. You might prefer a site where you're sure to get someone who really has convictions. And whereas mainstream online dating sites do match women interested in women and men interested in men, the larger population of the big sites is heterosexual. Because not all people live a heterosexual lifestyle, if you don't, it makes more sense to seek out an online dating site that has an emphasis on your sexuality, whatever it may be. Gay and lesbian dating sites are good examples of places where a comfort level can be established within a group of potential partners who share your lifestyle and values.

In most ways, lifestyle sites are very much like Match or Yahoo! Personals. They're able to assemble listings from people who want to find a mix of interests and backgrounds, even model shipbuilding, but they share a common sexual, experiential, or religious persuasion.

Lifestyle dating sites can also be about politics, parental status, age, job category—yes, we could go on, but we won't. Suffice it to say, there are many options. For example, if you're a creative person and work in advertising, design, or the arts, you may want to meet someone with whom you can talk about work or hash out ideas and who can share opinions with you about workday experiences. A lifestyle site for creative professionals, such as Media Bistro (shown in Figure 1.5), offers a personals section to match up people who share this lifestyle.

Some other examples of lifestyle sites are the following:

> ▶ Jdate.com is a site for Jewish singles.
> ▶ PrimeSingles.net is a site for singles over 40 and seniors looking for dates.
> ▶ Date-a-Doc.com is a site for health care and science professionals.
> ▶ SingleParentmeet.com is a site for, well, single parents.
> ▶ U.S.MilitarySingles.com is a site for, yes, singles in the military.
> ▶ SingleRepublican.com is a site for red state-ers.

The benefit of lifestyle dating is that you can meet a diverse group of potential daters within a broad lifestyle category. Lifestyle sites include personals, but they also provide content, message boards, and other features that make them a great place to find kindred spirits.

Figure 1.5
Lifestyle sites, such as
www.mediabistro.com
for creative
professionals, offer
personals to connect
people with a shared
occupation or
sensibility.

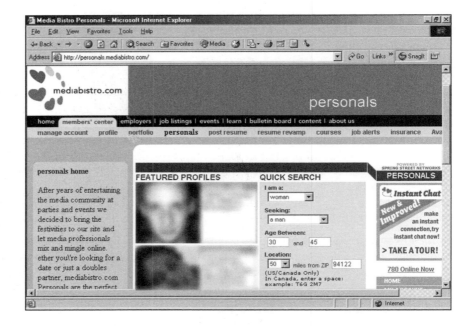

Very Special Friends Await

One of the big complaints you hear about online dating is how many inquiries daters get from people who are "only interested in one thing!"

People looking for sex partners are a big part of the online dating world. And it's not just men wanting to find women to sleep with them—women are looking to get action, too! If you're online, chances are you'll find some replies that make it very clear that sex is the topic du jour and you're the intended main course. Or maybe you're the one doing the ordering… .

As with so much of the online dating experience, the goal is to put the right message in the right place directed toward the right person. If someone is looking for a hot one-night stand, chances are that Match or Yahoo! Personals is not the right place to look. Most people on mainstream or non-sex-based affinity dating sites are looking for a relationship first, sex later (and it's true, we all have our own definition of "later," which could be "later tonight").

If you contact a person who simply wants to be friends first or is looking for a long-term relationship and you hit her with sex speak, it rarely works and just wastes time for both of you. For those people who want sexual partners or a relationship where sex is the cornerstone, there are an amazing number of online dating/sex sites where all the gloves come off (and hopefully go on during certain acts). These sites have no restrictions on what is shown in profile photos or the language that is used (see Figure 1.6).

Sex and swinger sites are big business and, in many ways, are just like traditional online dating sites. Preferences are listed, photos are important, and you can wink, e-mail, and IM people who

Figure 1.6
If you're looking for sex rather than a relationship/friendship, sex dating sites, such as www.adultfriendfinder. com, serve up nothing-left-to-the-imagination profiles.

match your particular tastes. The difference is that it's probably not someone's face or education you're trying to match up with.

Sex dating sites categorize preferences in a much more complex manner. Rather than "seeking friendship" or a "serious relationship," you'll find long lists of specific preferences, such as woman seeking woman dressed as man, 1-on-1, 2-on-1, group, fetish, S&M, bi, and probably a few categories you hadn't heard of before.

The photos are explicit. Men primarily show close-ups of their penises and women show their "best" attributes, which can range from full nude portraits to something their OB-GYN has locked in her records. If you're offended by full-blown sexual content, you may wish to pass on visiting such sites.

Like the old saying, "There's something for everyone," this is certainly true in the online dating world. Rather than having sex-starved people pestering timid little souls, sex dating sites are all a part of matching up the desires, needs, and interests of people to serve a need.

Old School Personals

Long before online dating, your local newspaper was matching up people with its "personals" section. In fact, it was the personals sections that gave us such now-famous acronyms as SWF and BBW. The cost of lines in print ads forced people to get pretty creative with abbreviating their ads, resulting in cryptic "only you know what I am talking about" personal ads, such as SWM seeks SMFs for LTR or ONS. Reply Louie at 75475… whatever that means.

Printed personals were the forerunner and model for much of the online dating experience. Blind box ads, photo personals, and the whole style of identifying the type of person you are and are looking for evolved in the back pages of our nation's newspapers.

Personals still thrive. In fact, the acceptance of online dating has given them even more legitimacy. Virtually all newspapers now offer online versions of their personals, making them great, free, local listings that may yield a few surprises. Many people who are still shy with online dating sites are comfortable with their local newspapers, and you may find people who are not listed on other online sites. Figure 1.7 shows an example of *The San Francisco Bay Guardian*'s online version of their personals section.

Figure 1.7
Local newspaper personals advertising is often offered online as well as in print, making them a great low-cost way to find locals looking for someone like you.

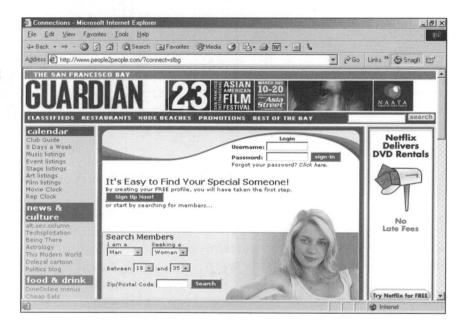

TIPS FOR FINDING A SITE

You're trying to decide what kind of site to use and what kind of sites might be out there for someone like you. It's easy to search for what you're looking for. From any of the Web sites with a search engine (Google, Yahoo!, MSN, etc.), type in what kind of site you're looking for with the words "online dating" after it. For instance if you're looking for a site for Jewish singles, type in **Jewish online dating**. A bunch of sites will show up. Or, if you're a single parent, try **single parent online dating**. A bunch of sites will come up. Yeah, it's not difficult. There are a lot of sites out there and, likely, a lot of sites for what you're looking for.

Local newspaper personals work a bit differently than online listings. As a rule, the person in the ad pays for the ad as well as for the replies. Sometimes you can contact them online or call a local phone number and leave a message but mainly you send paper mail to a box number.

One of the things about newspaper personals is that they tend to be very short. Newspapers charge by the line, so you may have to read between the lines to find the real story.

Things to Expect on All Dating Sites

There are things that all dating sites have in common. Whether you're on a mainstream site like Match, an affinity site like Winesingles, looking for action on Adult Friend Finder, or talking shop at Media Bistro, you'll see the following features:

- ▶ Profiles are written by the person posting the listing.
- ▶ Photo posting is offered and encouraged.
- ▶ The dater is asked to check off a number of boxes, indicating her basic information and preferences, allowing searches based on preferences and attributes.
- ▶ The profile will provide space for the dater to talk about herself in her own words, as well as to explain what kind of person she's looking for.
- ▶ There is almost always a lot of space dedicated to describing one's physical attributes.
- ▶ Daters are almost always asked for their idea of a perfect date (if you can answer this without cliché, they'll beat a path to your door).
- ▶ The site can "match" you with other daters based on each of your preferences.
- ▶ You can search by location, age, race, religion, and even how recently someone has been online.

Because most online dating sites share these traits, it's pretty easy to create a profile on one site, and then use the photo and text from it on a number of other sites. Each has its own flavor and special lists of preferences, but once you use one site, feel free to try others. Go to where you get results, and where you feel comfortable.

One of the most important features shared by all good online dating sites is the ability to maintain your privacy. Anonymity is essential. Just as with newspaper print listings, one of the things you pay an online dating service for is to keep your e-mail address, name, phone number, and any other ways of identifying you completely confidential. It should be entirely up to you when and to whom you wish to reveal your identity. This is both sensible (who wants to have that guy whose wink you've been ignoring for three months suddenly turn up at your office?) and a safety issue (nor that stalker…).

From a practical point of view, you should also expect good online dating services to have an easy way for you to determine their cost and for you to subscribe. Most sites have "free trial" or "free to browse" plastered all over their sites, but if you want to find out how much it costs to become a full member, on some sites you may have some trouble. Sometimes you may even have to register for their "free trial" before they'll tell you what you might ultimately have to pay. Their goal is to get you in (gosh, I already went through the trouble of registering) and hook you (wow, her profile was really great) so that when you see the price, you'll just go for it. It's just good luck that most sites make it very easy to actually go ahead and pay for your subscription. Another key factor to notice is how easy it is for you to cancel your paid subscription. Many sites "auto-renew" your paid subscription, and it's up to you to know when to cancel or to pay for another month.

Site Specific

Regardless of your comfort level or lifestyle, there is an online dating site that will help you find the type of person you want to contact. Online dating sites allow you to "shop" a bit by browsing or searching listings first and then subscribing to make contact. Take your time during your free browsing period to really explore each site. You want to make sure the selection is broad enough to give you lots of options to pick from. You want to be sure your fellow customers on the site are really looking for the same kind of relationship you are. And you want to pick a site that's going to make you feel comfortable and satisfied when shopping there.

By experimenting, browsing, and eventually finding the right online dating site; you can use your time, and your money, wisely in the search for that special person.

GUY SAYS

If you like sports, one of the problems with local television is that they only broadcast local teams. If you live in Chicago, you are going to see a lot of Cubs, Sox, Bulls, and Bears, but what if you love other teams?

Sure, you could stick with local cable, but if you really love sports, chances are you simply have to have Dish or DirecTV. They have sports packages featuring most teams in the country. If you live in Chicago but grew up in New York, you can watch as much Mets baseball as you want.

Online dating, to me, is a lot like having Dish or DirecTV sports packages—it helps you find someone who is on the right team. It helps you find the person you really want—not just the people who are nearby. I live in a small town, and online dating opens up a whole world of interesting women whom I would never meet any other way. It's awesome!

As I visited online dating sites, I learned that some sites have a better lineup than others. I am a big believer in changing the channels when needed. I also think it's good to be on more than one site. There is one magic person out there—I want to be sure that wherever she is, she can find me and I can find her.

Sure, the sports packages cost a lot more than the local stations included in most cable or satellite packages. Subscribing and trying different online dating sites costs more too—and it amazes me that a guy will shell out $50 a month for the big sports package, but will hem and haw at spending the same to meet the love of his life. What team is he rooting for?

—*Terry*

CHICK SAYS

Okay, not to go crazy with a stereotype, but I'm a woman and I'm a shopper. I can spend hours wandering an outlet mall or every shoe store in the city. And the fact is that my mom can do this, too, as can my sister and my best girlfriend. There are exceptions to this rule, but I think it's safe to say that women are shoppers. We're raised with it, we're encouraged in it, and we're well taught by our mothers. So why shouldn't we use this extraordinary skill to benefit us in the world of online dating?

There are so many sites out there it will make you dizzy. But haven't you ever spent hours scouring through online shopping sites looking for that perfect pair of boots you know you saw somewhere but can't remember where? Doesn't your dream man deserve the same dedication?

So sit down at your computer, make sure you're well hydrated, and leap in. Try on the different sites for cut and fit. If you don't like the color (or off-color in the case of sex sites), then put it back on the rack, hit the Google search button, and move on. But make sure you've taken a good look at the selection. You don't want to miss a good deal.

The key to this shopping excursion, like any other, is that if you find something really cute but not exactly what you were looking for, don't put it back on the rack. Try it on, turn around a few times, and who knows… maybe it's just the perfect fit after all. Just because you weren't looking for him, doesn't mean he might not be exactly what you should have been looking for. Keep an open mind.

Most importantly, don't get discouraged! That dream man, just like the perfect pair of black pumps, is out there somewhere. If you just keep looking, you'll find him.

—*Alyssa*

Chapter 2

Searching for Love, or Knowing What You're Looking For

*N*ow that you've browsed through some online dating sites, assessing their benefits, checking out the talent, finding a few friendly faces, it's time to knuckle down. Enough of being an innocent bystander, a wallflower, a casual observer. You need to get your feet wet. And maybe even your ankles, knees, hips—you know where we're going. You need to start searching for love. And to find it, you need to know what it looks like. And how to search for it.

The good news is that online dating sites have search engines. They're huge databases that allow you to pick what basic information and even specific qualities you want to find in your potential date. It's like a card catalog in a library. You just need to specify a subject, a title, or an author, and the catalog will tell you where to find the book you're looking for. Tell the catalog that you're looking for a 35 year-old, non-smoker, no kids, within 50 miles of you. Here you go; here's your lovely hard-backed non-fiction title… you knew it was on the shelf there somewhere.

Most online dating sites encourage you to search, offering it for free without making you register. They want to lure you in, show you all the pretty faces, throw open the doors to the smorgasbord—just as long as you don't eat anything. But some sites will ask you to register and sometimes even to post a profile before you're able to look around at all the tasty goodies. Ideally, you'll have a chance to look at the product before investing your time, but in order to get a good feel for a site, you really do need to do some searching to see what's out there. So if you've found a site that seems like it might be the right one for you, go ahead and register and do a basic profile if they require it. You can always delete it later.

Once you've browsed some different sites and have gotten a good feel for what they're like, you're likely to have discovered one that stands out to you. One that seems to have a lot of people of the sort you're looking for. Now you're ready to take the time to narrow your search and start looking for real matches. You should see at least a few people who get you excited before you decide for sure that you want to commit. Remember, you're going to have to pay to contact these people. You don't want to discover that there's not really anyone who's quite right after you've spent your hard-earned cash. And you really don't want to discover after subscribing that there are more interesting people on another site and end up having to pay for two or more sites. What are you, made of money?

Using Online Dating Search Engines

It's pretty easy to search for people on an online dating site. After all, that's what the site is there for—to easily connect you with someone you want to date. Each site is a bit different, but the basic process is as follows:

1. Indicate what gender you are and what gender you're looking for, such as woman seeking man. Many sites, such as Match and Yahoo! now have same-sex matches, such as woman seeking woman, as well.

2. Select an age range. You'll need to decide what your comfort zone is—some of us don't mind robbing the cradle and others are looking for a father figure. You need to make your mind up at this point.

3. Enter the Zip code where you live. Or they might ask for a city or state name or even an area code. This gives your search a starting point.

4. Indicate how far away from you your date can be. Usually you're asked to enter a number of miles. The search radiates from the center of the Zip code or city and works in a circular pattern from the center. You can often choose to search only within your city, as close as 5 miles, or you can even leave it unlimited.

5. Most online dating sites also allow you to choose to be shown only profiles that have a picture. If you don't choose this option, you'll get profiles with and without pictures. Most searchers prefer to see their potential dates, so you'll probably want to check this option.

Figure 2.1 shows a basic search screen that uses the above criteria. These screens are usually featured on the entry screen of the service.

Figure 2.1
Basic searching is usually available from the entry screen of most online dating services. This screen will allow you to do a quick search based on gender, age, and location.

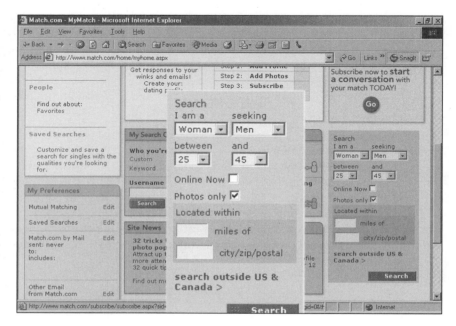

After entering the above criteria, clicking on the Search button will return profiles that match your selections. There may be cases where no profiles are returned. If you're searching in a rural area, or the service you've chosen is very strong in one locale (not yours), such as a city personals site, it's possible to get no matches. Or instead of returning no matches, they may return matches that don't quite fit the criteria you asked for, so make sure you take a closer look.

Refining Your Search

Now, with the basic search you've just done, chances are you've got a lot of profiles to look through, including a lot of smokers (if you're looking for non-smokers) or people with kids (if you're looking for someone without), etc. This phase of the search makes no assumptions about the sort of person you're looking for beyond the most basic information. And since you're probably not interested in every woman of a certain age within a 50-mile radius, you'll probably want to refine your search a little. You'll learn that if you're browsing, the basic search will show you lots of profiles, and will help you spot newcomers to the service. But if you're doing some real looking, the refined search is the tool of choice in the hunt.

Refining your search allows you to get a lot more specific about the person you're looking for. You can specify everything from body type to star sign to body piercings. And you can choose how much you want to refine it. Maybe all you want is a curvy girl with long red hair. You can specify just that. But maybe you want a 5'8" curvy girl with long red hair, hazel eyes, democrat, Sagittarius, non-smoker, never married, with no kids, has body piercings, dry witted, who likes to walk/hike, is a vegetarian, drinks socially, works in the arts, lives alone, and has no pets. Yes, you can search for her. Whether you'll find her... well, maybe if you're lucky. You'll get more results if you specify less, but if this is exactly what you want, if she's on the dating service, this search will find her.

Figure 2.2 shows a typical refined search screen. The choices are culled directly from the entry form when a user fills out his profile. This allows you to make incredibly detailed searches.

The more you search, the better you'll get at refining your searches. Often a process of trial and error, you may find that you'll have to modify your criteria as you go along, simply because there are too few profiles that match or that you have already seen them one time too many. Simple modifications, such as changing the age range or body type, will open up a new group of profiles for you to view.

SEARCH TIPS

Start specific and broaden your search from there. There's nothing wrong with going for the perfect match. But if you run out of candidates, slowly start expanding your search by adding other characteristics and interests that you're willing to be more flexible about. If you find that the service has too few matches after you've compromised on everything you're willing to compromise on, rather than further expanding your search to include people who just aren't right, it may be time to try a larger search area geographically. Keep radiating out in the number of miles to search to see if that helps. If those methods fail to return a good number of matches within a reasonable range, you may want to try another service. The one you're using may simply not attract the type of person you're looking for.

Figure 2.2
Refining your search
allows you to use the
equivalent of a laser
guided missile to locate
the exact type of person
you're looking for—if
they are on the service.

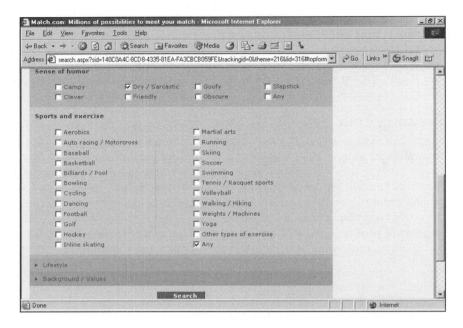

Saving Profiles You Like

So you've been doing all this searching, and hopefully it's resulted in some promising prospects. But now that you've found them, what do you do with them? Well, hopefully you don't lose them. And rather than go through the whole search process again, you'd like to put them somewhere where you can come back to them later. You can, but you're going to have to sign up first. One you've signed up with the service (this doesn't mean you've given them any money, only registered), then you can put all the lovelies you've discovered into your Favorites or Saved Profiles folder.

Most services offer a Favorites section so you can keep track of the good profiles you've seen (see Figure 2.3). They'll usually let you save up to 50 profiles, and they'll remain in your Favorites folder until you delete them or they leave the service. It's very important to keep track of people, something you probably discovered after one browsing session. For some reason it can be very difficult to re-find someone you've seen before unless you remember his user name. And frankly, how memorable is Sfdude60937?

Usually at the top or bottom of each person's profile there's an option to save them to the Favorites folder. Make sure you click it before you move on to someone else. Then you can usually return to the folder from anywhere else on the site or from the Home page.

Figure 2.3
When you find a profile you like, you can store it in a "favorites" area on the service. This allows you to come back later and not have to re-find people you already are interested in.

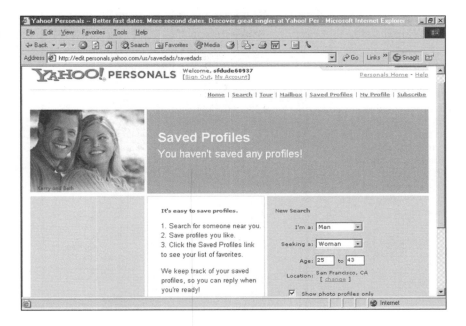

Thinking about How Your Profile Will Be Searched

Having done some searching, you now have a pretty good idea how searches work. Now think about how your profile will respond to searching.

As you have learned, you can refine a search by any of the multiple-choice fields in the profile. Some fields are mandatory. They will include:

▶ Age

▶ Location

▶ Gender

▶ Screen/User Name

In addition, there will probably be a few other required fields, depending on the service, such as:

▶ Weight or Body Type

▶ Hair Color

▶ Ethnicity or Background

Most of the above fields will be multiple-choice, with you clicking the box that corresponds with your personal qualities. Most of the sites are very thorough and have come up with virtually every option you might need to choose from. For location it will most likely expect a Zip code. And you'll have to come up with a user name. See Part II of this book for a discussion of how best to do that.

Once you complete all of the required fields, you'll then be asked to check off boxes in a long list of optional fields that describe your interests and preferences. Figure 2.4 shows a typical profile form and how easy it is to work with. You simply go down the list and start clicking the answers that best describe you and who you're looking for.

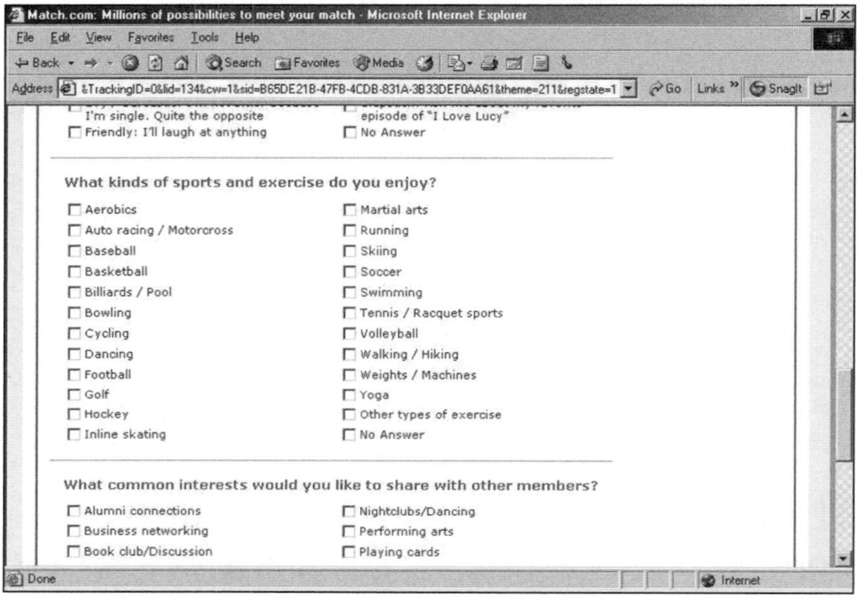

Figure 2.4
Services such as Match.com allow you to create a searchable profile by having you answer multiple-choice questions that describe you and the type of person you're looking for.

In the movie *Don Juan DeMarco* (with Johnny Depp and Marlon Brando), the infamous lover is asked by his newly found love just how many women he has slept with. Unwilling to lie to his true love (hey, he read an advanced copy of this book!), he proceeds to tell her how many and in some detail. Just before he does, in a voice-over by Don Juan looking back on that moment, he says, "This would have been a good time to lie."

In a book about how important the truth is, we'd like you to give pause at this moment and consider what poor Don Juan was trying to convey. The truth may set you free, but you may find yourself free… and alone. There's such a thing as a white lie or stretching the truth. Assuming you've reached dating age, you probably have a good idea about how that works. Do these make my butt look big? NO! Do you think she's pretty? NO! Does size matter? NO! You have to compromise the truth a bit sometimes, or at least put it off. Some things may be insensitive, better left unsaid, or left to be revealed at a later time.

You should never lie about yourself in your profile questions. However, when you're checking the boxes about what kind of person you're looking to date, keep in mind what you may be signaling to others about yourself. Say you describe your fantasy date, your perfect dream girl in the following way. Terry really loves tall women. He puts that he's seeking someone over six feet tall. And he thinks women with really long hair are hot, so he says he wants someone with long hair. Then he gets to the questions about occupation and income. "Hey," he thinks, "it would be great if my date made a lot of money—we could split the check," so he puts down that he wants to meet someone who makes more than $100,000 a year. Finally, he kind of thought his ex was a little too heavy, so it might be nice if he could date someone slender. Terry just defined himself as someone looking for a supermodel. So he effectively shut out nearly everyone online, unless Naomi Campbell is on the market and prowling the Web.

Maybe Terry would, ideally, like someone who fit that description. Hey, wouldn't most guys? But think about what kind of a message he's sending. Consider that probably 99 percent of the women reading his profile don't fit his description of the ideal woman. And what do you suppose these average-sized women with cute little haircuts and entry-level jobs are thinking when they read his profile? Well, if they searched for someone who matched their interests and preferences, they wouldn't ever see Terry's profile. But if they did find it and looked at his woman wish list, they would disregard his profile. At best they might think they're just not compatible with him. At worst they'd think he was a pig who only wants to date supermodels. (Incidentally, Terry's not a pig and would never create such a profile... sorry Terry.)

The boxes you check at this stage of your profile-making are the means by which others will search for you. If you want to meet a good person, don't limit yourself unnecessarily. Keep an open mind. If you can handle more than 1 percent body fat, open up your criteria to include average, athletic, even curvy or full-figured. If you thought that girl you saw the other night on the train had a cute little bobbed haircut, open yourself up to other hair-lengths. Don't be so materialistic when it comes to her salary. And maybe 5'9" or so wouldn't be so bad. Be flexible, or you'll never find someone. And that's true for after you've found her, too. Few people want to date someone who doesn't budge in his or her opinions.

From Don Juan De Marco we learn that there is a time and a place for the truth. This may not be one of them. There are preferences, and there are prejudices. In the click-the-button multiple-choice fields of profile building, your preferences may read like prejudice.

So you've looked through the multiple-choice questions and come up with some reasonable answers, using good judgement and some soul-searching. Did you make choices on all the questions? Really, you skipped a few? Why would you do that? Don't you know your own mind? Because that's what readers of your profile are going to think. It's always better to answer a question than not to. And it's usually better to come up with some choices rather than just checking the Any or No Opinion boxes. While you shouldn't be inflexible, you also shouldn't seem disinterested. I know some of the questions may seem silly to you, but you'd be surprised at the difference they might make to someone. Here are some examples of the more interesting multiple-choice questions you might be asked:

▶ What are your turn-ons/turn offs? (Body piercing, tattoos, thunderstorms, erotica, candlelight, etc.)

▶ How would you describe your sense of humor? (Goofy, dry/sarcastic, clever, slapstick, etc.)

▶ What sports/exercise do you enjoy? (Aerobics, martial arts, walking, billiards, bowling, etc.)

> ▶ What are your interests? (Book clubs, fishing, playing cards, video games, volunteering, etc.)
> ▶ What describes your diet? (Meat and potatoes, vegetarian, junk food, etc.)
> ▶ Which pets do you have/like? (Birds, reptiles, cat, dog, etc.)

These may seem silly and unimportant, not worth bothering with. But consider this—what if your dream girl, yes, even Terry's supermodel, has a cute little heart tattoo somewhere and you've said tattoos are a turn-off? What if you absolutely adore anything with Adam Sandler or Jim Carrey in it, but the girl you end up meeting hates goofy humor? What if you're a die-hard meat eater, and you meet a sensitive, vegetarian guy? What if you're allergic to dogs, and he has a St. Bernard? While you don't want to alienate anyone, there are some things that should be made clear. Again, try to keep things as open as possible so you can get the largest number of search responses, but don't compromise on anything really important to you. You need to show a preference for something, or no one's going to match up with you. And really consider anything you're going to call a turn-off—because on the right person, your turn-off could be a turn-on.

Working the Hot List

After you've been on a site for a while, browsing and searching, chances are you'll have seen everyone who fits your criteria. Suddenly you're seeing all the same faces and wondering if that's it for you. Is that all there is? At this point, you may decide to back off from your round-the-clock vigil in front of your PC, Doritos in hand, and take a break. "Maybe there's no one out there for me!" you cry, cramming more Doritos into your open maw. Some of us reach this stage of despair earlier than others.

However, a few hours later, hormones raging, curiosity calling you back, you wisely decide to resume the hunt. "There's got to be someone out there for me!" you cry, cramming your hand back onto your mouse. But rather than go back through the browse and search patterns that weren't working so well for you, you can modify your search. You can look for people who are new to the service (meaning you probably haven't seen their profiles yet) or for those who have been active only recently.

This will help you find brand new people as well as people who've had their profiles hidden from view but recently opened them up for public consumption. And by limiting the search to people who have been active on the site within the last week or month, this will help you to find people who are actually still using the site. A fair portion of the people on online dating sites are people who tried it for a bit then stopped or people who found a relationship but forgot to remove their profiles. It's disappointing to have your wink sitting out there without a response because the person hasn't been on the site in six months.

Finding People Who Are New to the Service

There is something to be said for the dew still being on the rose. The flower is fresh. The petals are just starting to reach out to the sun. There's no wilting, no browning of the leaves, no getting smashed under foot. On the other hand, people who have had their profiles online for quite awhile may be getting a little dried up, a little exhausted or jaded by the experience. Maybe they've had some dates that didn't go well or just had no spark. Maybe they've run through all the likely candidates but are still online, just hoping they'll find someone beyond all expectations. We're not saying all people who've been online for a while are tired of the process—but some may be.

New people, on the other hand, are full of hope and energy. They're excited and optimistic, if a little nervous and uncertain (but that's okay). They're hoping for a great experience. They haven't been on dates with people whose profiles didn't match who they really were. They haven't been profile spammed. They haven't been propositioned by someone who didn't even have the guts to post a photo. So far they've been spared rude behavior and broken dreams. There are many people who like to get to people before they have had any bad online dating experience. Too much time in online dating is a lot like a relationship in itself. Steve Martin describes such a situation in one of his early stand-up routines:

"I think you need to really know and love someone before you use and degrade them."

You may really know and even love using online dating, but you might start to feel a bit used and degraded if you hang out long enough. It's sort of like waiting for a longtime boyfriend to pop the question. You wonder how long you're willing to keep waiting and wasting your time if you're never going to get that ring on your finger. For this reason, most online services help new members find someone by putting a New or Recently Added symbol next to their profiles or photos. This will help you identify newcomers and will help them get lots of responses.

So, gentle reader, if you find such a profile, please make his experience a good one, okay? We don't need more wilted roses out there...

Going for Recently Active Profiles

One of the key searches is for recent activity (see Figure 2.5). You want to identify people who are online now, looking, and serious about finding someone. If someone hasn't been "active" in, say, a month, there's probably a good reason why; and you may find you're spending a lot of time trying to get in touch with her without a reply. Figure it out! If she hasn't logged in to the service for a long time, it means she's moved on. She's not even seeing your winks or reading your messages.

The lack of recent activity may hint at a change in her life. She may have met someone whom she's currently dating. She just may not be quite to the point where she wants to say, "I love you so much I'll never look at anyone else, so I'm taking my profile off!" Keeping that profile active is a not-so-subtle way for people to avoid commitment, keep some distance, or keep their options open. You don't want to be in the middle of some half-baked-I-can't-commit romance, do you? Or maybe she met someone online and just didn't bother to remove her profile. It's not costing her anything, so why bother?

Either way, you needn't bother with her. You want to get in touch with people who are actively looking. A good dater will check the service every day—or once a week at a minimum. Recent activity is a barometer of interest and need.

Figure 2.5
Most services show how long it's been since someone logged on to the service. Match shows this at the top of the listing because it's an important thing to consider.

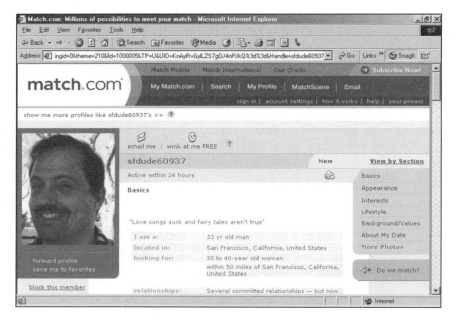

When you do finally wink, break the ice, or e-mail someone, you'll find that the Recent Activity field is even more important. Let's say you found someone you like. You e-mail them. You wait patiently in front of your computer. You're sitting there, Doritos in hand. A day goes by, then a few more. Soon it's a week later, and you start rationalizing: "She's not around," or "Her computer's broken."

Recent activity can also be just the reality check you need. You go back to her listing, and it says, "Active within 24 hours." And you think, "Curses! She *is* online! She got my e-mail! She's not interested, and she's online right now looking at someone else's profile!!!"

Well, at least now you can get up from the computer and wash off that Doritos dust. Recent activity. Sometimes you love it. Sometimes it's like Don Juan. The truth can hurt you.

Summary

After browsing for a bit, using the search tools on your dating site of choice will help you find the right people. Searching will also help you to understand how important your own profile choices will be in helping the right people find you when they're searching. Filling out your profile completely and honestly and being flexible in your choices are all key ingredients leading to your dating success. Using all the tools at your disposal, including finding new members and only pinning your hopes on active members, will lead to your greatest success. Using searches will help you find the right person at the right time.

GUY SAYS

When I first started online dating, I made some stupid mistakes when I created my profile. First, I didn't fill in a lot of the profile fields. Second, the ones I did fill in I didn't take too seriously. I was online to browse and find someone, not fill out forms.

I was finding lots of people that I wanted to contact and would send them e-mails, but I wasn't getting many responses back. Finally, someone did send me an e-mail saying that they loved how I looked, but they didn't know too much about me and then proceeded to ask me a bunch of the same questions that were on the profile questionnaire. Even worse, I was only getting responses to the ones where I made contact first. I wasn't getting winks or e-mails from women who made contact first.

Getting ticked and ready to cancel my subscription, I thought about the one e-mail where the woman said she didn't know much about me. Then I thought about how I found people when I searched. I didn't have the information in my profile that I would use to search on for my matches. So I went back and redid my profile, answering as many questions as possible, and filling in all the descriptive fields with a good amount of detail.

The result: Lots of replies, and lots of winks and e-mails coming to me from people I didn't even know about. The change in my profile helped women learn all about me and find me easily.

My final awakening was one person who actually wrote me and was offended that I found piercings and tattoos a turn-off. She said except for that, we'd be a good match. That sent me back to my profile to be a bit more open about choices others make. I can handle a ring up in the navel!!!

—*Terry*

CHICK SAYS

I'm a great searcher. When I'm on Yahoo! or Google I can find anything I want within a matter of seconds. I know the tricks, I know how to phrase things, I know what I'm doing. When I'm on Amazon, I can find that CD I've been wanting to buy but can only sort of remember the words to one of the songs. I can find a polka-dotted slingback with a kitten heel. I can find that old movie starring that woman with the hair and the guy with the mustache. When I'm on CNET, I can find the review I remember reading a couple of months ago about that gadget that had Bluetooth and a digital camera or that news story I remember about the guy who invented the thing for cars like a GPS but not…

So why can't I find the guy with the sheepish smile and goofy hair who likes Green Day and Ella Fitzgerald and calls himself a geek because he works in Silicon Valley? Well, because you can't search for those things. Online dating is practical in many aspects. There's no goofy hair option. There's no geek box to check.

So when I search, I have to be creative. The sheepish smile might imply a dry/sarcastic sense of humor. The goofy hair could be called wind-tossed or teased. Maybe I can't specify groups or singers, but I can look for someone who loves music and concerts. And a geek who works in Silicon Valley probably makes well over $50,000 a year.

The trick is figuring out how to get the search tool to work for you. Just like finding those kitten-heeled slingbacks, I have to know how to ask for what I want. And once I find him, I need to make sure he fits, that he's my style, and walk around a little with him to make sure I'm comfortable. Then I'll make my purchase.

—*Alyssa*

Chapter 3

Baby, Now That I've Found You–Sending Winks, Icebreakers, and E-mails

*Y*ou've been browsing, searching, checking boxes, and modifying your own profile (you'll learn all about how to create your profile in Part II of this book), and you've saved all of the people you wish to contact in a Favorites section. You're almost bursting with the excitement of finally starting a dialogue with someone. Only, well, how do you start that dialogue?

Making contact is the mainstay of online dating. It's how online dating services make their money. As you've seen, you can browse and search for free. You can even post your own profile and have it listed at no charge. In most services you can even send a little free "wink" to someone, letting him know that you're interested in him (if you have your profile posted). But the people running the online dating sites are nothing if not business-people. They won't let you get to any real contact or have any kind of real conversation with the person you're interested in unless you pay to subscribe. That's the real world for you—so much for fairy tale romance. Your fairy godmother is a capitalist.

Online dating services really know what they're doing. They understand that once they get you in and you take a look around, you'll find someone special you're willing to pull out the credit card for. That's why they allow you to post your profile for free. Your free profile helps populate the service with lots of members. They don't doubt their ability to draw you in with the smorgasbord—they'll have you bellying up to the buffet soon enough.

So you're ready to take the plunge and say hello to that hot babe you've been eyeing. Well, in this chapter we're going to tell you how to do that. We'll take a look at the ways you can start talking with people using the communication tools found on most online dating services.

Using Winks and Icebreakers

Whether you're a paid or a non-paid subscriber to an online dating service, most sites give you a quick way to send a note to another subscriber to tell her you're interested. A common term for this is sending a "wink" (the name used by Match.com) or an "icebreaker" (the name used by Yahoo! Personals).

The *wink*, as we'll refer to it from now on, serves two purposes:

First, it lets a non-paying member send a note to another member indicating interest. And the other member can wink back, showing that the interest is mutual. Or, if she's a paying subscriber, she can send an e-mail back to get the ball rolling.

The second purpose is more human than financial. It allows a paid member to show she's interested without going out on a limb. If the person she's winked at responds in kind, then the paid member can send an e-mail in return. But the wink allows her to test the waters first, before investing too much time or affection on someone who might not be interested.

Figure 3.1 shows a Match.com Winks page containing people who have winked at you, and also "mutual" winks—in which both people have winked at each other.

Figure 3.1
The Winks page from Match.com lists all of the people who have winked at you, and it also has a symbol for people who have returned your wink.

Let's say Alyssa's been running around Match for a while, and she returns to the profile of a guy she's looked at about 10 times. She thinks he's really cute, really smart, clever, and has a great sense of humor. She's been eyeing his profile without making a move because she thinks he'd never go for her. Maybe she doesn't perfectly fit the choices he's marked for the qualities he wants in a date. Maybe she's not quite the right height or body type or he loves sports and she doesn't. But there's just something about him she keeps coming back to. Finally she thinks, well, what can a wink hurt? He probably won't wink back, but what if he does? No one dislikes being told he's interesting, right? So she winks. And she waits. And whether she gets a response or not, all she's done is wink. She could have written that long e-mail she was considering, detailing all her wonderful qualities, her life story, telling him how much she loooooves him... but it's really a good idea that she didn't. Besides making her sound desperate, it could have been a waste of time and a build-up to a big let down. At least if he doesn't wink back, she hasn't spent hours agonizing over the proper wording for how much she looooooooves him. Sometimes a short e-mail is a good idea, but starting with a mutual wink is better. At least both parties know they're interested, and that's a good place to start. (And by-the-way, Alyssa's NOT desperate—we would never suggest such a thing.)

You're never able to personalize a wink by writing something specific to send to the person you're interested in. The wink is usually a simple comment—I'm interested in you or, as a response, I'm not interested in you. But some services have taken the basic wink and made it a little more interesting for sending and replying to initial messages by giving you another multiple-choice option. Yahoo! Personals, for example, allows their version of winks to contain one-phrase messages that help send a certain message to your intended. Examples of messages for first time contact include:

- ▶ I like your photo. Let's talk.
- ▶ I like your smile. Want to chat?
- ▶ Are you busy tonight? Let me know.
- ▶ Wow! You're cute!
- ▶ We have lots in common.
- ▶ Hand me my flip-flops cause you've knocked my socks off.
- ▶ Call the fire department—you're smokin'!

Being able to send a brief message to get someone's attention and to give him an idea of how you're approaching contact with him is a pretty good idea. These messages do a good job of telling someone if you're generally interested or if it's a call to action. They don't go so far as to say, "Come on over, baby," but they do give you an opportunity to show a little of your personal style and approach.

For people who get one of the above winks, they can choose to reply using one of the pre-written responses. These include:

- ▶ Thanks, I liked your message.
- ▶ Thanks, but I've just met someone and want to see what develops.
- ▶ Thanks for getting in touch. Have you got a photo?
- ▶ Your profile is starting to look interesting. Would you mind adding more details to it?
- ▶ Thanks! Are we a good fit?
- ▶ Sorry, but we're definitely not a good fit... Good luck.

The replies run from polite to pretty cold, and they are effective for interests and rejections. The messages are clearly crafted to help get non-paid subscribers to pony-up and buy a subscription to move things to the e-mail level.

Other services have their own flavor of winks, so you should check to see how effective the method they use will be for you. Most services only allow one wink/icebreaker per member you wish to contact. You can send them to just about every member, but limit one per member please. This keeps wink spammers at bay.

ONE PER MEMBER

Winks and icebreakers are great for starting a dialogue, expressing interest, and seeing if the interest is mutual. Remember that you will only be able to send one wink or icebreaker to each member, and they can only send one back to you. If you wish to communicate further, you will need to move to a paid status and escalate the communications to the e-mail level.

Although we don't think it's worth the bother, creating a new profile with the same information and pictures easily gets around the one-wink-per-member rule. With your new user name and profile, you could go wink at the same people again. However, if they weren't interested the first time, they probably won't be the second, third, or hundredth time. And do you really want to keep track of all your different memberships?

E-mail Communications: Say It Loud–I Subscribe and I'm Proud

So you've winked at some cuties, and hopefully you've gotten a bunch of winks back. Now you're going to want to start sending e-mails. That's the way relationships work—pass one stage then take the next step. In the online dating metaphor, winks are a hello and e-mails are the first dates. E-mails can give you encouragement and allow you to learn about the other person, or they can shut you down pretty fast.

We know that in the online dating world there are two different types of daters: paid subscribers and unpaid members. It's a pretty simple concept. If you're an unpaid member, you have limited access, you can't e-mail anyone, and you can't respond to anyone's e-mail. If you're really serious about finding someone and pursuing a relationship, you should be a paid member. You wouldn't think of using another service in your life, like a plumber or a physical therapist, without knowing you'll have to pay for them. Online dating sites are offering you a service—do you expect to get something for nothing? Well, we don't expect it, but we always do sort of hope to get something for nothing. That's why it's often a game of cat and mouse between two people, both interested in each other—who will break down and pay for the subscription to get things started?

As you will quickly learn, any personal identity information about members is strictly hidden from other members. The sites make a lot of noise about how this is to protect the privacy of members (and it really does). But it also ensures that the service gets subscribers. Without using the service's e-mail system, there is almost no way for members to communicate with each other or contact each other outside of the service.

GUYS PAY FOR DINNER, AND PAY TO COMMUNICATE. SORRY FELLAS!
It may not be fair, but it does seem that in the online world, women expect the man to pay for a subscription. Then it's up to the man to find some way to send her his e-mail address or phone number if she is not a paid subscriber. This may be a holdover from the days when women weren't supposed to make the first move. Only recently have women been encouraged to take command of these situations. It's still ingrained in them to let the man make the first move. Even when women are paid subscribers, it will probably be up to the man to start the e-mails flowing.

Note that we said *almost* no way.

As you will learn later in this chapter, there are a number of simple tricks for sending e-mail addresses and contact information to non-paid members. This saves one party from having to pay for a subscription. Some members will even try to sneak in their e-mail address or their contact info in the text of their profile, which is a risky option to avoid a small monthly fee. It's not something the sites allow, and you could have your profile removed from the site.

Subscribing Allows You to E-mail Members

As shown in Figure 3.2, when you attempt to answer an e-mail from a paid member, or just initiate an e-mail, you will be prompted to purchase a paid subscription.

Figure 3.2
Even if a paid member sends you an e-mail, chances are the service you're using will require you to be a paid member to e-mail back.

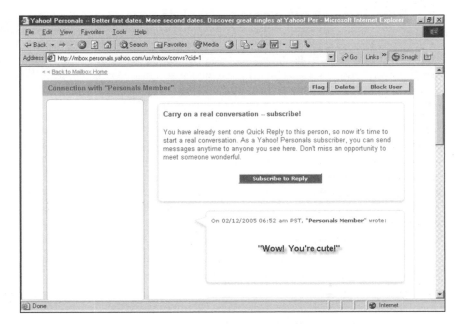

Being a paid member will allow you to initiate e-mails to any member, even if they're not paid members. It also allows you to respond to any e-mails that are sent to you. It is good to remember that when you e-mail a non-paid member, they will not be able to reply back. Many people get frustrated that they paid to be able to e-mail people they're interested in, only to learn that the members they're interested in can't reply. We need to remind you again—online dating services are businesses, and they count on both parties paying for membership. It's a fact of life in the online dating world.

You've made the decision to subscribe, so let's put aside the issue of whether the people you want to e-mail are going to be able to e-mail you back. We'll give you some ideas of how to deal with that later. For now, let's concentrate on the subscribing process. Your first big decision comes right away. How long of a subscription should you get?

Most online dating services have subscription packages offering you unlimited features and e-mail options for periods such as one month, three months, and six months. The price per month goes way down when you opt for the longer subscription packages. For example, a service will charge $24.95 for one month, $39.95 for three months, and $59.95 for six months.

That means you can pay 25 bucks for one month, or 10 bucks a month if you purchase six in advance. It all boils down to how good of a catch you think you are—and how many prospects are on the service. It's really a numbers game in that sense, and that's why it's important to browse and search a bit before you decide to subscribe.

Deciding on the Subscription Package

Chances are you're not going to find the right person in one month. Sorry.

But here's a good way to look at it. If you purchase a six-month package, and you meet the love of your life after three days on the service, then it was money well spent. It's really not about the money. You want to be able to be calm, take your time with people, communicate in a relaxed and friendly manner, and not be under the pressure of closing the deal in 30 days.

What makes choosing the length of your subscription package a hard one is that online dating services rarely have a cancellation policy where they return the unused portion of your paid subscription. When you subscribe, they make it pretty clear that there are no refunds. Your best choice is going for the value package. Assuming that you may be online for at least two months, you can see that the pricers at the dating sites really know what they're doing. Two months at $24.95 each is really almost the same cost as a six-month package. Why not go for the Costco jumbo-sized package of dates? Unlike buying the Costco-sized package of toilet paper, at least storage isn't an issue for you in this case.

It's hard to make the commitment when you aren't even sure what type of response you'll get. Combine that with the no-refund policy, and it's a tough call. Luckily, the services often have a way to help you out.

Taking Advantage of Free Trial Offers

To help you get excited about the other members on the service and to see the response you'll get as a paid member, many services offer a free trial offer. Yeah, baby!

Services such as Match.com will offer you, right from the front screen, a free three-day membership that is the same as if you were a paid member. You'll be able to get on and e-mail away to every dream date on the service.

Reality check.

Three days is a great start. During that three-day period, you can wink and e-mail as much as you want. If the service has instant messaging, you can IM everyone who is online. If the world was a perfect place, you would be able to browse and search for a few days, get your favorites list together, sign-up for the free trial, e-mail every one of your favorites, and then cancel before the end of the trial.

It's not a perfect world, and the online dating services know that.

Yes, you will be able to e-mail a large number of people, and yes, you will get some responses. But most likely many of the people you e-mail won't be checking the service every day. And even if they are, they won't know you're using the free trial and only have a three-day window to communicate. Also, they may not yet be paid members and able to get back to you. It may be your magic profile and e-mail that prompt them to subscribe, but you'll be off the free trial by the time they do! Oh the tragedy!

TRIAL TIPS

When you send someone an e-mail, you can come right out and tell her you're on the three-day trial because you're checking it out, and you hope she'll get back to you during that period. Make it clear that you're trying the service out, not cheaply trying to get something for nothing. You don't want her to think she's not worth spending the money on.

During your browsing and searching, be sure to select the people who have been active within the past 24 hours—these are your best bets. Activity within the last week is also worth a shot. Spend your free trial e-mails and time on recently active members, not ones who haven't been online for a while. You need someone who will get back to you quickly.

Be sure to tell the person to send you a wink if she's not a paid member and can't e-mail back. Indicate that you'll send her another e-mail with some way of getting in touch if you get a wink or icebreaker from her indicating she's interested.

Free trials are simply a way to help you decide if the service offers value to you, and also to help get you some initial responses to whet your appetite. If you use the tips listed above, you may even grab the brass ring and get a good e-mail dialogue going in the trial period. Chances are you'll feel encouraged and want to continue on as a paid subscriber.

When you sign up for the free trial, the service will collect your credit card billing information and ask you to agree to a subscription period (of whatever length you choose) as a part of the free offer. It will be up to you to remember to cancel the subscription before the trial period ends. If you don't, you will be billed, and it's a non-refundable offer. Figure 3.3 shows a typical free trial sign-up screen. You'll need to decide on the subscription term and agree to a contract and payment terms before the trial offer kicks in.

Figure 3.3
Free trial periods almost always require a credit card number and commitment to a subscription if you don't cancel your subscription by the end of the free trial period.

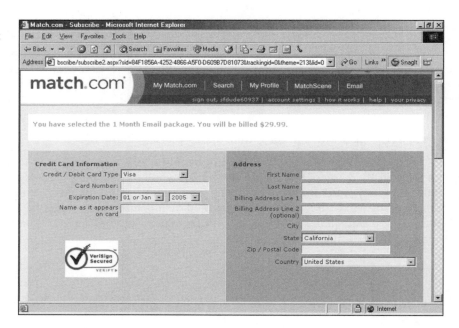

If you cancel before the end of the trial period, your credit card will not be billed, and you'll return to non-paid member status. Your profile will remain, and you can continue to browse, search, and send winks as before—but you won't be able to e-mail, including people who read your e-mails from the trial period and are getting back to you.

If that happens, you can always purchase a subscription. Not a bad deal when you look at it that way.

One thing you won't be able to do is take advantage of the trial offer again—at least not with the same billing address and credit card. Services are smart about users canceling after the trial, then creating a new profile with a new user name and doing it all again. They track the subscription offers by your credit card number not your user name. There are some workarounds (we'll be getting to that), but it's pretty hard to get around this process.

Mastering the E-mail Process

There are a number of things to understand about e-mails sent within the confines of an online dating service. They include

- ▶ The service wants you to continue paying, and will often "strip out" your personal e-mail address from within an e-mail sent within their service. If you were able to send your outside e-mail address to non-paid members, the non-paid members wouldn't have to pay for a subscription to contact you. They could do it from their regular e-mail accounts.

- ▶ Some services allow an e-mail going to a paid member to have e-mail addresses within it, but strip out the same for non-paid members receiving the e-mail. You won't know which service does which at first, so it's a tricky business.

- ▶ Web addresses (URLs) are sometimes stripped out as well, for the same reasons as e-mail addresses. Sending someone to your personal Web page where you can have your e-mail address or phone number is the same as sending her your e-mail address.

- ▶ Most of the time you will not be able to tell who is a paid member and who is not. Some "adult" services indicate that a member is at a tier of service that indicates a paid membership, but you will need to check with the features and terms of a service to be sure.

The ability to e-mail is the value that online dating services offer, and they guard it carefully. Some services will even strip phone numbers out of e-mails. The automated systems look for any text with a ".com" or an "@" symbol, as well as any text string with "www." in it.

Those automated systems are smart, but they aren't as smart as you or me. This is a free country with free speech, and darn it, even if the e-mails aren't free, you should be able to say what you want. And you can. As long as you can outsmart a machine (and we're not talking HAL here).

Sneaking In E-mail Addresses and URLs

Your online dating service may strip out e-mail addresses and URLs, or they may not. You can't be sure. So here are some practical tips on sneaking your e-mail address or URL into the body of an online dating service e-mail that goes through their filtering system.

First, spell things out a little differently. For example, here's a way to say your e-mail address is johndoe@mail.com:

"Hi, in case you aren't on a paid membership right now, here is my e-mail address so we can get in touch. I heard that they sometimes leave out the e-mail addresses, so I'll give it to you as is, and also spell it out. Just put it together as a standard e-mail address without any spaces and replace the symbols, and we'll be in touch in no time. It's johndoe@mail.com, or if that's not showing up, it's john doe THEN THE AT SYMBOL followed by mail THEN THE DOT COM THING."

When you want to send someone to your Web page, you can use an equally effective method, such as

> *"Check out my site at www.johndoe.com or, in case that's not showing up, put this together as a Web address without spaces: w w w dot john doe dot com."*

People are smart. They'll get the idea and figure it out. When it comes to getting in touch with the right person, it's good to put the power of technology to work for you—your personal technology of stealth e-mails and URLs.

Setting Up Free E-mail Accounts

A big part of being safe online is not revealing too much personal information to people you don't know. For this reason, it's good to create an e-mail account only for online dating correspondence. Also, if you give out your everyday e-mail, you might end up with a lot of angry, unwanted e-mail in your inbox if you decide you're not interested in someone. It's a lot easier to get a free e-mail account and cancel it or simply stop using it if that happens.

Most mail services (including AOL) allow you to have more than one e-mail address. You could create a new account and dedicate an e-mail address for online dating. If that doesn't work for you, it's a good idea to get a free e-mail account from a service such as Hotmail.

It's easy to set up a free e-mail account—chances are you've already done this at least once. Free e-mail accounts are useful for signing up for contests or registering on Web sites when you know there's a good chance you'll end up getting spammed. There are a lot of sites where you can do this. The aforementioned MSN Hotmail, Yahoo!, Google, and Excite are just some of the sites that offer free e-mail accounts.

We'll use Hotmail as our example. Figure 3.4 shows Hotmail's registration screen.

We'll guide you through the basic steps:

1. Go to www.hotmail.com, and click on the Sign Up button. This will take you to the Registration page.

2. The first thing the Registration page asks for is your name. Here's where you want to start lying. This is the only time we're going to tell you to out-and-out lie in this book. The main purpose of having a free e-mail account is to hide your true identity. There are a lot of hackers who can find your personal information if you put it out there. So we're telling you not to put it out there. You can use a random name, like Sylvia Plath (though be aware of what this says about you). Or whatever user name you're planning to use, just break it up. If you were going to sign up as Sfdude60937, then make your first name SF and your last name Dude. Your "name" will be on all e-mails you send, so make sure it's something you can live with.

Figure 3.4
Hotmail is one of many sites that offer free e-mail with registration.

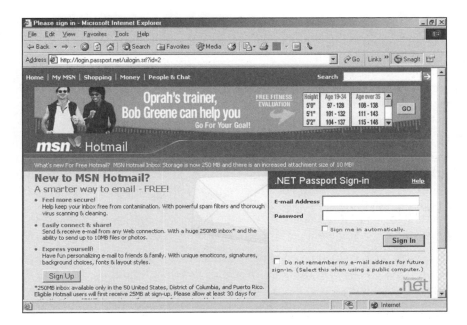

3. As you go through the Registration page, you can tell the truth or not about things that don't really matter, like country, time zone, gender—none of it is information that someone could use to track you down with any accuracy. Just don't get too specific about things like your date of birth, your address, or put in an alternate e-mail address.

4. You'll need to choose a user name for your e-mail address. Choose anything you like, again being aware of what it says about you, but don't use your real name. If you don't understand why we're saying this, go back to Step 2 above.

5. When you're done, it will ask you to enter your last name as an agreement to their terms and conditions of service. Make sure you remember to use your fictitious last name, or it won't work.

Okay, you're done! Wasn't that easy? Just like falling out of bed, as our mothers used to tell us. And now you have a safe e-mail account dedicated solely to your search for love. But here's a little tip for you—make sure you check your account. Not only does Hotmail delete your e-mail account if you don't log in for more than 90 days, but do you really want an e-mail from your potential spouse languishing in your Inbox without your realizing it? When you have multiple e-mail accounts, it's easy to forget to check them all. Don't neglect your Inbox of Love.

Creating a Web Site to Send People To

One nice option to tell people more about yourself prior to even communicating with them in e-mails is to create a Web site that tells them more about you. Your personal Web site can include information that the online dating service doesn't allow you to include, and you can even display pictures of art you've done or that you like, links to other sites, lists of music you like, or anything else you want. It's your own personal Web site—it's all about you and what you want to put out there.

We're not suggesting you use your personal Web site as a means to show pictures of body parts best left covered until later in the relationship, or to show pictures of your kids or exes (things we strictly forbid later in this book), or to talk about your favorite sexual positions, your ugly little fantasies, or your youthful suicide attempts. Just because you're off the site and not actually sending these things to someone directly, it doesn't mean you can throw caution to the wind. Remember some things are best shared later in a relationship—or sometimes not at all. You're trying to attract someone you want to date, not scare them away from dating for life.

Also with your Web site, you should remember the same things about safety that we mentioned before. Don't use your full name, though if you want to put up your real first name, that's okay. Don't show pictures of where you work or live. Don't include your home address or phone number. Don't include identifying information like your date of birth. You want to share who you are with your potential dates, but you don't want to share where you are or your bank account with these people. At least not yet.

Most Internet service providers allow you to create your own Web site at no charge, and this is a fun way to help people learn a bit more about you. These services offer free design tools and templates, so you don't need to know anything about creating a Web site. It's very easy, a lot like writing a profile on an online dating site. They give you fields to fill in with your interests, hobbies, etc. Go to your service provider, for example Earthlink or MSN, and look at what tools or services they offer their members. There should be an option to create a Web site or for free Webhosting. You can make your site as simple or as complicated as you like—they usually offer a quick Web page that you can have up and active within 10 minutes. There are other providers of free Web sites, such as Yahoo!, GeoCities, and Tripod, though you'll likely have ads on your site as that's how they can offer the sites for free.

Figure 3.5 shows an example of a very simple one-page personal Web site created specifically for online dating.

Summary

You've found a dating site you like, you've found a lot of people you'd like to contact, and you're ready to reach out. You have to decide at this point how you want to proceed. Consider your options, and make your start in whatever way seems best to you. We suggest you start with a wink to determine if someone's interested in you. It's quick, free, and very easy. And a mutual wink may be all the incentive you need to go ahead and open your wallet and join the service. Once you've joined, you can e-mail to your heart's content, using the methods we've described to

Figure 3.5
Creating a simple Web page to give potential dates a little more information is a great, creative idea.

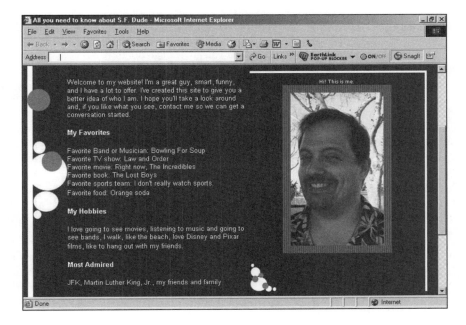

get the most out of each e-mail. Go ahead and make use of the trial period, but know that it will most likely lead to that same wallet opening. You may continue to wish you could get something for nothing. But the fact is, there's no free ride in life or online dating. Consider what finding the love of your life is really worth to you. Then take the leap and pay up.

GUY SAYS

I'd like to tell all the guys reading this that online dating is not fair—you probably won't get as many inquiries and e-mails from women as you send out.

It may be a generational thing, but my experience has been that if there were to be any contact, the guy needed to make it happen. Women do like to be courted, online and off. It will be up to you to send a wink, and it will also be your job to sign-up and e-mail first.

I used the trial period deals, and they did help a lot. If anything, it got me used to writing e-mails and learning how to take the lead and get the dialogue started. And it's hard. Sending out winks and not getting any back can be discouraging. Sending out an e-mail and not getting any reply, not even a wink back, can be ego-crushing.

One thing is for sure, if I didn't wink or e-mail the profiles I was really interested in, those women wouldn't have made contact first. When I took initiative and took a few chances, I did hear back from women I was interested in, and they were glad to hear from me.

The other thing that happened is that I went through a lot of what I think women experience: I got winks and e-mails from people I wasn't interested in. It was pretty frustrating because it seemed that the only attention I got without initiating it was from women who just were not matches in any way. They were nice, but mostly I felt they hadn't read my profile or checked what I was looking for.

That taught me to wink or e-mail profiles that were a really good match to my interests and where I fit what they were looking for. I am someone who replied to all inquiries and said thanks, but I don't think there's a good match when that was the case. When you get enough of those, it's a lot of work and truthfully, it's no fun sending out "no thanks" e-mails.

So guys, before you start sending a wink or e-mail to anything with a skirt, think about what you would do if you started getting the same from women who aren't good matches. Why send out a lure when you don't want fish for dinner?

—*Terry*

CHICK SAYS

I'm a little younger than Terry so maybe that's why I've had a slightly different experience. I'm a woman, and I wink online all the time. What the hell? What does it hurt?

While in daily life I'm a little more reserved, I see no reason not to take a chance online. You're not face to face with the person you're winking at. There's no danger of getting that up-and-down look, and then a "no thanks" in a slightly disdainful voice. There's no danger of the drink you bought him being returned. There's no awkward silence while he thinks of a good reason why he can't go out with you Friday night.

When you wink at someone online, the worst you can get is no response. It's the not knowing that's hard, but ultimately you can assume that he's just not interested. The best you can get is a wink back, showing he's curious enough to take the next step. The first time you get that mutual wink, your stomach will do a back flip. It's the same sort of flutter you get when you get a return smile from across a crowded room. Only in this case, it's the crowded Internet.

As women, we've likely had it ingrained in us that men should make the first move. It's the man who's supposed to walk through a room full of people to talk to you. It's the man who's supposed to pick up the phone. It's the man who should send the wink—because part of each of us is still living in the 50s.

Listen up chicks—it's the 21st century and the world has changed. You know it, I know it, even our mothers know it… deep down. You want the same pay as a man, you can do the same job as a man, you want to be an equal in decisions in your relationships… so what are you pussyfooting around about? Make that move, send that wink, pay for the service, and send out some e-mails. We don't need men to do anything for us that we can do for ourselves. So come out of the 50s, chicks. Join me here in century 21, and enjoy the freedom.

—*Alyssa*

Chapter 4
Subscribing and Taking Advantage of Free Trial Subscription Offers

*S*ince there are so many types of online dating services, you may wish to diversify and place yourself on as many as possible; the large sites like Match.com, the affinity sites, and even the lifestyle sites, all beckon: "Post your profile and find love." It's a good idea to try more than one service—you never know which one your true love is signed up with.

As you have learned, posting your profile is free on most services, but the ability to communicate through e-mails is a paid member benefit. With all those monthly fees, your love life can become an expensive proposition, even before your first date! It would be easy to spend between $50 and $100 per month if you belong to several services.

One of the best ways to find out which services work best for you is to

> ▶ Browse and search the large services first.
> ▶ Browse and search affinity and lifestyle sites next.
> ▶ Create profiles on the services you like.
> ▶ Send winks or icebreakers to people you're interested in.
> ▶ Take advantage of any free trial offers.
> ▶ Send e-mails to a good sampling of members on each service on which you have a free trial, then follow-up with an e-mail to anyone who winked back at you.

Although the free trial periods are seldom long enough to conduct any meaningful dialogue, they will teach you how much activity you get with any particular service. There are no rules of response. A lot of the activity you get will be based on the quality of your profile, the number of people on the service who may be interested in you, and your geographical location. Later in this book, you'll learn how to create a good profile that should get you the response you want. After that, it's about trying the service—without breaking the bank.

Understanding the Free Trial Period

There are no free lunches and, sorry, no free rides on the dating sites. The "free" trial offers are really paid subscriptions that essentially allow you to cancel your paid subscription within a certain period of time. Since most online dating services have a no-refund cancellation policy, it's worth trying. If you read the fine print at many online dating sites, there are services on which you can cancel your paid subscription, usually within 24 hours or as much as three days after signing-up. But usually once you've paid, they've got your money, and it's not coming back. You may as well make the most of it.

Figure 4.1 shows a typical trial offer/subscription signup form.

Figure 4.1
There may be a big box telling you about the free trial, but you're signing up for a paid subscription.

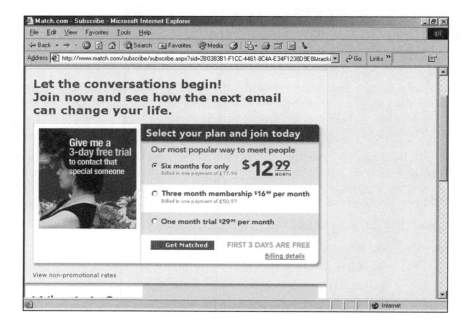

Here's how most free trial offers work:

- ▶ First you must become a member by creating a profile—even if it's not open for public viewing.
- ▶ Next, you must use the Special Offer button, not the regular subscription process, to take advantage of the free trial offer.
- ▶ You'll need a credit card or other form of payment, such as your checking account, because you'll be creating a paid subscription that you may cancel if you choose to within the specified period of the offer.

▶ Finally, you'll need to select the subscription offer (such as one month or three months) and agree to pay for it if you don't cancel by the time specified for the free trial offer.

▶ It will be up to you to keep track of when the free trial offer starts—and ends.

It's a good idea to read all the fine print associated with any subscription or free trial offer. Each service has unique terms and conditions about how you're billed and how to cancel a subscription (regardless of the refund policy). Some services, for example, require that a cancellation must be done in writing and sent to them via certified mail. Funny, they don't make you subscribe or pay them that way. Figure 4.2 shows a typical terms and conditions page, including fine print.

Figure 4.2
Be sure to read all of the terms and conditions any time you subscribe to an online dating service. Privacy, renewal, and cancellation policies are all worth checking out before you subscribe.

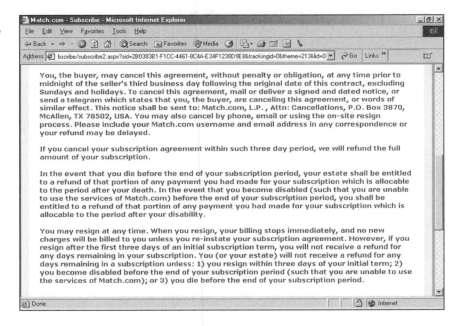

The most important thing you can do is to write down or calendar the time and day the trial offer ends. You'll need to notify the service prior to that time if you don't want to subscribe. The service may also bill your credit card as soon as the trial offer begins, and then refund the full amount if you cancel.

Using the Service after You Cancel the Trial Offer

Don't worry about your membership if you cancel your subscription before the end of the free trial offer. Your profile, winks, icebreakers, favorites, and other member profile data will all remain active. The only change is that you'll return to non-paid member status.

If you sent e-mails and you get e-mail responses after you cancel, you'll still be able to read them—but you won't be able to reply to them. The good news is that you can always subscribe to the service after all and begin replying and sending your own e-mails. It's worth the money if someone you really like has e-mailed you back.

Some services turn off your posted profile when you cancel. Some may ask you first if you wish to keep your profile active, even though you're canceling your paid membership. If the service deactivates your profile, making it active again is simply a matter of signing on to the service again, choosing to activate and post your profile again, and continuing to use the service as a non-paying member.

Circumventing the System

If you have gotten some good responses and made contact during the free trial offer, it may be tempting to cancel the subscription, wait a while, and then take advantage of the free trial offer again. Ah, if only it were that simple! Online dating services are aware of that strategy, and make it pretty hard for you to take advantage of a free trial offer twice—using the same profile and user name.

As you browse through member profiles, occasionally you'll find the same picture and profile under a different member name. Chances are this is a member who took advantage of the free trial offer, then wanted to do it again but discovered that it doesn't work more than once with the same profile and user name. They simply created a new member profile with a different member name, then used the same photo and profile information. At that point, they were able to use the free trial offer one more time.

This method of circumventing the system is getting harder and harder to do. Online services, such as Match.com, have some pretty strong measures in place to prevent it. They keep a record of your user name, and it's good for one free trial. They also track the free trial offer by the payment method, such as your credit card number. If you create a new profile and try the free offer under that different name but use the same credit card number, you'll be told to contact customer service. That means you've been caught.

They probably won't take your profile down, but they will explain their policy to you and try to get you to pay for a subscription.

Subscribing and Canceling

Subscribing is easy. Of course it is. The online dating services want you to subscribe. It's the whole purpose of their existence, to make you subscribe. So they make it as simple as possible. There is a link to subscribe on virtually every page, sometimes several links. Once you click on one of those links, it takes you straight to the subscription page.

If you're already signed in to the site, it takes two pages to subscribe:

1. Choose your subscription (one month, three months, six months).
2. Fill in your credit card information, your name and address (it's okay to put your real information on this page), then click the Subscribe Now button, or some version thereof.

On the page on which you entered your credit card information, you might have noticed a little statement, usually not very obvious, that says your subscription will be automatically renewed. This will usually happen at the end of your subscription, depending on what amount of time you chose. However, some sites will auto-renew 24 hours before the end of your subscription. Make sure you read the details carefully when you're signing up.

So if subscribing is that easy, surely canceling your subscription must be just as easy. Sadly, no, poor deluded dater. While it benefits them to make subscribing easy, it does them no good to have you leave their service. So you'll have to work a little to cancel. Figure 4.3 shows a typical cancellation page.

Figure 4.3
Online dating sites are nearly as good at guilt as your mom. They want to know why they weren't able to make you happy.

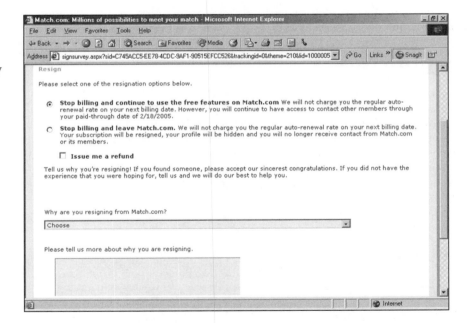

You can usually find the information on how to cancel your subscription under My Account or the equivalent on the site you're using. They'll guide you through the process, even though they'd rather not. It usually includes telling them why you're leaving and choosing whether you want to continue as a member or if you'd like to be removed from the site altogether.

CRAFTY TIP

Match has a tiny chink in its armor. When you subscribe, which automatically includes their free three-day trial, you sign up, but they won't bill your card until after the trial is over. Once you've subscribed, you can immediately go to Account Settings and click on Resignation. Once you've resigned from the service, no more than 30 seconds after subscribing, they'll tell you that your account won't be auto-renewed, but you're paid up for the next three days. So you still get your trial period, but you don't have to worry about remembering to cancel before they charge your card. Cool, eh?

You may be tempted, if you have a friend using the same online dating site as you use, to share a subscription. While seemingly a budget-saving move, it just makes you look cheap. Whoever uses his credit card and user name to buy the subscription is getting the better part of the deal, as no one will know he's splitting the cost. But if you're the one piggybacking on his membership, you'll end up having to explain to everyone you e-mail why you're not who the e-mail claims to be. And again, you can't explain that without looking cheap. And don't take a picture with both of you in it and try to share the subscription that way. It will only serve to make anyone you e-mail think that she'd be dating both of you. It's tacky. Don't do it.

Summary

The expense of subscribing makes it important to find one or two main services that work well for you. You can use free trial offers to test the effectiveness of an online dating service. After browsing and searching, you can use the free trial period to send out e-mails and see how many good responses you get. The trial period is a short one, and not a substitute for a long-term subscription. The services make it hard to use a free trial offer more than once, so if you're getting good results, the next step is to purchase a paid membership. Be sure to understand the privacy rules, the automatic renewal process, and the cancellation policy before clicking on the Subscribe button of any service.

GUY SAYS

It only took one e-mail from a woman who said, "I'm only on for the three-day trial so let's talk" to decide that I would never send that message to anyone. It's just tacky to tell someone that the only way you would get in touch with him is if it were free.

That doesn't mean I didn't use the free trial offers. I did, and they really helped me learn about how the e-mail service worked, and I even got a few nice e-mails. I actually subscribed because I was able to try the service first with the ability to cancel if I wasn't happy with the response I was getting.

I liked subscribing. It took all of the stress off; I could browse, and when I found someone, I was able to write a nice short e-mail. That let her know that I wasn't some person who gets on for free and winks away at every member. Paid membership seems to say, "I'm serious about this. I'm serious about you." That's a much better message to send.

It was hard to decide which subscription offer to purchase. They really make it hard to just buy one month. The one-month deal is expensive, and the six-month, by comparison, is a real bargain. I remember thinking to myself, "I sure hope I don't need to be on here six months!"

I chose the one-month subscription, even though it's not a good deal. More than anything, it made me feel that if there was someone out there, we'd find each other pretty quickly.

The wheels of online dating don't really work that way. It does take time, surely more than a month, for men to get enough responses and e-mails going for anything to happen. Maybe women get lots more activity and can pick and choose, which may make it faster, but by the time you wink, e-mail, wait for a response, and then establish some level of trust to be able to call or meet, the month has passed, and you're into a renewal period.

Looking back, it would have been better to get the six-month subscription first. If I had met my true love one day after subscribing, I think the price of the six-month subscription would have been well worth it.

—*Terry*

CHICK SAYS

I've ponied up some cash here and there. It's hard to make that commitment, especially if you're choosing the best and most cost-effective subscription—the six-month option. That's a lot of money to spend all at once—$60 or $70, or even more. You think, as Terry did, surely it won't take six months. I'll just take a month and see how it goes. Then your month is up, you're facing another $25-$30, and you wonder why you didn't go for one of the better deals. Sometimes love comes quickly, but there's no guarantee.

And while it may be true that women get more winks more quickly than men do, the quality of those winkers can be sketchy. It's usually the guys who are looking for sex, looking for love desperately, or who don't have much to say for themselves who contact you early on, just after posting your profile. The quality men, for some reason, take longer. Maybe it's that they have good jobs that keep them busy so they don't have as much time to search through profiles; maybe it's that they're dating around already and again don't have time. Or maybe it's just that the good ones know they're good so they're a little pickier, which makes their dating search pool shallower, and they're less likely to find you.

So you need to stick it out for a while. And going back to a previous tip—you need to make the first move. You need to search the sites during your paid subscription time and find those good guys. If you've only paid up for a month, make that month count. Take your usual shoe-shopping or movie-watching time and spend it searching for Mr. Right. You can give those things up for a month if it means at the end of that month you'll have someone who might admire those shoes and watch those movies with you.

—*Alyssa*

Part II

Presenting

Yourself Online

Chapter 5
Putting Your Best Face Forward

*B*y now you've probably visited a number of online dating sites and have done some window shopping, marveling at the eye candy (or lack of it). As you've seen, pictures are a huge part of the online dating experience. C'mon, admit it—you liked looking at the pictures, and you got excited about some people simply based on how they looked.

That's not shallow, is it?

Shallow or not, it's human nature. The one thing we can say about responding strongly to the way people look is that it's a very basic response and everyone does it. Anyone who has been in business or advertising will tell you that first impressions are critically important.

You only get one chance to make a good impression. Especially in the online dating world.

When you last did a search on a dating site, you probably scanned many pages of profiles. (Of course, you chose to only view ones with photos, right?) Now think of how long you spent on each one. Maybe on the first page, you actually looked for a few seconds at each one. They are usually pretty small pictures, so they do require a close look. Then, as you moved on to following pages, you probably just scanned each page looking for someone who caught your eye.

That means that you're probably spending less than one second with each photo.

Each of those casually glanced at photos represents a living, breathing, hopefully decent human being who is calling out to you, looking for your love and your attention. Behind that photo is years of love and heartbreak, hopes and dreams, longing and passion. Then it all comes down to being evaluated and judged in less than one second, based on less than 4KB of digital image data on some computer screen.

Ouch. Online dating is a tough town.

In the online dating world, others will judge you on how you look. You did it when you looked at their profiles. The people you want to meet will most likely judge you the same way. If your photo catches someone's eye, she'll click on your profile to learn more. If you don't have a photo, or the photo isn't very good, the chances of having your profile viewed goes way down. Most online dating sites say that profiles with photos get viewed about 10 times more often than profiles without. So what choice do you have? You have to post a photo because…

...It's All about How You Look

Read that heading again. It's all about how you look. Not about how good-looking you are. Those are two very different things.

When you post a photo of yourself online, you will have a "look," which can be any one of the following or a combination:

- ▶ Pleasant (I'm easy to be around.)
- ▶ Funny (I just love to find the humor in any situation.)
- ▶ Cute (Hey, I really am a cutie.)
- ▶ Serious (Life's too short for games. Date me.)
- ▶ Flirtatious (C'mon in, the water's fine.)
- ▶ Happy (Pretty well adjusted, actually.)
- ▶ Sad (C'mon and save me. I'm listening to Aimee Mann, and I'm ready.)
- ▶ Unhappy (What am I doing here?)
- ▶ Difficult (Do you really want to go there?)
- ▶ Sexy (Oh, baby! Are you in for a treat!)
- ▶ Desperate (I'm available right now. Call. I'll fly across the country.)

Unfortunately you can also look manic, goofy, disinterested, or out of date. Posting a picture is important to get your profile viewed. But which photo you choose to use is just as important, as it determines who looks at your profile and what impression they get of you.

In a perfect world, the photo you post should match the message in your profile. If your nature is funny, then your picture should reflect that carefree, have-fun-with-things attitude. If you're a serious person, then a somewhat more serious photo may be called for.

Your photo, more than anything, sends a message about you. It's not about how you look; it's about who you are.

The Picture Is the Thing

Your picture is what will get you noticed, send a message about what you're like, and hopefully attract the right type of person to you. It's that last part, attracting the right type of person, that is really worth considering.

As you will learn, there are profile spammers. These are people who send winks, icebreakers, or e-mails to just about anyone who is on the service. They play the numbers game, much like the guy in a bar who thinks that if he hits on every woman, statistically he will score with one of them eventually. You will learn later in the book how to do some spamming of your own, and that will help you spot other profile spammers. Discounting those types of contacts—people who don't care about how you look or who you are, just as long as you're breathing—how do you attract the right type of inquiry?

Common sense when choosing or taking a picture of yourself will go a long way toward attracting the right person. For example, you may be a very sexual person. You may be pretty hot, with a great body and model looks. If you use a photo that shows that side of you, who will you get a response from? People who are going to judge you almost entirely on how you look? People who are just looking to get laid?

The way we think of ourselves, and the way we have come to posture ourselves in photographs may not be in harmony with our personalities or our experiences. You can be a very sexy person who takes a smokin' photo, but if you're looking for a serious relationship based on mutual interests, and sex is the last thing on your mind right now, that is the message you need to send.

The One-Second Evaluation

So, we've told you that your photo will most likely have about one second to catch the eyes of most people on the service you use. So take a good look at the pictures you're trying to choose from for your profile, and conduct your own one-second test.

Take your pictures (including those you don't even plan to use) and, if possible, have a friend with you. Next, take some little pieces of paper and write basic categories on the pieces such as happy, sad, funny, serious, romantic, or any other looks you think will attract the type of person you want to date.

Now put the pieces of paper on a table, take a handful of your photos, look at each one for a second, then throw it into one of the piles. You can do this, or you can have your friend do this. Once you're finished, whoever did the throwing sits back, and the other person looks at each pile and confirms the impression. You or your friend take the pictures from the happy pile, and make sure that the pictures are indeed happy pictures of you.

The most important part of this exercise is to sort the pictures quickly. You want to go with that "one-second judgment" that is so much a part of making a first impression. This will help you sort out pictures by the message they send rather than how much you like the particular photo. Figure 5.1 shows the process of sorting through photos with a friend, looking for one that sends the right message.

The one-second exercise will help you not only with existing photographs, but also with the photos you'll take to use for your online profile. Start thinking of your pictures as messages you're sending to the person you're looking for. You can attract the right person if you send the right message.

Judge Yourself the Way You Judge Others

It's hard to be objective, or honestly critical, about yourself. We all have an image of ourselves we've honed over years of having good and bad pictures taken. That self-image may not be the best image for attracting someone. For example, your favorite pictures of yourself may be at the beach when you're looking fantastic in a bathing suit. Even though those photos may be the best pictures of you, a picture of you in a bathing suit may send the wrong message to potential daters.

Figure 5.1
Get together with a friend and conduct a "one-second evaluation" of your photos, sorting them out by the messages they send. You'll be surprised at the outcome.

In selecting photos to use with your profile, you need to judge yourself the way you judge the pictures of other people. Think about what you would think if you ran across your photo online. What reaction would you have?

Then think about your reaction to the photos of people you liked when you were browsing an online dating site. Did you like the photos of people who were happy? The sexy ones? The sad and deep types?

The pictures you respond to online, the people you find attractive, can be really helpful in deciding which picture or what type of picture you want to use in your profile. The people you like, the people you want to attract to your profile, are sending messages to you that you like. Maybe you should be sending a similar message to them with your photo.

Kindred spirits will find each other. You're sending out vibes. There's a soul mate for everyone. No matter how you word it, the way it really works is this: You want to connect with someone you like, and you have that one second to do it, so you need to get it right.

Photos That Work Best

Online dating services have some pretty good empirical data about what type of photos work best. Making their customers satisfied and getting results is their business. Nearly all online dating services recommend certain types of photos that work best, and they have guidelines for what should, and shouldn't, be in a profile photo.

A Headshot Is a Must-Have

Even if you don't send them a headshot, chances are very likely that the online dating service will crop any photo you submit into a headshot.

It's human nature to want to see someone's face. Even the people looking just for sex want to see what type of person they're about to hit on, so they look at headshots. Don't you want to look into someone's eyes before you invest yourself? Your face, your eyes, and your expression all speak volumes about you. For this reason, headshots are the primary photos used for profiles. Figure 5.2 shows a good headshot.

Figure 5.2
A good headshot that sends the right emotional message works wonders in attracting the right responses.

With any type of photo, there are good headshots, and there are ones that don't work as well. Your first instinct may be to hurry off to a portrait studio and have a formal portrait taken. That may be okay, but it's really not the type of headshot you want.

Studio portraits are just that: Studio portraits taken by a professional photographer. The lighting may be great, and the photo of excellent quality, but studio portraits are so formal and stuffy they often make you look like someone you're not. You're better off having a friend who loves you take the picture as they make you smile with dirty jokes. Or find a shot from that beach party when the weather was just perfect and that cute redhead had just winked at you. People like more casual, candid photos. You look like yourself. A good snapshot of your face that projects the right message, you looking like the best version of yourself, is probably a better choice.

If you do go to a photo studio, you can ask for a casual, candid portrait using a natural background (such as a nature scene). It will work better than a portrait background, such as the gray or blue seamless backdrops photographers often use. Make sure that the photographer knows that you want a natural-looking photo without the "studio" feel.

CROSS REFERENCE
Chapter 6, "Taking Your Picture and Getting It into Digital Formats," explores how to take your own pictures.

Chapter 6 will teach you how to take a decent photograph of yourself, or help others take some pictures of you, and you'll probably get the best results using the advice given in that chapter. Professional photographs aren't required for success in online dating. You can take your own pictures and get great results. Using the "message you're sending" strategy discussed above, you'll be able to take lots of pictures of yourself, sort them by the messages they send, and find one that works for you.

ELEMENTS OF A GOOD HEADSHOT
Headshots are classic portraits. They show you from the shoulders up, and your head fills most of the frame of the photo. Avoid facing directly into the camera. Instead, look slightly off to the side, but keep eye contact with the camera. Use natural light (meaning room lighting). Avoid pictures taken in bright sunlight, and, if at all possible, do not use the flash on the camera. Direct sunlight and flash photos create harsh shadows that can be unflattering.

Body Shots Make a Good Second Picture

In addition to a great headshot, it is good to have a tasteful body shot. No, not the body shots you do at the bar when they turn you upside down and fill some crevice or surface with some gooey liqueur, then someone you've never met comes over and licks it all up, leaving an even gooey-er mess behind. Oops, sorry, we're having some bad bar flashbacks... Why do you think we started online dating?

In many ways, the body shot is just as important as the headshot. People will be taking a close look at it to see if your description of yourself (as in "slender," for example) matches up with your body shot (as in maybe a few extra pounds). As with everything in online dating, it may be temping to alter time, space, and physics and put up a body shot of you from some bygone era and a galaxy far far away, but don't mess with the space/time continuum. That never ends well. Put up a nice photo of yourself taken within the last few months, saddlebags and all. There's just more of you to love. Figure 5.3 shows a good body shot.

Later in this chapter, we'll cover things you should not include in your photo, and be sure to follow those suggestions. The body shot will tell a lot about you—how you take care of yourself, how you dress, the setting you put yourself in. It shows your comfort level and how you feel about yourself. For this reason, if you know you fall into the "a few extra pounds" category, don't shy away from the body shot. Sure, you may not look the way you wish you did. But be bold, be comfortable in your skin, and show yourself as flatteringly as possible. If you take a good body shot, a lot of people will accept you no matter what your body type. And though some people will eliminate you based on those pounds, isn't it better to know now rather than later?

The most important thing is to be honest. Choose a picture that is attractive and flattering to you, but not one that doesn't look like you do in real life. If you should arrange a meeting, nothing stops a prospective date cold like a surprise. If you look dramatically different than your body shot, you'll surprise your date, and you'll have some explaining to do. This will speak to your

Figure 5.3
The headshot will get you noticed, but you'll be judged—both online and if you ever meet—by your body shot. Make sure it is recent and a good representation of how you actually look.

honesty and also to your self-image. If you don't feel okay with yourself, how will your date feel about you?

ELEMENTS OF A GOOD BODY SHOT

Body shots should include you and only you. Stand with your body slightly angled, away from the camera, so you're not facing it directly. Keep eye contact with the camera, and smile or have a pleasant look. Wear comfortable, everyday clothes, and don't be too revealing in your attire. The picture can be a snapshot, such as one taken on vacation, in the backyard, or a park, but indoor pictures can work equally well if the background doesn't show where you live or work. Stand naturally, and put your hands on your hips if possible.

Having a nice headshot and a good body shot will help you get lots of responses, and if you choose the right pictures, the responses will be from the types of people you want to hear from.

You can include more than one picture on most online dating services. Some allow up to 10 pictures to be uploaded. The two basic shots are virtually required, but you may want to show different aspects of yourself by putting more photos online. If you follow the basic rules discussed so far (the messages you send, current photos, and not revealing too much about your location or identity), click and upload away.

Image Editing Can Help Your Pictures

Just about everyone today knows about image editing programs, such as Photoshop. It's no secret that you can take a picture and doctor it to make yourself look better—or even like someone you're not. As great as the temptation to improve on Mother Nature may be, avoid it.

But image editing programs *can* help your pictures. They can correct brightness and contrast, remove red eye, allow you to crop your photo, and even remove things like signs that can give a clue to your name or location. But stop there. Anything else is cheating.

Figure 5.4 shows a photo before and after editing. Editing allows you to crop the photo to a tighter headshot, get rid of the cars in the background for a more pleasant feel, and lighten a dark photo.

As with the advice for taking body shots, showing yourself realistically is very important. If you start removing wrinkles, changing your hairline, slimming down your waist, or one of a hundred other tricks you can use to make yourself look better, you risk painting an unrealistic portrait of yourself—a portrait of someone who isn't proud of how they look, a portrait of someone who'd rather lie than take a risk with the truth. That's not a pretty picture.

CROSS REFERENCE
Chapter 7, "How to Photo Edit a Picture," explores editing your pictures.

Figure 5.4
An image editing program, such as Photoshop Elements, will help you improve the quality of your photos and remove unwanted elements that may give away your identity.

Chapter 7 will show you how to use image editing programs to correct the quality of a photo and remove unwanted information. Use one of these programs to improve the quality of your photos and control their content, but don't alter your appearance in any significant manner.

Photos to Avoid

If you're tempted to use existing photographs, or if you plan on taking some new pictures, you'll want to pay close attention to the following rules.

There are strict "no-nos" for pictures you use in online dating services. The best picture of you ever taken may include one of these rules, and you need to put it back in the photo frame. The rules cover items that may give away your location or identity, but mostly these are pictures that can be a turn-off or send the wrong message. Let's take a look at photos to avoid.

Pictures of You and Your Ex

Big no-no number one is never use a photo of you and your ex (as in ex-spouse or ex-significant other).

First, it's not fair to feature someone in an online dating site without her knowledge and when the profile isn't about her. Next, it's tacky. A prospective date may be saying to herself, "Hey, that could be me if he dumps me!" Finally, it's not a photo of you as you are today. You're no longer in that relationship, and you're single now (we hope).

Photos with your ex also send a message about what type of person you've been attracted to in the past. So if that tall, sexy person checks you out, and they see you with that short dumpy ex of yours, he may think, "Hey, I'm not what she's looking for." Or he may even think, we're sorry to tell you, "If that's the best she could do, there must be something wrong with her." That would be, well, too bad for all of you.

Pictures of You and Your Kids

Beyond not being a picture of just you, it's always a little dangerous to put pictures of your children on a public site. Too much information. Too risky for your identity and theirs. You don't know who might be trolling a dating site, looking for just such an opportunity. When you combine a bad person with the name of your town and your kids' picture, you're creating a recipe for disaster. In just one scenario, the bad person could stop by your kids' schoolyard (how many schools are there for kids their age in your town?), spot them, and then follow them home to learn where you live. We don't want to scare you, but you don't want to end up on the evening news.

Your kids are the center of your universe. Keep them there, and don't put them online for everyone to see. And actually, we do want to scare you—a little. It's for your own good.

Group Pictures

Okay, which one are you? The one in the back? The one in the disco outfit? The one holding TWO cocktails?

There is no better way to confuse someone than with a picture of you with a group of friends. It's hard, if not impossible, to figure out who you are in the group, and you also end up putting pictures of people online who shouldn't be there. And think of this:

What if they think your friends are hotter than you are?

Ouch.

Most group shots tend to be from parties or at nightspots. Everyone is laughing and has a drink in hand. You may think these shots make you look fun. But consider this—do you want all potential daters to think you're a party animal? Do you want them to think all you do is go out drinking? Do you want them to think you're still a frat boy/party girl, like you were in college? Do you want them to think you'd rather be hanging out with your friends than be with your partner? Are there people of the opposite sex in these pictures? Do you want your potential date to wonder how many of the people in the photo you've slept with and may still be sleeping with? We're not saying you can't show yourself having fun. But there are better ways to do it.

Pictures out of Magazines

You may not think anyone would do this, but people do flat-out lie, taking pictures from magazines of attractive people and using them for their profile photos. Now, before you start to think to yourself, "Hmm, I never thought of that, it's not a bad idea really... "

Aside from flat-out lying, this is also illegal. If you aren't proud of yourself, don't like the way you look, or are afraid to put your picture online and so you resort to this level to get responses, you may want to reconsider being online or attempting to meet someone. You're not ready. You've got some problems you may want to work out first. Hold on, I think we have a number of a therapist here somewhere.

Pictures That Aren't of You

Some people choose to put pictures and graphics in their profile that are not pictures of themselves at all. They may put up a picture of a place they love (such as the beach), a painting they did, a snapshot of their pets, or some image that has a special meaning.

Such pictures can fill the additional picture spots in your profile, but they should never take the place of the headshot and body shot. As a primary picture, such images are a no-no. Are you suggesting we date your dog? If you are, there's probably an affinity site for that somewhere you should be using instead.

Old Pictures of Yourself

Not to put too fine of a point on it, but never, never, not even if you're terribly lonely and will do anything for a date, *never* should you post an old picture of yourself from when you were much younger. You don't look like that anymore, and you never will again. It's not fair to your prospective date, and it's not fair to you.

The farthest back you should go in using an older picture is one year. And if your weight, hairstyle, or general appearance has changed since then, even that old is not acceptable.

An old picture may be how you think of yourself. It may be from a better time, a better hair era, a greater firmness, but it's just not fair. It's not telling the truth. Take a new picture. That's the person you are, and that's the picture everyone wants to see. You'll get responses with a new picture, we promise. You'll feel good about yourself when you do, and you'll feel less nervous meeting that person if they've seen the real you.

Summary

The pictures you choose to show people online say as much about you as your profile text. You should always use current photographs and include a nice headshot and a body shot. Avoid photos that aren't just of you, and respect the privacy of others by not featuring them in your photos. Judge your own photo the way you judge photos of people you're looking at online. Be sure your photo is sending the message that will resonate with the type of person you hope will respond to your profile.

GUY SAYS

There's nothing worse than finding a woman who looks great in her picture, and then finding out when you meet her that she doesn't look anything like the photo. That's bad news.

After reading the profile, exchanging lots of e-mails and then phone calls, you think you know something about the person. Then you meet, and you don't know if anything she's been telling you is true. Maybe it's all like her photo—it really sets things back big time.

Women think guys only go for profiles with hot chicks. Some guys may be like that, and sure those photos get attention, but I always responded best to photos of nice people. Nice, friendly, pleasant, and also serious ones. Those are the qualities most of us look for, and those photos always got my attention. The last thing I wanted was to find someone who only cared about her looks.

When I chose photos of myself, I looked for ones that fit what everyone said about me—nice, warm smile, beautiful eyes, mister artiste. In my headshot, I actually used a bit of a profile shot, since it did the best job of showing my smile and my sparkling eyes. To be fair, I added an extra headshot of me front-on. It was good too, and it proved that, yes, I was a real cutie.

The body shot was a tough call. After my breakup I gained some weight. Not bad, but I didn't look like my pictures from even six months ago, so I took some new ones. It was hard to upload them, since I was starting to reduce my weight, but I figured if I met someone, it was better for them to see me at my worst and pleasantly surprise them.

One of the things that I liked about my pictures was that they really showed what I was like. I'm easy going, gentle, and an artist. I was able to find pictures that showed me that way. And it worked. I met my girlfriend using those photos, and she is a delicate flower type, and very much the artist. We were drawn to each other. Her photo was very dramatic, very deep, with great eye contact. I am like that a lot, too. It was different than most headshots, but it told me that she was a lot more like me than other people on the service, so it worked for both of us.

—*Terry*

CHICK SAYS

As I've tiptoed through the various dating sites, there's one thing I've discovered that strikes me more than anything else—a great big genuine fabulous smile. There is no bigger draw for me, no picture that makes my toes curl more than one of a man whose happiness is bursting through. It doesn't matter what he looks like—if he's happy, the picture makes me smile back. And anything you can do to make a browser pause and smile at your photo will give you an advantage. Remember that one-second rule we were talking about? Catch a woman's attention with a great smile, and she'll take the time to see what else you have to offer.

When I was first posting my profile, I had been broken up from my ex for a little while but was still hesitant about the idea of dating. I just wasn't sure if I wanted to be back out there, but I was curious to see who else was out there with me. So I posted a profile with no picture. I got a grand total of zero responses. I think when I returned to my profile a couple of months later, I'd been browsed about 10 times. This is not a good result.

I came back to the idea of online dating after a while and decided maybe I should update my profile and maybe be so bold as to post a pic. I *still* wasn't absolutely sure I wanted to be out there (it was a pretty bad break-up), but I wanted a better idea of how this online dating thing really worked. So I updated my very cautious profile to make it a little more upbeat and posted a sort of contemplative photo of myself. I got browsed more often. And I even got a few winks. I could see the appeal of this online dating thing, I supposed.

A couple of months later, again, I came back to my online dating profile. There had been a clear shift in my attitude. The skies had cleared, the wind had changed, and suddenly the idea of dating again brought a big ol' genuine smile to *my* face. So what could I do? I posted a new pic to my profile—showing that big ol' I'm-ready-to-start-kissing-some-boys-again smile. And what do you know? I got a lot of responses. A lot of new boys. And I was ready for them.

—*Alyssa*

Chapter 6
Taking Pictures of Yourself for Your Online Profile

*I*f you want to be successful at online dating, adding a really great picture of yourself to your profile is essential. Nothing will get you more responses or say more in the first few critical seconds when someone views your profile than a good photograph.

The term "subjective" best describes a profile photograph. A photo that may look good to you may not be attractive to the magic person you're hoping to meet. Chapter 5, "Put Your Best Face Forward," detailed why it's important to have a good, honest headshot and body shot, and this chapter will take you through the process of taking those photos. With some helpful advice and a bit of patience, you'll be able to take pictures of yourself that capture your personality, make you look attractive, and will send the right message to prospective sweethearts.

You can use either a conventional film camera or a digital camera. Digital cameras have a big advantage here. They create an image that can be uploaded instantly to the online service. And you can see the results of the picture-taking almost instantly, as well as take as many pictures as you need until you get a few winners. Film cameras require a trip to the store. And the cost of film and processing is pretty expensive, so you're less likely to take a lot of shots. The good news is that if you do use film, you can get a disc of the pictures in digital format, which will allow you to upload them easily.

For now, let's look at the basic steps in taking a picture of yourself using a digital camera.

Starting with a Digital Camera

Profile photos are not fine art—you can use any current digital camera, even a low-end model. The picture that you'll upload to the online service will be very small, and you don't need a top-of-the-line model to get good results.

If you have (or have access to) a digital camera with a memory storage card, here are a few things you should look to see if it has:

> ▶ Built-in flash
> ▶ Tripod socket

▶ Self-timer

▶ LCD screen to view the pictures

▶ Exposure settings or manual settings

Not all cameras will have all of the above features, but most digital cameras over $100 being sold today do have most of them. The following sections outline what you should know about each feature.

Controlling the Built-In Flash

You'll learn that it may be best to avoid the use of a flash, but it's good if your camera has one—especially when you're taking pictures outside. Built-in flashes are notorious for creating artificial, harshly lit portraits. The flash washes out features, removes all shadow details, creates harsh shadows in the background, and allows little control over the lighting of your pictures. Flashes also produce the infamous "red eye," where the flash actually illuminates the back of your eye. With your pupils wide open in dim light, they can't close quickly enough when the flash is fired, and you end up looking like a deer or cat in the headlights of a car at night.

If your camera has settings to force the flash to fire, or not fire, you're in good shape. You'll want to familiarize yourself with the settings on your camera that allow you to control how the flash is used while taking pictures. Specifically, you'll want to learn how to turn the flash off. You can take some simple steps to avoid flash pictures on cameras that don't allow control over the flash. One simple technique is to put black electrical tape over the flash as shown in Figure 6.1. It will fire, but the tape will block the light.

Figure 6.1
If your digital camera doesn't allow you to turn off the flash, you can simply use black electrical tape to block the (visually) harmful rays of the flash.

Finding the Tripod Socket

You may find that the best person to take your picture is you. If you're shy or don't have someone to take pictures of you, you can use the self-timer on your digital camera to take your own pictures. One important tool for this technique is some form of tripod.

You can use a table or a stand of some sort to place the camera on if you don't have a tripod, but they don't offer the same controls as a tripod when it comes to correctly positioning the camera for a good picture. A simple, small tripod can be purchased for as little as $12 at a store such as Wal-Mart. It will allow you to position the camera at the best distance from you and at the right height. It will also keep the camera steady at the low light you'll be taking pictures with, since you probably won't be using the flash. If you choose to use a tripod, turn your camera upside down and make sure that it has a tripod socket, as shown in Figure 6.2.

Figure 6.2
To find out if your camera has a tripod socket, turn it over and look on its bottom for a round threaded hole. This is where the tripod will attach to your camera.

Using a Self-Timer

Most digital cameras have a self-timer. When you turn the self-timer on and press the shutter release, you'll have a short period of time (usually 10 seconds) to run in front of the camera before it takes your picture. Most cameras have an audio signal that will beep slowly until the last two seconds when the beeping will speed up to let you know the picture is about to be taken.

Depending on your camera, finding the self-timer controls may be easy or hard. Some cameras have a dedicated self-timer button. Some force you to scroll through a series of menus to find it. Since each camera is different, be sure to search for this feature and to learn how to use it. Try it a few times while holding the camera in your hand. Get used to the sound, and look at the front of the camera to see if there is a visual indicator in addition to the audio indicator. It will work the same way—blinking slowly for the first few seconds, then more rapidly just before the picture is taken.

Some cameras will have two time settings for the timer, such as one setting for 5 seconds, and one for 10 seconds. Be sure to learn how to choose either timer, and get comfortable with the audible and visual indicators.

Figure 6.3 shows the self-timer symbol in the window of a digital camera. The final thing you'll need to learn is if the self-timer function stays on until you turn it off—or if it needs to be set each time you wish to take a picture with it.

Figure 6.3
When you press the shutter release while using the self-timer, a symbol will usually appear as an icon in the display window of a digital camera.

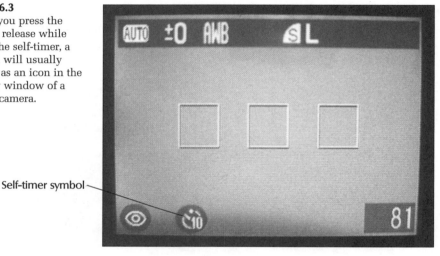

Self-timer symbol

Previewing Pictures on the LCD Display

One of the nicest features of today's digital cameras is their LCD displays. These admittedly small displays allow you to compose your pictures—and to see the results as soon as you take the picture.

As nice as the LCD displays are, they are so small and limited in how much detail or quality you can see in a picture that you should consider them a "thumbnail" of your picture. It may look good on the LCD screen, but not so great when you view the picture on your PC or when you make a print.

It's a good idea to get used to how well your LCD display does at previewing the pictures you take. Some LCD displays allow you to zoom in on the detail of the picture so that you can check focus and details. If your camera has this feature, be sure to learn how to perform this function prior to taking your pictures. As with all things regarding your camera, learn all the basics now—not during the photo session. You'll want to spend your time taking a great picture, not messing with your camera.

Making Adjustments to Exposure and Other Settings

Some digital cameras will allow you to adjust all settings manually. Other, simpler cameras, will force you to use their automatic settings. Whenever possible, it's best to be able to manually control the camera. Check your manual, or the menus of your camera, to learn if you can control the following settings:

▶ Flash on/Flash off

▶ Exposure

▶ Shutter speed

▶ White balance

▶ Compression level

Such controls may sound complex and intimidating, but they are very simple functions that will help you take a good picture.

For example, being able to turn the flash on or off will allow you to decide if the flash is helping your picture or hurting it. When you choose to turn the flash off, manually controlling the exposure will help you get the right exposure using your own lights. When you use your own lights, such as table lamps, you may find that you have the exposure setting set to let in as much light as possible, but the picture is still dark. Changing the shutter speed will keep the shutter open longer, letting in more light (but you'll have to stay pretty still). Using incandescent bulbs from table lamps may require you to change the white balance to avoid a yellow or orange cast in the color of your picture.

Finally, to get the best quality at any time or to help you fit a lot of pictures onto your memory card, you'll want to learn to change the compression levels on your camera. Compression allows you to store more pictures on your memory card, but it does this by compressing the picture, which results in a lower-quality picture. In your portrait shoot, you'll want to use the best quality setting, which uses the least amount of compression.

Figure 6.4 shows the way most digital camera menus look for these settings. When you press the Menu button on your digital camera, you'll most likely see settings for all of the above, and you can change the settings as desired. It's a good idea to experiment with and test these settings before taking your pictures. If you're not comfortable doing this, or the results are not too good, you can always revert back to the automatic settings that your camera offers.

Once you have learned to control your camera, it's a good idea to practice taking pictures using a variety of the settings. Take a few self-timer shots. Try turning off the flash and using the manual settings. Learn how to get quality results where the picture is under *your* control—not the camera's.

You can take pictures of yourself or of a friend. After you take your test shots, be sure to preview them on your PC or by making prints—not on the LCD display of your camera.

Figure 6.4
The Menu button on your digital camera allows you to reach all the camera settings, including those for exposure and compression.

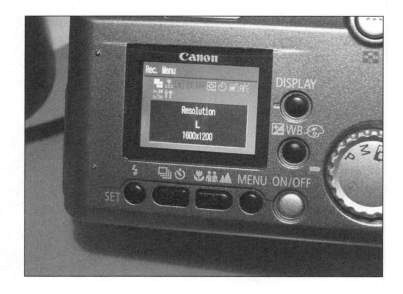

Getting Ready to Take Your Picture

Once you have gained control of your camera, and you have joined the ranks of the Richard Avedons and the Ansel Adamses as per your technical abilities, you're ready to tackle a much harder task: taking your picture.

The reason to get all of the mechanical issues of picture-taking under your belt is to allow you to focus on your picture, not on the camera settings. As you will learn, a good picture is not just the pose you strike, it's the lighting used for the photograph, the detail of the image, and the overall composition, all working together to make you look, well, like you!

Most people have had lots of bad photos taken of them. If you're like most, you've had pictures taken in which the flash fired and you looked horrible, or the flash didn't fire and you were just a shadow against a perfectly lit background of the Grand Canyon. Your head may have been cropped off, or you were just some little speck against a huge wall.

There are a million mistakes that can happen when pictures are taken. If you follow some very simple procedures and rules for taking your photo, you'll get that million-in-one picture you need to land that special someone.

Lighting the Shot

Of all the things you can do to help your picture, some simple lighting rules will get you the best results. Most pictures are poorly lit. If you've ever had your picture taken professionally, you have noticed that professional photographers make huge investments in lighting equipment. They have light stands, umbrellas that reflect the light, strobes, and they spend a good amount of time setting up the lighting of any shot. They know what they're doing, so learn from them.

It's rare that a pro will ever point a camera with a flash at you and click away. A flash mounted on a camera will only do one thing: blast you head-on with light. It will properly expose the picture, and you'll see every little pore or wrinkle and all of the blemishes that you might prefer to hide. A flash portrait is ruthless—to the point of being unflattering to any person. Figure 6.5 shows the same person's picture taken with a flash—and with natural lighting. You can see how much nicer a portrait looks when you avoid using a flash.

Figure 6.5
The portrait on the left was taken using a camera-mounted flash. The portrait on the right was taken using natural light without a flash.

In the real world, we never look like we do in a flash picture. We don't have red eyes. Natural light creates gentle shadows that help give our face shape and three dimensions. In real life, we look much gentler than in a flash picture, so the challenge is to take a picture without a flash that helps us look like we really do in most situations. This is a book about telling the truth, and flash portraits lie.

To capture the "real" you, turn off the flash, and use the same simple lighting techniques pros use to take great portraits of people. Here's how it's done:

1. Position yourself about 4-6 feet from any background, such as a wall, making sure you have enough room in front of you for the camera and some lights.

2. For a headshot, sitting in a chair is best, so find a simple, low-back chair. A kitchen chair works great for this purpose.

3. Position your camera on a tripod or a small table in front of you. The camera should be about 3 feet away from you and at roughly the same level as your head. This is easy to do when you use a tripod. If you're placing the camera on a table, you can use a box or even phone books to achieve the correct height.

4. Select two lamps that use incandescent bulbs (regular light bulbs—not fluorescents). Standing lamps work best, but table lamps will also work fine though you may have to have a couple of small tables to elevate them to the correct height. Use a 40 watt bulb in one lamp (your "fill" lamp) and a 100 watt bulb in the other lamp (the main lamp). Remove any lampshades and leave the bulbs uncovered.

5. Position each lamp about 2-3 feet in front of you, each off to your side (think of them as being at 45 degrees from you on each side). If both the bulbs are the same brightness, move one lamp a bit further away than the other. Each bulb should be about the same height as your face or slightly higher. If the bulbs are too high, they will create shadows under your eyes. The goal is to have the 100 watt lamp light your face, and have the 40 watt lamp "fill-in" any shadows. You can keep moving the fill lamp toward you and closer to the camera to soften any shadows.

6. Make adjustments. The only way to effectively determine the lighting is to take a test shot of yourself to see if the lighting is flattering, or if there are any unpleasant or unnatural shadows. Move the lights to create a natural lighting effect. Keep trying. Change the position and the height of the lamps as needed. Sometimes adjusting the height of the lamps can create a more pleasing effect.

7. If the pictures you're taking using your lights result in a picture that's too yellow, orange, or blue, be sure that your camera is set to "Auto White Balance." If the pictures still result in artificial color, try the different white balance settings or even move to a different background since the camera may be making color adjustments for walls or light reflected off of other objects.

8. If your camera has a zoom lens, don't use the "wide" setting since it may distort your face a bit. It's better to use a mid-range zoom setting.

Figure 6.6 shows a typical "makeshift" home lighting setup. It may not be as glamorous looking as the lights in photo studios, but you'll get a similar effect.

Figure 6.6
Your makeshift photo studio will allow you to take a natural-looking portrait right in your own home. Be sure to keep moving the lights until you get them right.

You could also take a photo using natural light. If the ambient lighting in your home is pleasing, you can certainly try it first and see the results. Natural lighting or lighting in a home tends to come from overhead, and overhead lighting tends to create shadows under your eyes, your nose, and under your lips. Although you may not notice that so much in everyday life, those shadows do seem exaggerated in a portrait. Shadows tend to add age to any person—it shows the effect of gravity over time on your face. The simple lighting technique described above puts the lights at the same level as your face to eliminate those shadows.

Depending on the time of day and the windows in your home, you can get nice results using natural sunlight. You could position yourself so you're lit from late afternoon light coming in through a large picture window. The soft, diffused lighting makes for a great effect—but it's not something that you can count on. You may work during the day or not have a window that lets in enough light.

Your headshot will include a bit of the background. Don't worry too much about it. It does not need to be well lit, and it will actually look better if it's a bit out of focus. You'll want to make sure the background is not too "busy." Avoid complicated backgrounds, such as bookcases or a wall with paintings or frames. Remember that the picture is of you—not the background.

Figure 6.7 shows a classic lighting diagram from overhead. If you can create a similar placement of yourself, background, lights, and camera, you're well on your way to a great headshot.

Figure 6.7
Try to replicate the placement of yourself, lights, camera, and background while setting up your portrait shot at home. Feel free to move the lights to get the most flattering effect.

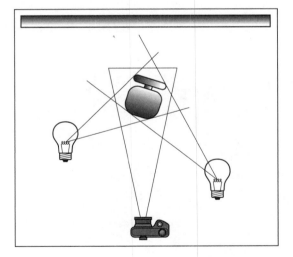

Deciding What to Wear in Your Picture

Once you have your lighting set up and you have taken a few test shots that look attractive, you should turn off the lights and begin to focus on how you wish to dress in the headshot. Although the picture is primarily of your face, you'll see a bit of your shoulders and chest, so what you wear is important.

For men, it's best to wear a casual, collared shirt. A polo shirt or casual dress shirt will do perfectly. You should avoid a dress shirt with a tie, and avoid T-shirts, tank tops, or other shirts without a collar. Leave the top button undone, and avoid a solid black or solid white shirt. Textures and small prints add detail and warmth. Choose a color that is flattering to your skin tone. Don't be afraid to try a few different shirts to find which one looks best in a photo. Ask a female friend for advice if you need help.

Women have a bit more of a challenge. The classic head shot will show the top portion of your chest, not the breasts, but the photo will hint at what your breasts are like. You'll want to choose a top that shows your neck and a bit of your chest—but not too much. You'll want to make sure you look fully dressed. The neckline of the top should be modestly revealing, but not show cleavage. A simple v-neck or scoop-neck will look great; it should fit comfortably when you're seated and not show bra straps. Avoid tube tops or any top that makes it look like you're not wearing anything. Avoid solid white or black, and, depending on your personality, flowers, lace, and small details are all good things. A simple necklace and flattering earrings are great accessories.

Some very simple rules for portraits: If you're a police officer, don't wear your uniform. If you're a nurse, don't wear scrubs. If you love wearing hats, don't. Men, you may spend your day in your trucker cap, but nobody will be interested in your loyal support of Bud or Skoal! Women, you may love wearing your Giants cap when jogging, your ponytail sticking out the back, but this is not the time for it. A hat is a form of camouflage. That's not the way to show off who you are.

Figure 6.8 shows how our model can go wrong, based on what she chooses to wear in her headshot.

Figure 6.8
Your choice of attire sends messages about you and also can mask your good looks. Simple is better, and avoid any hats or T-shirts.

Working with (All of) Your Hair

After selecting your attire, you'll need to take a long look in the mirror and decide what to do about your hair.

First, you'll want to make sure your hair looks its best. A good day to take your portrait shots is when you're scheduled for a haircut or styling. A good practice is to let your stylist know you're going to be taking your picture, and have him help style your hair to work best in a photo. You'll want to be sure that hair is not covering your face, and that the style is natural-looking and pleasant.

The goal is to show what you really look like. If you have long hair and wear it back all the time, don't be afraid to pull it back for the photo. If you're a man and you're balding, hey, you won't be able to hide that when you meet, so don't play games and make yourself look silly by combing your hair up from the back and down onto your forehead. Be proud of yourself, and show that you're comfortable with your hairline.

Women should avoid trendy or radical hairstyles. Sure, you may use red streaks now and then. You may try different styles for special occasions. In your picture, choose the hairstyle you wear most often. The one that looks like you do most of the time. Everyone gets a great "do" for a wedding or social event, but that's not how you'll look when you meet at Starbucks for your first coffee together. Set some realistic expectations by showing how you look everyday—which is beautiful, right?

For men, stay away from five o'clock shadow. It's a good idea to be clean-shaven. Unkempt facial hair can be a turn-off for some women. But if you wear a beard or mustache all the time, don't shave it off for the photo just to attract more chicks. Look like yourself., If you do have facial hair, be sure it's trimmed perfectly and that you look neat and groomed.

While on the subject of men, you may have hair that pops up all over, including your chest. If you're hairy, and your hair pops up out of your open-necked shirt, you may want to consider trimming it a bit or buttoning up all but the top button. Hairy chests can be a turn-on or a turn-off. Why take the chance of turning off someone when all can be fixed later with a wax job or an electric trimmer, if that is an issue? And no matter what your chest hair situation, do NOT unbutton your shirt down to your navel. This wasn't a good look in the '70s, and you won't win any dates with it now, either.

Doing Your Make-Up

This section will mainly apply to women, but men—read on and learn, too.

Make-up is something that can really help you, or really hurt you, in a photograph. As with any fresh application of make-up, too much may simply be too much. Lips that are too dark, rouge that is too strong, eye shadow that is too noticeable—these will all be exaggerated in a headshot. On the other hand, depending on your skin type and the make-up you use, even too much make-up may not be enough. You may find that you need to use more make-up than normal.

Some women do not use make-up at all, or they use very little. It's important to use make-up in a photo even if you normally don't wear very much. Unfortunately, the camera can be unforgiving and make-up can help make you look more put together. Here are some things you'll want to consider as you prepare for your picture:

▶ **Avoid shine.** Gloss lipstick will reflect the lights and tends to look too *Playboy*-like. Get as much shine off of your skin as possible by using powder or a matte foundation, especially on the forehead and chin.

▶ **Don't line your lips.** Adding a liner around your lipstick gives your lips a hard look, and also looks like the make-up used by *Playboy* models.

▶ **Be gentle with rouge.** Use it, but make it soft, blend it in, and keep it high on the cheeks.

▶ **Remove any shadows under the eyes.** Use any number of cosmetics designed to remove bags, circles, or wrinkles. Photos and lighting tend to exaggerate under-eye shadows, so be sure to counteract that effect by working on this area of your face.

▶ **If you use eye shadow, keep it natural.** Avoid blues and greens or anything metallic. Your eyes will be the most important feature in the photo, so you want them to look natural and pretty.

▶ **Add detail to your eyelashes.** Mascara is enough, but curl them if that's what you're used to, and use a good eyeliner. Don't clump or overdo it. Beautiful lashes will add to your eye appeal.

▶ **Keep your eyebrows soft.** You may want to go dark with eyebrow pencil, but be sure that it doesn't add hardness to your look. Thinner eyebrows are better than thick in your photo.

▶ **Don't worry about a few laugh lines or wrinkles.** If they are appropriate to your age, they're fine.

▶ **White teeth will help your smile.** There are a number of bleaching products for your teeth, so if your pearly whites are a bit dingy, give whitening strips a try.

The best advice for applying make-up for your photo is to start subtle. By taking test shots, you can gradually build up enough color and detail so your picture looks natural and not overly made-up. Cameras tend to wash out colors and details, so don't be afraid to keep adding make-up as needed. If you add too much, you can always remove it and start over.

Being Honest with Yourself

After all of the above preparations, the final test is to take an honest look at yourself in the mirror—or with a simple test shot with your camera.

Be honest. Does it look like you?

The most important thing is to take a picture of the person your prospective date will eventually see when you actually meet. This book is about truth in dating—be truthful in your picture so there won't be any surprises on that special day when you finally meet each other.

You can improve on nature through make-up and photo retouching (as you'll learn in Chapter 7), but the love of your life won't be dating a photo, they will be dating you. Look at yourself, and make sure that the clothing, hair, make-up, and your overall appearance do a great job of showing you in a pleasant way that matches how you look most of the time.

You'll be glad you did. And so will the love of your life.

Taking Good Pictures of Yourself

Lights? You've set them up. Camera? You have yours at the ready. Action? Well, the actions you need to perform next will have a huge impact on the success of your picture.

Selecting the right attire, hairstyle, and make-up are all-important, but what happens next is even more important: your attitude.

We all have "photographic history." We've had pictures taken through the years, and many of them are not flattering. Most people cringe at having an important picture taken of them. They instantly think of all the bad snapshots, of all the silly expressions, and of all the times photos made them look bad rather than good.

If you feel that you're not photogenic, or that pictures taken of you in the past have been terrible, here's a way to think of it using the dating metaphor. Maybe those photos were just taken by the wrong person. If you use the simple rules presented in this chapter, you'll have no one to blame but yourself. In the privacy of your home, or with a good friend helping you, you'll be totally in control of your photo taking, and you'll be able to take as many pictures as needed to get good results.

The first rule of a good photograph is to have a positive attitude. It will show in the photo, big time! If you're comfortable with yourself, like in how you have made yourself up, and have taken care of all the technical issues involved in your own personal photo shoot, you'll get a great photo of yourself.

And think how important that photo is—how important it is in sending the right message to that special someone out there. This is your chance to say, "Here I am, and it's pretty nice!" It's what will get you attention and what will get potential suitors reading your profile. In the online dating world, it's the shingle you hang out to represent your heart.

With your great attitude, the next task is to make sure the camera captures it. If you're ready and feel good, here's what to do next.

Taking Your Headshot

You've taken your test shots, your hair and clothes are perfect, and the lighting makes you look stunning. Now, all you really need to do is sit down in the chair and position yourself calmly while the self-timer clicks away and your pictures start to fill the memory card of your digital camera.

Taking your own picture is a bit tricky for two reasons:

▶ You'll be taking a photo of yourself, and since you can't actually see yourself in the camera viewfinder, you'll have to learn how to pose yourself through a series of trial-and-error pictures to find the right pose and expression.

▶ Since you'll be using a self-timer, you may start to fixate on when the shutter will fire rather than how you're looking at the camera.

Taking a self-portrait using a self-timer is something you'll just have to learn to do through trial and error. Don't be discouraged if the first dozen or so attempts are complete disasters. By simply standing up, clicking the shutter, then sitting back down, you'll get into the rhythm of the self-timer and the technique. What's important is that you look at each picture as you take it to see what's working or not working.

Once you get used to having your picture taken with a self-timer, you can then begin to concentrate on how you look and on composing the shot. For your headshot, try the following suggestions:

1. **Position your body.** Sit at a slight angle to the camera. Your body should be facing "off" to either side of the camera. This is best done by sitting with your knees and shoulders facing to the right or left of the camera. One of the benefits of placing yourself at a slight angle to the camera is that is slims your body profile. Your body should be comfortable; it will show if it's not.

2. **Turn your head to the side.** Just as with your body, you'll want your face to be facing ever-so-slightly off at an angle. You should avoid facing directly to the camera, or facing too far away. Most faces look better seen from a slight angle. Your face will slim down a bit, and your features will photograph better when seen from an angle.

3. **Maintain eye contact with the camera.** It's natural to turn your face directly towards the camera when you're making eye contact, so you may need to practice keeping your face turned slightly, while your eyes are directed at the camera. Although you can have a portrait in which your eyes are facing the same direction as your face, you'll lose direct eye contact with the person viewing your photo. Remember: You want to look directly at your viewer and establish eye contact.

4. **Tilt your head.** The tilt of your head is also something you'll need to experiment with. Some people look better with a slight upward tilt—it reduces a double chin and looks more attentive. Some people will also have a nice look when their head is tilted down ever so slightly. A sideways tilt will also produce a friendly, informal look. With all portrait shots, you'll need to experiment with the positioning of your head to find a flattering look. Try a number of poses, and go with what looks best to you.

5. **Smile at your true love.** There are two things that make or break a headshot on your profile picture: your smile and your eye contact. Be sure to smile and look happy! You're about to meet the love of your life—let her know you're glad to

meet her. Each person has a special smile, and you need to find a warm, inviting smile that projects your personality. A big, broad smile may work best, or sometimes a soft, gentle smile will do the trick. It's good to show your teeth, as closed-mouth smiles can often look like a smirk or grin. A good trick for smiling at the camera is to think about sex! Ah, fond memories…

6. **Laugh a little.** It may sound funny, but if your smile pictures don't look natural, try laughing a bit. Laughing creates a natural smile, and your eyes will twinkle. When all else fails, think of sex again, only this time think about your first time and how good you were. That should get you laughing.

Figure 6.9 shows a picture that brings all of the above elements together: clothes, hair, make-up, lighting, position in front of the camera, and a great smile and eye contact. The end result is natural, not formal like a studio portrait, and friendly. You should end up with a picture you feel good about, and will make others feel good about you.

Figure 6.9
A classic online dating headshot is something you can do yourself at home. Keep trying until you bring all of the rules for taking a good photo together for a perfect picture.

Taking Your Body Shot

If you decide to add a body shot to your profile (and it's a good idea to include one), you can use the same lighting and background that you did for your headshot, or you can even venture outside on a nice day.

If you use your in-house lighting setup, remember that you had positioned the lights to work with you when you were sitting on a chair. Since the lighting of your face is critical, even in a body shot, you'll need to adjust the lights higher to primarily light your face. They will also light your body quite well.

Taking your full-body portrait outdoors is trickier. Bright sunlight casts harsh shadows that may make your face look bad, or add shadows to your body that can be unflattering. One technique for bright sunny days is to use the flash on your digital camera to "fill-in" the shadows. If your camera has an "always" flash setting, use it and see if it helps the shadows.

A better way to take a full-body portrait outdoors is to take the picture late in the afternoon or on a very overcast day. The softer light will fill-in and remove any shadows and will gently light your entire body. If you're shooting in such conditions, be sure to turn your flash off. It's still a good idea to use a tripod because if you're taking a self-portrait, you'll need to position the camera and use the self-timer.

As with the headshot, you'll need to take a few test shots to see how you look and if the lighting is flattering. If you're comfortable with the setting and the lighting, you can then concentrate on your look and positioning your body.

The choice of clothes is very important in a full-body portrait. In addition to all the rules of appearance in the headshot, you should carefully choose clothing that says positive things about you. Here are some simple rules to consider:

> ▶ **Men: Think corporate casual.** A nice polo shirt or casual dress shirt and a pair of Dockers always look good. You may be a biker, you may be an aging hippie, you may feel most comfortable in T-shirts and jeans, you may be a wild and crazy guy—if you choose to project those traits, you probably will remain a lonely guy.

> ▶ **Men: Keep it under wraps.** You may have an awesome six pack and you may be well-endowed. Cover it up. If you keep it special, it will be a special treat. If you put it all on display, your true love may think you're too willing to give it away. Women tend to be turned off by bare chests, bulges in tight jeans, or bathing suit shots, and you shouldn't take the risk that your tight abs really look more like a beer belly. All will be revealed later at the right moment. This isn't that time.

> ▶ **Women: Less is not more.** Just as in the rule for guys, you won't look hot by wearing less. Bikinis and swim suits, tube tops, short skirts, low-cut blouses, or transparent attire may send the wrong message. Think about the image you want to project. If you want to show what a nice person you are, dress nicely. You're a mystery waiting to be revealed, so wrap yourself up like the nice present you really are.

> ▶ **Women: Guys chase skirts.** One of the things women can wear that makes them special is dresses and skirts. They are extremely feminine and, unlike the clothing described above, can be in extremely good taste and allow you to show off your figure and great legs.

> ▶ **Men and Women: Good taste and attention to detail go a long way in a full-body portrait.** Casual clothes that fit well will always make you look good. Nice accents, such as a good watch or other jewelry, will add detail. You can even get away with a super casual look, such as jeans and a nice top, if that represents you in everyday life accurately, but think twice about looking too casual. Finding a true love is not a casual affair. We hope!

Once you've selected a great outfit that makes you look comfortable and confident, you're ready to step in front of the camera. Try keeping the camera low—not much higher than waist-high. The lower camera position can make you look taller and flatter your body. However, this can make some women's hips and thighs look big, so experiment with the camera until you find an angle that is flattering for your body type. Sometimes a higher angle will be better. Avoid using the widest angle setting on your camera if you are using a zoom lens as this may distort your figure.

Standing in front of the camera, here are some simple tricks that work perfectly for this type of picture:

> ▶ **Face to the side.** Just as with the headshot, turn your body off to the side slightly. Your face will continue to look at the camera, but your body should be angled about 10 degrees away from the camera to the right or left. The angle will slim your body, create a better shape, and is generally more flattering than a picture in which you're fully facing the camera.

> ▶ **Maintain eye contact.** With your body angled slightly away from the camera, you should keep your face pointed towards the camera and make direct eye contact with the lens. It's okay if it's facing slightly away from the camera, as long as you maintain eye contact with the lens.

> ▶ **Hands on hips.** One of the best tips for body portraits is to put both hands on your hips. Keep them lower on the hips if possible—just to the point where they would slide down if you weren't keeping them in place. Arms are gangly and awkward in most body portraits, and although you can hold your hands together or put them in front of you, the hands on the hips really helps show your shape and creates interest. People are looking at the picture to check you out, so it is a pose that shows your body well. Try it. You'll like the results.

> ▶ **Good posture pays off.** This is a picture of you—all of you. Stand straight and tall, and don't slouch. Good posture projects confidence, and it makes you look taller.

> ▶ **Smile and laugh.** This one is simple: look happy. Smile, laugh, show your dimples, and make your eyes sparkle. People want to be with people who are happy with themselves. If you can look happy while you're having your picture taken, that speaks really well for you.

Figure 6.10 shows a great example of combining casual clothes with a perfect pose. Eye contact is being maintained while the body is angled slightly away from the camera. Hands are on hips, creating a nice shape and showing all the curves the right way.

It's easier to take a full body portrait with a friend. It's hard to position the camera and use a self-timer. The constant running back and forth to the camera will throw your position off, and you will not have much time to set up the pose. If you have a good friend who is patient, have her read the above suggestions and work with you to get the picture right.

As with headshots, one of the benefits of using a digital camera is that you can take lots of pictures. Take as many shots of any pose as you can, and remember, the above suggestions are just good starting points. You can try as many different poses as you want.

Figure 6.10
Great body shots are not
hard to take, once you
get the lighting right.
Tilt your body away
from the camera while
putting your hands on
your hips, and maintain
direct eye contact with
the lens.

Working with a Film Camera

If at all possible, use a digital camera. They're cheap, and so many people now own them that
chances are you can borrow one from someone. The advantage of a digital camera is that you can
take a lot of pictures quickly and cheaply, and most importantly, you can see the results
immediately. This is not true with a film camera.

If you do have to use a film camera, use every suggestion and rule listed above meant for taking
pictures with a digital camera. It will be much harder to "frame" your shots or determine how the
pictures will look, since you'll need to take the film to the one-hour photo processor near you. A
good technique is to set everything up, take a roll of pictures, then zip off to one-hour processing.
When you get your prints, you can return home, take more pictures, and make any needed
adjustments.

Since film is a slower process, and you can't get results immediately, plan on the whole
procedure taking longer. Since the expense of film and processing can actually run into some
serious cash, consider this: Five rolls of film and their processing (which is about the minimum it

will take to get great results in the trial-and-error process you're working with) will cost a bit over $70. You can purchase a pretty decent low-end digital camera for about the same price as film and processing.

You may want to buy a digital camera instead of using your film camera.

If you do use film and have prints, you'll also need to get your photos into a digital format that you can upload onto the online service. There are two basic techniques you can use.

First, if you have a scanner, simply scan your prints to JPEG files.

Second, if you do not have a scanner, take your prints to the place where you get your film processed and use their "photo station." This is essentially a scanner that most stores now have that allows you to convert your prints to digital files. When you complete the process, you'll be given a CD-ROM or floppy disk with your pictures stored as JPEG files. If the store does not have a digital photo station, chances are they can have your prints converted by sending them out to a service that can do it for you. Most stores, such as Target or Walgreens, have self-standing digital photo stations where you can convert prints to digital files for about a quarter each, plus the price of the disc they will be stored on.

Although most photo processors offer CD-ROMs of your photos from your film when it's processed, this usually is not a one-hour service and takes a day or two. Since you're running back and forth with your lights set up and your make-up and hair just right, go for the one-hour processing and then make digital files from the prints later.

Summary

With some simple planning, learning to light a photo shoot, and paying careful attention to your appearance and the message you want to send, you can take great photos for your online dating profile at home and by yourself, if need be. Using a tripod and the self-timer on a digital camera, you can effectively take a headshot and a full-body portrait that will get you attention while sending the correct image of what to expect if someone meets you.

GUY SAYS

Okay, it's not a big deal to me... but a long time ago I used to be an art director and photographer, and I worked for *Playboy*. Yes, I took pictures of naked women, and I still take some pretty hot photos of the hosts of TV shows I produce for Good Time Networks. I know a lot about taking pictures and the effect those pictures have on guys.

Here is my take: If guys want to see hot bods and lots of skin, they can buy a magazine or rent a porn DVD. Every guy wants to meet someone who is sexually attractive, but most guys looking for a girlfriend also know that looks are only one part of the attraction.

Maybe because I used to take pictures of naked women, I really find a photo of a woman fully clothed to be sexy. I like the mystery of what is underneath the clothes, and I want to be the only one who gets to see it. That's how guys really think. They are territorial, possessive, and protective by nature. Play to those instincts. *Playboy* does. Every centerfold includes pictures of the model at work or out on the street in everyday clothes. That's the fantasy. That incredible body and all that hot sex is waiting there beneath the oxford shirt and the simple skirt. Wow!

Too much skin, too much make-up, too much attitude. Leave that for guys huddled up with a copy of *Playboy* at night all by their lonesome. You'll want to tell the real story. Show your smile, show that you're nice. Show that you're proud of yourself, and don't put yourself on display too easily. That is a big turn-on for most men.

When I look at pictures, I look at the smile and the eyes. I look to see if the person is happy and inviting me into her world. A picture should always be about the person—not her body.

When I took pictures of myself for my profile, I used one of my best assets: my smile. Every response I ever got said, "I love your smile, and that's why I'm writing to you." I am a nice person, and my photos captured that niceness. It worked. I met the love of my life—she loved my photo, and she was attracted to my smile and the twinkle in my eyes. I loved hers too, and all she showed in the photos were her two amazingly big beautiful, luscious eyes.

—*Terry*

CHICK SAYS

No offense, but guys can be clueless. Some of the pictures I've seen in men's profiles online would make you blush… or laugh. And I'm not talking about the ones on Adult Friend Finder!

For some reason a lot of men don't seem to understand what it is that women are looking for. So guess what, guys… I'm about to tell you. Actually, first I'll tell you what we're not looking for.

We're not looking for a shot of you in a Speedo. We're not looking for your sexy-guy look, leaning back in a chair with your shirt unbuttoned to reveal excessive chest hair (or any kind of chest hair). We don't want a come-hither look. We don't care about seeing you standing next to your car or motorcycle.

We want that sweet, funny guy smile. We want that "I've got something devious in mind and I can't wait to tell you about it" look in your eyes. We want you wearing a nice shirt. We want to see your head, hair or no, and your eyes (no sunglasses). And we want you to look confident and comfortable in your own skin.

I've said that there's nothing I like more than a huge grin in a guy's photo. Add to that a well-fitting shirt that brings out the color of your eyes, stylish glasses that make you look like you might be solving the US financial crisis, and a confident pose that says "go ahead, snap my picture, I can take it"—and I'm hooked.

Guys, listen up. I think you're misguided. I think you've been told by your frat buddies and football teammates that chicks dig tough guys and a big motorcycle. I think some girlfriend in your past dumped you for a six-pack with a cool car. I think your high school buddy said only geeks wore glasses and paid attention in school.

Women want intelligent, funny, sweet, nice, individualistic guys. We want guys with character. We want you to be as smart as we are. We want you to respect yourself enough to be yourself instead of some adolescent theory of who you should be. Show who you really are in your photo.

And you may not believe this, but some of us hate motorcycles, think it's stupid to pay $75,000 for a car, and couldn't care less about a six-pack. We're the ones you want to date. We're the ones who want to date you, not the you you think you should be.

—*Alyssa*

Chapter 7
Using (Not Abusing) Photo Editing Software

*A*fter you've taken your headshot and body shots, you can probably improve them a bit by using photo editing software. Programs such as Photoshop, Windows Paint, and the handy freebie Picasa2 from Google are all very handy for image editing.

Be warned: There's always the temptation to fool with Mother Nature when you get a powerful image editing program in your mitts. All of a sudden you have the power to slim your waistline, brighten your teeth, remove a mole or two, and tweak yourself into someone off the cover of *Shape* magazine.

Stop right now and look at the cover of this book. Look at the title—*Truth, Lies, and Online Dating*. Your unedited photo is the truth. If you retouch it in any significant way, that's a lie. Good relationships are built on truth, so don't lie in your photo no matter how good you are with the airbrush in Photoshop!

That doesn't mean you shouldn't correct some very basic things in your photos. Image editing programs are great for

> ▶ Cropping your photos
> ▶ Adjusting contrast and brightness
> ▶ Correcting color
> ▶ Removing unnecessary information when needed

The final step in creating a great online profile photo is to use image editing to adjust the quality of the pictures you took so that they look good on a computer screen. The following steps can improve or fix problems that are common to most digital camera photos—especially ones you took of yourself.

First, take a look at some programs that are free and how they can solve your photo problems.

Cropping and File Format Changes with Windows Paint

If you're a PC user, you're in luck. Windows comes with a simple, but effective, image editing program called Windows Paint. You can find it from the Start menu by choosing All Programs, then Accessories. In that menu, Paint will be waiting for you and your photos. (If you're a Mac user, you're in luck since your Mac comes with iPhoto! However, our explanations are going to focus on Windows, since Microsoft still rules the world.)

Paint is a bitmap image editing program. Photo files can be saved as bitmap images, and you can use Paint to make cropping and file format adjustments to them. Many people think Paint is a painting or drawing program, and it is. Paintings on PCs are made of pixels, just like photo images, so it can work with photo or graphics files.

Your digital photos most likely will be JPEG files. From the Paint File menu, choose Open, then find where your pictures are stored and open one as shown in Figure 7.1.

Although Paint is pretty limited in its photo editing capabilities, it will allow you to make the two most basic adjustments to your photo: cropping and saving the newly cropped version. Figure 7.2 shows this important function. In Paint, a photo of Terry has been opened and the goal is to convert this body shot into a headshot by simply cropping the photo to remove the body and background.

Figure 7.1
Choose File, Open to locate and open your photo file in Windows Paint. You'll be able to manipulate the photo, then save it with a new file name so you have both the original and edited versions.

Figure 7.2
A full body shot of Terry is cropped down to a headshot by using the Rectangle Selection tool and selecting the area of the photo that will become the headshot.

Paint is fairly crude, and you'll have to do some of the heavy lifting yourself. In the case of cropping a photo, you simply use the Selection tool to copy the selected portion, then open a new document and paste the selection into it. You do this by selecting Copy To from the Edit menu, and then creating a new document by giving it a name. The selection that you copied becomes a new image, allowing you to save the cropped document without harming the original.

You can also use the Selection tool and simply click anywhere on the original photo. Small selection boxes will appear at each corner and midway through the sides, top, and bottom. You can click on any of the selection boxes to crop the photo—but this is not recommended. When you crop in, you can't crop back out! It's simply better to copy and paste into a new document due to this limitation.

In addition to cropping, you can also use Paint to save your file to a different file format. For example, if you have a JPEG and your online service requests a BMP file, you can open the file in Paint, then from the File menu select Save As and choose to save the file in the new file format from the Save As Type menu as shown in Figure 7.3.

Paint will help you crop and change file formats, but not much else. Since it's free with Windows, you can't complain about the price. If you have more complex image editing fixes to be done, you can download a really handy image management program called Picasa2, free from Google.

Making Masterpieces with Picasa2

Continuing Google's world domination plan to organize your computer in every way possible, they have begun to offer a free image management program called Picasa2. It allows you to catalog all of your picture files—and has some really easy-to-use image adjustment tools that just about anyone can master. In fact, the image editing tools in Picasa2 are some of the best freeware image editing tools anywhere, and the results are spectacular.

To get Picasa2, simply go to Google and select Images from the menu bar. On the Images page you'll see a link for downloading the program. If by some chance the link has moved by the time you read this, the URL for the program is http://google.picasa.com or simply type **Picasa2** in the Google Search box.

Once you download the program, follow the installation instructions and let the program work its magic with your image files. The first thing the installation process will ask you is if you want it to search your computer for picture files. When you say yes, it scours your files and catalogs every image and photo file into pristine thumbnails that allow you to see all of your pictures in a very organized and visual manner, as shown in Figure 7.4. By cataloging your pictures, it allows any future searches to be quick and painless. You'll enjoy browsing all your files, but right now you'll want to scroll to the online dating pictures you took and stored on your PC to edit them in Picasa2.

Image editing starts by simply clicking on any of the thumbnail images shown in the library. The image will open in a View and Edit window, as shown in Figure 7.5.

Figure 7.4
Picasa2 starts by cataloging all of your picture files and allows you to quickly sort and find them using high-quality thumbnails organized by libraries.

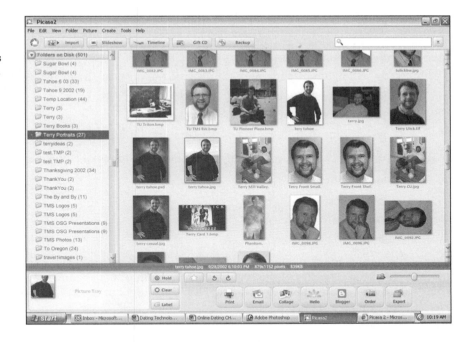

Figure 7.5
By clicking on a thumbnail, you move to a View and Edit window where you can make a wide range of image adjustments to the quality of your photo file.

From here, you can make a number of corrections and improvements to the quality of your picture—but not go in and actually change the subject. The basic fixes included are

- ▶ Cropping your photo.
- ▶ Straightening the photo if it's crooked or if the image needs slight rotation.
- ▶ Red-eye reduction.
- ▶ Auto contrast or auto color adjustments.
- ▶ Adding "fill light" to correct common lighting problems.

In addition to the basic fixes, the Tuning tab allows you to make adjustments to

- ▶ Highlights.
- ▶ Shadows.
- ▶ Overall color cast.
- ▶ Fill light.

Each of the tuning adjustments uses a slider with a real-time preview. This allows you to view the changes to the intensity of the highlights, the depth of the shadows, and changes to the overall color cast of the photo. By playing with the sliders in the Tuning tab, you can improve the overall image quality of your photo.

All of the above adjustments require you to decide how much of an adjustment you want, so they are largely manual procedures. Picasa2 also has extremely powerful effects that automate a number of adjustments that can add complicated effects to your photos. These include

- ▶ Sharpening your photo, which adds detail to any photo.
- ▶ For artistic types, a quick conversion to black and white or sepia.
- ▶ "Warmify," which adds a warm, natural quality to photos, especially those taken with a flash.
- ▶ Saturation adjustment, which adds or removes the intensity of colors.
- ▶ Soft focus, which allows you to select a portion of the image to remain sharp and soften the focus of the surrounding area. This is very pleasing with headshots.

Figure 7.6 shows starting the process of working with the same image as with Windows Paint, only now using Picasa2. The first step is to crop the image. Here, the cropping is intuitive, and the image cropping can be changed at any point in the process and saved in the cropped format.

To see how your cropped image will look without the surrounding area, click Preview. The cropped image will fade in and fill the image area, then fade out again to the entire image with the cropped area highlighted. If you wish to change the cropping, simply click and drag within the image again until you get the correct crop. Once you're satisfied, click on the Apply button, and you will then be working with the cropped image. You can choose Recrop once you have completed the first crop if you change your mind later. Neat!

Figure 7.6
To crop a picture in Picasa2, simply choose the Crop button from the Basic Fixes menu. Click and drag on the image to obtain the desired crop. Choose the Manual crop rather than the standard photo-sized crops that are also available.

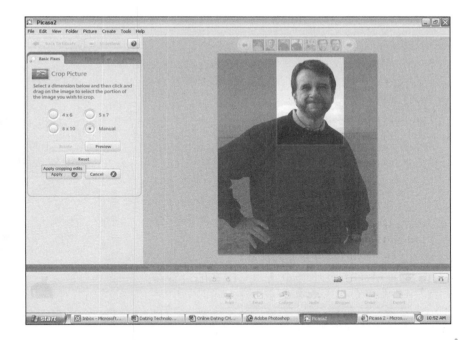

Using the Basic Fixes tab, play with Auto Contrast and Auto Color. You'll be able to see if these adjustments improve your picture. If they do, apply the change, and if not, undo the change from the menu at any time. For many photos, these adjustments will do the trick, but as important as your photos are, you'll want to use some of the other fixes that the program offers.

The Tuning tab will allow you to adjust brightness and contrast and overall color cast. By moving the Fill Light, Highlights, Shadows, and Color Temperature sliders, you'll be able to tweak your photo until it looks like the cover of some glossy magazine. You can play as much as you like because all changes can be reversed at any time. Figure 7.7 shows the Tuning Tab menu and the cropped image undergoing some adjustments to its shadows.

After making adjustments in the Tuning tab, you'll want to see how sweet you can make your picture by working with automated adjustments in the Effects tab. Many of the effects are more suitable for prints, but a few are really important for your online profile pictures.

Start by clicking on the Sharpen button. Your picture will instantly look better. It will have more detail and look crisp and alive. There may be times when you don't want a sharper picture. If you have lots of freckles or wrinkles, it's likely that the Sharpen button will accentuate those features. So go ahead and try it, and if you don't like the effect, cancel it.

Figure 7.7
The Tuning tab allows you to make precision adjustments to brightness, contrast, color temperature, and highlights by simply moving sliders and seeing the effect in real time.

Two other effects will round out your image editing. First, use the Saturation button to make adjustments to the color saturation of your picture. This feature can remove too much overall color or add color intensity to a picture that lacks deep, rich color. As with all adjustments, you should experiment until the image looks better. If you don't think playing with the saturation makes the picture better, cancel the effect.

The second effect you should try is the Soft Focus effect. It's not a good idea to ever completely soft focus your picture. A soft focus will imply that you're softening age lines or wrinkles or simply trying to hide things. The nice part of this effect is that you can select which area of the picture remains in focus and add a soft focus to areas that are not important to your portrait. This allows you to place complete emphasis on your face, for example, and blur out the background.

Figure 7.8 shows the Terry picture as a body shot with the background made into a soft focus while keeping Terry's face and most of his body in focus. The effect makes Terry the center of attention, no matter how beautiful Lake Tahoe was on that day.

All of the edits to the picture done in Picasa2 focus on the image quality—not changing the image. It doesn't let you "airbrush" the photo or change your basic appearance. This works for most pictures and keeps your pictures honest!

After you've used the program to enhance the quality of your pictures, you should choose Save a Copy from the File menu to save the changes while keeping the original intact.

Figure 7.8
Using the Soft Focus effect allows you to emphasize your face or body and blur out the background in a photo, which is great for body shots where you wish to downplay the background.

Going All the Way with Photoshop

There may be times when you really need to make some major changes in a photo. If you find that you need to remove something such as a sign, another person, or any clue to your identity from a photo you really want to use, then you'll need to use a powerful image editing program, such as Photoshop (or its little sibling, Photoshop Elements).

PHOTOSHOP ON THE CHEAP

Programs such as Photoshop Elements cost about $100 (it's more like $600 for the full version of Photoshop), so it may be cheaper to take another photo if all you want to do is edit out a small section of the image. The good news is that you can often download a trial version of programs such as Photoshop Elements to use for about 30 days. Some functions are turned off in such trial versions, but overall a trial version may do the job for you. And if you just need it long enough to make your photos perfect for your profile, the 30 days should do it. You can check it out at www.adobe.com.

With all of their power, true photo editing programs often are just too tempting. You really can work a photo to the point where it's simply nothing like what you started with. Figure 7.9 shows a photo that will be manipulated in Photoshop, and just look how powerful such a program can be in the hands of a skilled photo retoucher.

Figure 7.9
Anything is possible
when you use a
powerful image editing
program like Photoshop.
To demonstrate how
much can be changed in
a photo, here's a simple
body shot.

The famous picture of Terry at Lake Tahoe used with Picasa2 is now in the even more powerful environs of Photoshop, and in Figure 7.10, some big changes are starting to take place. Using the Eraser tool, we have totally removed the background. Gone are the blue skies and the sparkling water. The checkerboard pattern behind Terry means that the background is transparent—nothing is there.

But more than that is going on. Notice how Terry has shed a few pounds around the waistline? Oh, not too many, but certainly enough to make you think he's slimmer than he actually is. Even more pounds could have been taken off, but this is an example of a little wishful thinking—just a little cleanup, or, well, the Eraser tool just got a little too close around the belly. That's okay!

Actually, it's not. But, this goes to show how easy it is to fool yourself (or another way of putting it is to lie about your appearance) when you're using such tools.

It's actually a lot of work to remove a background or take off pounds. It requires a steady hand and a lot of practice with Photoshop. Once the figure is outlined, just about anything can happen. For example, on the safe side, let's say that Terry didn't want it known that he hangs out at the casinos at Lake Tahoe, but he liked the photo a lot. One of the things that you can do with such a program is remove the background to avoid revealing too much about yourself.

Figure 7.11 replaces the Lake Tahoe scenery with a classic faux portrait studio background. The background was created by using effect filters in Photoshop, lighting effects, and lots of blurring of the background image. Even though Terry's a bit slimmer than in real life, the photo is still pretty representative of Terry and does mask his choice of hangouts. That may be a good thing to

Figure 7.10
Major retouching begins by totally removing the background behind the figure—and trimming the waistline a bit to reduce a little midriff bulge. The lies begin.

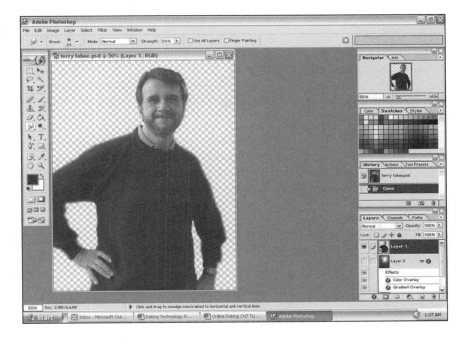

Figure 7.11
Terry didn't want people to know he spends his days at the lake rather than toiling away at his PC writing books, so he replaced the Lake Tahoe background with a studio backdrop. That's fair.

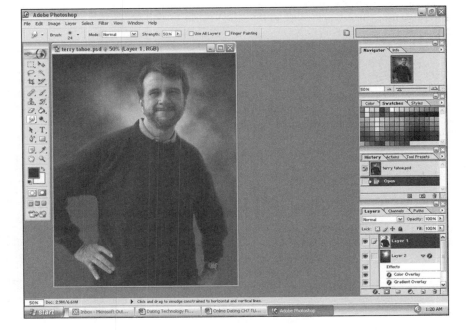

consider. You may have a photo of yourself in front of your home or place of work that's a great photo of you, but you don't want to show your haunts. With Photoshop, you can get rid of the background.

So far, the worst that can be said is that Terry cheated a bit on the waistline—and not much at that. He blames it on the sweater and too many burgers that weekend, and he assures himself that rather than lying, the photo now looks just like him. Oh, what a wicked game we play with the power of image editing...

But the real story is that Terry is off to New York for a few weeks and wouldn't mind meeting some dazzlers while he's there. So, he thinks about how he took out the Lake Tahoe background and how easy it was to replace it with the studio backdrop. Wheels turn, and the New York trip looms. He hasn't had much luck meeting someone in the Tahoe area (probably because they saw him with the burger belly sticking out, wolfing down a few more burgers, and know he used Photoshop to edit his profile picture), so the light bulb goes off over his head.

It's the type of inspiration that led the first male primates to pick up a bone and use it to hit some poor she-monkey over the head. He decides to post a profile that says he lives in New York, and he can change his photo to prove it! That way he can check to see if the great women in NYC are ready for a smooth operator like him.

Figure 7.12 shows just how deceptive a photo can be.

Now, the online dating services are buzzing all about the new listing from that handsome guy in front of the Statue of Liberty. Thanks to a little skill with Photoshop, Terry is a new man—in a new town. And it begs the question: Is any photo we see online real?

Figure 7.12
This is how easy it is to move from Lake Tahoe to New York—and he didn't even have to rent a U-haul.

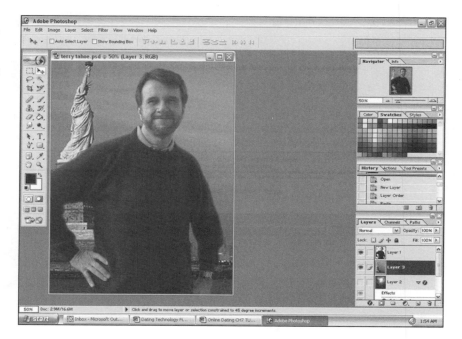

Lucky for all of us, Terry was just showing off his Photoshop skills and assures us that he saw the movie Spiderman and agrees that, "With great power comes great responsibility." Photoshop and other programs like it offer great power. They can change how you look, where you live, and create a whole new reality. You have to use that power responsibly.

As you will learn later in the book, the above example of just how much any photo can be manipulated is something to think about. What if the photo of the person you're interested in has been doctored in Photoshop? How can you tell? We'll show you how later in the book, but for now think about how such a program can help you make more appropriate changes, such as removing the background, as shown in Figure 7.11.

Summary

Even the best photos may need a bit of technical tweaking to make them "pop" online. Using a simple program such as Windows Paint allows you to crop a photo or save it in a different file format. A more powerful program such as Picasa2 will help you organize and technically enhance your pictures so they are sharp, crisp, and cropped correctly. For special situations, such as removing unwanted information in the background of a photo that may reveal where you live, you can use powerful image editing programs such as Photoshop—as long as you use that power to present an honest portrait of yourself.

GUY SAYS

Most guys are probably okay with how they look, so the idea of editing their photos may not seem important to them, but I would suggest that it is.

I'm a big believer in using image editing programs to make any photo perfect. You can crop, correct color, add sharpness, and even take a color photo and save it as black and white if you want to get creative.

Most pictures taken with digital cameras are good—but not perfect. I'm a photographer, and I use a few basic image editing tools on just about every photo I take.

First, I use the Sharpen tool to bring out detail in my photos. Next, I always adjust the contrast and the brightness. You can always make a photo look better by making this adjustment. It adds highlights and creates rich, deep shadow detail.

Finally, I play a bit with the color temperature. Some programs have "auto color," which takes a look at the picture, and if it's full of skin tones, corrects the skin tones for you. It's a great tool that you can play with manually if you choose.

If you think of yourself as a dull guy who is not very sharp, then use the picture right off of your digital camera. It will be dull and not very sharp, too.

If you're bright and very sharp indeed, we've taught you how to improve your pictures by adjusting color, contrast, brightness, and applying the Sharpen Picture filter. Do this, and don't be dull.

After all the trouble you went through finding a polo shirt and a pair of Dockers for your portraits, it's worth a few more extra steps to look your best.

—Terry

CHICK SAYS

Yes, we chicks have issues. It's widely documented. Women, more so than men, have all kinds of body issues, hair issues, face issues, lip issues, eyelash issues, you name it—we've got it.

In my circle of friends, I have one who thinks her lips are too thin and always lines them bigger and fills them in with lipstick. I have one who thinks her breasts are too small and wears a waterbra whenever possible. I have another who thinks her arms are too big and refuses to wear tank tops. I have another who thinks her pinkies look fat. Okay, that last one is me.

So the temptation, when faced with Photoshop, is to fix these things virtually, the way you try to fix them in life. Enlarge your picture, and play with the drawing tools to make your lips look bigger. Add some shadows and make your breasts look bigger. Thin those arms and those… well, really, would I ever be so insecure as to thin my pinkies? No, but does anyone know a good exercise regimen for that?

Tempting though it may be, that's not who you are. It's not truth in advertising. And no matter how many body issues you may have, this is not the place to release those demons. Just keep snapping photos until you take one that you're happy with. Don't use Photoshop to make the picture look like you imagine you should look.

Use Photoshop to make your picture clearer, brighter, or to fix color contrast issues. That's what it's there for. And that's all I'm going to give you permission to use it for. Your body image I leave in your own and your therapist's hands. I think you're beautiful the way you are, and you'll find someone else who agrees with me, I swear.

—*Alyssa*

Chapter 8
Truth in Advertising: Reviewing Your Message

*W*e've talked about how important it is to tell the truth, so when you finally meet someone special, you have nothing to hide and no stories to change. Online dating starts with the combination of words and pictures that comprise your profile. The emphasis in this book so far has been on planning and taking your picture, since pictures are worth a thousand words. At this point, however, it's important to start thinking about how to actually tell the truth in your story of you.

It's not always as easy as it sounds.

In creating pictures of yourself and in preparing to write your profile, it's just human nature to want to present yourself in the most flattering way. The things that you leave out or conveniently forget to mention are part of that process. For example, you may be a smoker, but you know that will limit who responds to your profile. You may feel that if you meet someone who's a nonsmoker, you can quit, or maybe once he gets to know you, he'll be okay with your choice.

That's why this isn't as easy as it sounds.

The little things that you choose to leave out may end up being deal-breakers. And even the truths that you choose to put in, that we encourage you to put in, may be trouble. You may like to have a glass of wine each night with dinner. When you fill in your form, you get to the "drinks" question, and you're faced with a decision: You drink everyday—but you really aren't a "drinker." How do you answer such a question, especially in a form that, as Figure 8.1 shows, only gives you the choices of "never," "socially," or "regularly," and no space to explain?

If you answer "regularly," many people may think you're a heavy drinker, but you're not. You may even just be following a doctor's advice. A glass a day keeps the doctor away these days.

As you write your initial profile, take your first pictures, and get ready to put it all together online, it's a good time to look at it all with fresh eyes. Make sure you've done a good job of "selling" yourself without painting an unrealistic portrait. This chapter will look at how to deal with the subtleties of truth in advertising—yourself.

Figure 8.1
Where is the box that allows you to explain the box you've checked? Surely things should not be so black and white.

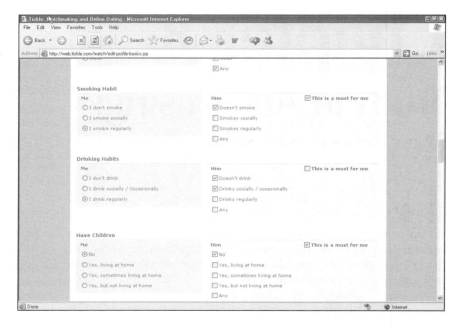

Turning Up Your Amp to Eleven

One of the great lines from the movie *Spinal Tap* comes when the band is told that their very blatant album cover art is sexist, not sexy. They realize that, "There's a thin line between clever and stupid." Well, there's actually another great line where Nigel tries to explain that Spinal Tap is the loudest rock group, since their amps go up to 11, not 10 like other bands, so they're "one louder."

Telling your story in a creative and attractive manner is clever. Changing the facts is stupid. So put on your tightest Lycra spandex stage outfit (or bicycle gear), turn your amp up to 11, and get ready to blow their minds with your profile. But first consider what is clever and what is stupid when it comes to telling the truth about yourself online.

Being Clever Is Smart

In the wine scenario we mentioned at the beginning of this chapter, you'll need to be clever while remaining honest. You could say, "Drinks regularly," and that would be the truthful answer. Getting clever would be adding a bit about this fact in the Describe Yourself area of your profile. You could explain that you enjoy a glass of wine with dinner each night, just like the French, and would love to share your wine cellar with someone special. You've been completely honest; you explained that the drinking is mild and that you view it as something you'd like to share. You didn't apologize for it, and you were able to explain it well. That's a clever and creative solution that helps "sell" your personality.

Many of the things you may wish to hide can easily be turned into pluses or at least into something that can endear you to the person reading your profile.

A good example is if you're a bit overweight. Oh sure, you could say that your body type is "average" and only use a headshot, leaving the body shot off the profile. But then when you meet someone, they'll think you lied about your weight. And it may not be the weight that bothers them, but the lie. Maybe there's a better, more creative way to turn it all up to 11.

Think about simply describing yourself as having "a few extra pounds" and then including the body shot. You could use a headline such as, "Love handles waiting to be held." Or in the text of your profile, perhaps you can say that you're looking for someone to walk or workout with as you get yourself in shape—assuming it's true. You're suggesting that you're starting on a healthier routine, and you're inviting them to be a part of it.

That's pretty clever, isn't it?

We are what we are. You can use your profile to explain that what you are is good, but you see room for improvement, and you're inviting that special someone to be a part of that—and to share in your life. Wow! And you were worried that the few extra pounds would be an issue—it's almost a selling point.

Being Stupid Is, Well, Stupid!

Ah, the thin line. No matter how you look at it, if you don't get the clever part just right, it just sounds stupid. We've all heard lame excuses and tacky lines such as, "There's more of me to love!" When clever goes wrong, it's pretty bad because you just sound stupid.

And some stories told in profiles are just that—stupid stories that will ruin a lot of things in a relationship. So here are some things that we advise you to avoid when you create your profile because they will come off as disingenuous, phony, smarmy, or tasteless.

- ▶ Anything that refers to your sexual appetite or your sexual abilities.
- ▶ Descriptions of your body parts.
- ▶ Commenting on how many partners you've been with.
- ▶ Bragging about how great you are.
- ▶ Saying that you're edgy, hot, or a bad boy/girl.
- ▶ Saying you're "just looking for fun" or "just want a good time."
- ▶ Saying that you're stubborn, hot tempered, or opinionated.
- ▶ Proclaiming that you're just there on a lark or because your friends dared you to.

Even if most of the above items are true (in your mind), they're simply stupid things to put out there. Some may be true but are inappropriate to bring up. Others may be true but aren't going to win you any points. Let's take a closer look at why these proclamations are stupid things that are not good truth-telling at all.

Bragging about Sex

In an earlier chapter we mentioned Don Juan. Do you think the world's greatest lover had to say that he was? No way. He was charming, bold, engaging, and he left it up to his partners to decide if he was a great lover. That's what makes saying you're a great lover a lie: It can only be determined by the person you make love to. When you say you're a great lover, you sound like an arrogant fool. And more than likely you sound like someone who may be sexually inadequate. Bluster is usually a cover for insecurity.

If you're on a swinger or sex site, then talk all about sex. That's what you're there to do, and that's what you're there looking for. On most dating sites, however, it's wise to avoid such bragging and to realize that if all you have to "sell" is your little love machine, since we all have 'em, that's not offering much to the other person.

Describing Your Anatomy

If you think that the size of your penis or the size of your breasts (you figure out which applies to you) is a selling point, stick to the sex sites where you can just take a picture of it/them, and get it over with. For most other dating sites, as proud as you may be of your 12 inches or those double Ds, it's not smart to reduce yourself down to a quick chuckle. Even if you're hung or stacked, who will believe you? Easy to say, but most people would doubt your claim or, even worse, think you're desperate for attention. If you decide to post a picture of or talk about your fabulous Figure 8.2 assets, you're sending a message you might want to rethink.

Figure 8.2
Yes, they're impressive. But are they the sum total of who you are? If you post this photo or describe them in detail, that's the message you're sending.

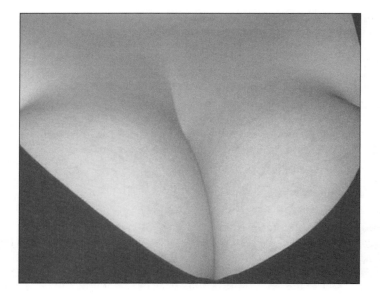

Most people are online to meet a person, not a body part. If you do have special gifts in the part department, wait a while and let that be a surprise your mate can unwrap later. Your patience will be rewarded.

Adding Another to the List of Conquests

One strange way people have of saying that people like them or that they're desirable is to talk about how many people they've "been" with. In a world where people are looking to find a special someone, it's pretty stupid to talk about how many conquests you've had. Does anyone really want to be another in a long list of probably disappointed lovers?

Experience is good. It's fine to have had past relationships. Stop there. And if you've had lots of lovers, you probably have a problem with commitment and need to think about that anyway. This may not be the book for you.

Saying How Great You Are

It doesn't take much to figure out that describing yourself as sexy, brilliant, sophisticated, or a laugh riot may not be the best idea. Those are opinions people form of you by getting to know you. If you say them about yourself, you sound immodest. And if you come out and say you're sexy, that's downright questionable—remember Don Juan. But you can say something like, "All my friends say that I'm cute," and that works fine. Don't brag about yourself, but if you do, let it be the opinion of your friends. If you don't have any friends who compliment you in this way, you either need better friends, or you need to rethink your vision of yourself.

Claiming That You're Edgy, Hot, or Bad

Someone who's attracted to someone who claims to be edgy, hot, or a bad boy or girl will be attracted for just about as long as it takes to get laid. You figure it out.

Saying You're Stubborn, Hot-Tempered, or Opinionated

Modern science has yet to figure out why primates of human form think that being a pain in the butt is somehow an attractive quality. Think about whether you would like to spend your time with someone who thinks that stubborn is a positive quality. Or hot-tempered. Youch! And opinionated? That's another way of saying you love to argue about everything. These are all statements that say, "I don't want a date." We're not saying you can't be any of these things, but using them as reasons someone should want to be with you is unlikely to get you dates with anyone but a masochist.

Proclaiming You're There on a Dare

If you really want to tell people you're not looking for someone, a good start is to say, "I'm just here because my friends dared me to." Exactly—you're not here to meet someone. You're not serious. Oh, and you're not good enough to get online and write a sincere profile like the many other people who are taking the online dating process seriously. As Joan Rivers is wont to say— "Grow up!"

Okay, all of the above are examples of how a well-intentioned attempt at being clever or describing some of your more interesting traits can end up making you sound stupid or simply unattractive in the personality department. Here are some great examples of how to turn each of the above around to tell the truth in a clever, not stupid, way:

- ▶ **Sex.** "I love how romance can lead to intimacy and passion."
- ▶ **Body Parts.** "My smile is just one of many wonderful features I'm lucky enough to share with you."
- ▶ **Conquests.** "I've had enough experience in romance to know what makes someone happy."
- ▶ **Everyone Loves You.** "People seem to think I'm funny and smart, but why don't you contact me and find out for yourself?"
- ▶ **Edgy or Hot.** "I'm a lot of things: Boring isn't one of them!"
- ▶ **Looking for Fun.** "I love a good time; I'm happy to start with that and see what happens next."
- ▶ **Opinionated Personality.** "I'm not a wallflower, and I'm willing to share my opinion with you… Let's see if we agree!"
- ▶ **Here on a Dare.** "Okay, my friends talked me into going online, but I love it now that I'm here."

Telling the truth doesn't mean that you have to be boring—or that you have to be crude or offensive. You need to find ways to describe yourself that communicate your qualities, not as your opinion of yourself, but in a way that others can understand and appreciate.

Think about that fine line between clever and stupid, and make sure you stay on the right side.

Using a Current Photo Is Essential

In this refresher course (and we know we've said it hundreds of times in the book), it's important to stress that you use a current photo of yourself—not just for any prospective dates, but for yourself.

A current photo is a key element in accepting yourself and sending the right message for you as well as to anyone who happens upon it. At some point, if you get a response and you go to meet your date, you'll feel much better about the experience when you know you're accepted exactly as you are. It sets the stage for moving forward and shows one of the best things that can happen in online dating: acceptance.

Online dates usually start with viewing the photo, so the hard part is largely out of the way. The fear of physical rejection, of being liked or disliked solely on appearance, is addressed largely by someone "previewing" your photo—someone you've never met who you'll never know has rejected you. When you do meet someone, if your photo is representative of how you look right now, you will not be rejected based on physical appearance.

If you use an old or "doctored" photo, you probably will be rejected.

When you think of it that way, using an old photo is an impressive setup for failure. To get a response, you use an older photo from when you were younger or thinner or felt you looked better. In getting more responses, you'll meet with more people, but since you may be rejected solely because you don't look like your picture, you face more and more rejection. It's a vicious circle where you can only lose.

Truth in advertising yourself is about accepting yourself. It's about knowing who you are, what your qualities are, and being comfortable with how you look. If you're okay with yourself, you'll be advertising that message to the world, and that's the best possible start.

Using a Photo from a Magazine or Copyrighted Source

One thing that some people do to enhance their profile is to use photos out of magazine articles, ads, or books. We've seen profile photos of models on the beach with great bodies and tiny suits. They are far enough away so it could actually be the person writing the profile, and it's simply too hard to tell. Sometimes the photos are outright model shots from a fashion magazine.

Beyond the total misrepresentation of who and what you are, you face more than a "truth" issue here: Using copyrighted photos from publications is against the law. You can actually be sued or fined in a civil action if you use such a picture.

Sometimes people will pull out a nice picture of a flower or animal from a magazine or book to put on their profile. Although it's unlikely that the publisher will take an action against you, it is still an illegal act. If you want to put a representative graphic of this nature in your profile, take the picture yourself, or buy a cheap disc of royalty-free stock photos at Wal-Mart or buy from an online source for this purpose.

If you have your photo taken by a professional photographer or a portrait studio, chances are they'll assign you limited rights to the photograph. Usually, there will be a "copyright" stamp on the back of the prints. Technically, you don't have the right to reproduce the photos in any way, so using them online is a no-no. Online dating services state that you shouldn't use professional photographs that are copyrighted, and you really shouldn't, unless you've obtained permission from the photographer or studio—in writing.

Changing Your Looks

Throughout this book you've seen or read about how image editing programs can alter reality or enhance the way you look. As tempting as this is, just as with using an older photograph, you aren't just cheating the person viewing you as a prospective date; you're cheating yourself and saying that you're not attractive enough to be seen without some major retouching. That's fine for *Playboy* models, but you? Hey, you're better than that.

In truthfully advertising yourself, you need to deliver on the promise. Most guys never meet those *Playboy* models, but chances are you'll go out with some of the people who see your retouched photo. It's pretty uncomfortable to have someone sit across from you and start to wonder where those circles under the eyes came from, where that shape went, or if that mole is new and something that needs immediate medical attention. That's not what a good date is about.

It's far better to take a great photo of yourself, as detailed in Chapter 6, than to take a bad photo and play with it in Photoshop or some other image editing program.

Looking Like You Do Everyday

We all can get dolled up and look great. ZZ Top said it best—"Every girl's crazy 'bout a sharp-dressed man." Woman, too.

In this refresher course, a good way to think of truth in advertising yourself is to consider the benefits of getting all dressed and made-up versus showing yourself as you look at most times and in most places. They each have their benefits, but overall you may want to take the "everyday" path.

First, if you look too made up and look great, you'll probably find expectations are high for you to match your profile photo when you meet. That's fine on a dinner date, but chances are your first meetings will be at a coffee house or some small daytime meeting out in public. That's not the time or place for hair, makeup, and elegant clothing (see Figure 8.3). You'll probably feel more comfortable if you've managed expectations by posting an honest, casual picture that shows exactly how you look when you're happy, having fun, or just tooling around town rather than on a night out.

With that in mind, consider that when the first date works, what may come next is that dinner date. Then you can really seal the deal with the major do and duds.

Figure 8.3
Terry's looking sharp. But is this really who he is? And is this what he would wear to a coffee shop first date?

Revealing Details

Sometimes too much truth can be bad for you. You may be a parent, but don't put your kids in the photo. You may be a nurse, but a picture of yourself in a major hospital corridor can reveal where you work. You may be into drinking, but you probably shouldn't be taking a drink in your picture.

Revealing details can help or hurt you. It all depends on the details. Some details are things you're proud of. Maybe being a nurse is the most important thing you've accomplished, and you love your work. Maybe you love your kids and are proud of your parenting skills. Maybe drinking wine is a passion, and you're practically on the cover of *Wine Spectator*. These are all things that may be tempting to include in your profile photo, but they really are better off in your profile text.

Anything that can reveal your job location or your identity is not to be included in your photo. Any pictures that have another person in them should not be used. It's not fair to the people in the photo with you—even if they're your kids, and they'll do what you tell them and like it.

A few little details that can slip into a profile photo are simple and fun. Like you make your own clothes, then wear them and reference it in your text (assuming they don't look homemade). If you love an outdoor location (meaning a very public place, such as the Grand Canyon) and it's not where you live, you can use a picture of yourself there. Figure 8.4 shows Alyssa in front of a really cool castle in Portugal.

Figure 8.4
If this was Alyssa's summer home, she wouldn't be showing it. Sadly, she does not live in Obidos nor in this castle, which is now a pricey hotel.

If you're a fisherman, sure, you can have a picture of you out on the boat for your body shot. But make sure it doesn't show the name or license number of your boat. Details are great, just don't reveal anything that might compromise your safety. Figure 8.5 shows a great leisure shot of a guy with a boat, without any indication of where he might be.

In general, a little common sense with any photo that shows detail will help you avoid the hassle of someone you don't want to meet up with finding out where you live or work.

Figure 8.5
Our sailing friend shows his lovely boat without showing its name or license. We've even eliminated the name and location that were written on a boat in the background to protect everyone's privacy.

Summary

After reading chapters about how to take your picture, write your profile, and send e-mails, it's a good time to do a reality check to make sure you're being honest with yourself and others. What may seem like clever, fun ways of describing or photographing yourself may come off as silly or even reveal too much about where you can be found. Take time after you create your profile (text and photos) to make sure that you have told the truth and tuned your message to be most appealing, while stressing all the good things you have to offer.

GUY SAYS

When I was getting ready to write my profile, I was full of ideas about what to say about myself. I was going to stress my previous career accomplishments (taking pictures of naked women, yeah, *that* will impress the ladies), talk about how many places I've lived (so… he's lived in 48 states—wonder how long he'll stay in this one?), and talk about how making love is my favorite thing ever (with who, mister?).

Oh, I wrote that profile. I even put it up for a short while. Then I went back to check out how great it was and read it.

What an idiot.

I wasn't working for the girlie mag anymore, I had settled down and lived in one place for a long time, and the part about loving the lovin' was just plain stupid—like I was the only one who ever figured that one out?

I hadn't actually lied about anything, but I certainly wasn't telling the truth. It's like seeing an ad for a new BMW for $20k. You get to the lot, and yeah, they had one for that price just like it said in the ad, but the dealer's son bought it last night.

Most of that first profile was tacky and made me look pretty bad. The things I was proud of were things that would be hard to understand if you weren't there (believe me, when you're doing a photo shoot with a model, you really have to be there to know that's it's not like on TV). Most of all, it didn't really tell much about me today or what I was really like.

So, by looking at my first profile, I was able to see that trying to impress is quite different than being impressive. I finally rewrote the whole thing to tell what the real truth was—I was a nice guy who had a lot to offer emotionally, and I was hoping to meet someone who was similar and valued the same things that I did. I went on to talk about what those were.

The results were much better, and most of all I was actually proud of what I said and looked forward to meeting someone who could spot the truth from the nonsense. That would be the woman for me, and I would be the guy for her.

—Terry

CHICK SAYS

There's truth, and then there's truth. Shall I make that clearer? There's such a thing as being too honest, to the point where no one will be interested in you. If you're the kind of person who just puts everything out there, chances are you make people a little nervous. When I was putting together my profile, I had to consider how much truth I was willing to give and which truths I was going to choose to tell. For instance, most online dating profiles ask you to pick a body type. They usually give the options of Slender, Athletic, Average, A Few Extra Pounds, Full-Figured, BBW, Curvy, Stocky, Heavyset, Other, or No Answer. What's really funny about this is—there are three ways of saying you're thin but twice as many ways of saying you're overweight. You're meant to choose whichever sounds most correct while sounding most appealing. So which truth should I go for? There are six different versions of the truth here.

Meanwhile, other multiple-choice questions don't seem to give you enough options. In the drinking question mentioned previously—how much do you drink?—you're usually given five options at the most. These are No Answer; Gave It Up; Non-Alcoholic Beverages Only; Social Drinker, Maybe One or Two; and Regularly. For me, none of these seemed quite right. I might drink once a month with friends, but there's a pretty good chance it's more than one or two if we're having a good time and the wine or margaritas are flowing. Sure, Social Drinker comes the closest. But it suggests a certain restraint that seems boring. I'd rather attract a social drinker than a regular or non-drinker, so that's the truth I choose.

And they ask you to pick your best feature, making you choose just one thing from a long list. What happens if I say eyes, but I also have great hair and lips? Is the guy out there looking for my great hair going to miss me? What if honestly my chest is my best feature, but I don't want to attract someone who's looking for that answer? I have to choose which truth I want to present.

The lie is a lie, no matter how you cut it. But the truth seems to have a lot of shades to it. Sometimes there's more than one truth, and you just have to decide which one works better for you in the situation. And while the truth will set you free, you don't necessarily have to set the truth free at every opportunity. Pick your truths wisely and tell them when it's appropriate.

—*Alyssa*

Chapter 9
Writing Profiles and E-mails–Watch What You Say

*Y*es, the photo you choose for your profile is very important. It's a visual world for most people. We want to see your look, your face, your hair, your eyes, your smile, and yes, even your body. We may not even look at your profile if what we see in your photo doesn't appeal to us. But that doesn't mean you can skimp in your profile. It is important. If you get through that early screening stage, your profile is all your potential date is going to have to go on. You have to be more than just another pretty face.

Once you get past the multiple choice questions you were asked to answer in the early part of your profile, as discussed in Part I of this book, you're going to be asked to do the hard part. You're going to come to the essay questions. Remember the essay questions? If you weren't an English major-to-be in school, you probably hated the essay questions. "Just give me some options to choose from!" you mentally screamed at your teacher. Even true/false was preferable. All that writing, all that worrying about structure, all that trying to remember your SAT words. What a miserable mess it was! And here you are being forced to revisit that nightmare. Wait, what's going on? I've never in my adult life used the geometry they made me learn, but you're saying I'm going to have to do essay questions? What kind of justice is this?

Get over yourself. This is important. What's geometry going to do for you but help you build the picket fence? These essay questions are going to get you the girl. They're going to find you your dream guy. They're going to change your life. So stop whining. Take a deep breath and jump in. You'll do just fine. Just follow some simple guidelines.

Say What You Want, Just Spell It Right

You may not want to believe this, but it's true, and it's important. We want to make this very clear. If you spell words wrong, you're going to lose points. Yeah, it's not fair. Not everyone spells well; we think it's genetic. But this is the computer age. If there are typos or misspellings in your profile, your potential mate will think you didn't care enough to spellcheck. Considering that spellcheck takes only about 30 seconds to use, you've lost a lot of effort points there. There's no excuse for not doing it.

Grammar is also very important. You may think you should write like you talk—but when you don't use correct grammar when you're speaking, you may just come across as relaxed and un-pretentious. When you don't use correct grammar when you're writing, you come across as uneducated and crude. And once again, there's no excuse for bad grammar. Spellcheck checks your grammar, too, and offers to fix it for you. How much easier can we make this? Take the time to do it.

The easiest way to avoid spelling and grammar errors is to write your essay questions in a word processing program, like MS Word or WordPerfect. It's likely that you have one of these programs on your computer. WordPerfect usually comes free with your PC. The steps are simple.

1. Open your word processing program, whichever one you have on your computer.

2. Type your essay question response to the question asked.

3. Find your spellcheck. It's probably under the Tools menu, as it is in both MS Word and WordPerfect. In Word it's called Spelling and Grammar, and in WordPerfect it's called Spell Checker. Click on it.

4. A box will open telling you what you've done wrong. In Word, it will tell you, in the same box, whether there's a spelling error or a grammatical error and give you replacement suggestions. In WordPerfect, you run a spellcheck first, then click on a separate heading to check grammar. Make sure you do both.

5. Don't automatically accept any changes offered by the spellchecker. Make sure that the word it wants to change your word to is actually the word you want. Make sure the grammatical change it makes still makes sense within your sentence. Remember—it's a computer. It knows the rules, but it has no subtlety.

6. Read your essay through at least once after the spelling and grammar check to make sure it sounds right. Reading it out loud often helps to make sure it sounds natural.

Figure 9.1 shows WordPerfect spellchecking an essay.

When you're done spellchecking and you're happy with your essay, just copy and paste it from the word processing program into your online profile. This process of writing in Word, then copying it into the online dating site is also useful in case of a timeout on the site. Some sites, like Match, will time you out after a certain period of inactivity. They'll make you log in again. If this happens, you may lose whatever you were working on if you hadn't saved it. If you've written it in Word, then you have all the time in the world to work on it, and only if you close the window without saving have you lost what you've written.

Some online dating sites offer spellchecking within their sites, which is usually a little box at the bottom of the profile. This is useful, but it will only check your spelling, not your grammar. Figure 9.2 shows a built-in spellcheck on a dating site.

Figure 9.1
WordPerfect offers both spelling and grammar checking. It also offers a thesaurus, if you want to choose a more interesting word, and a dictionary so you can make sure you're using the word you meant to use.

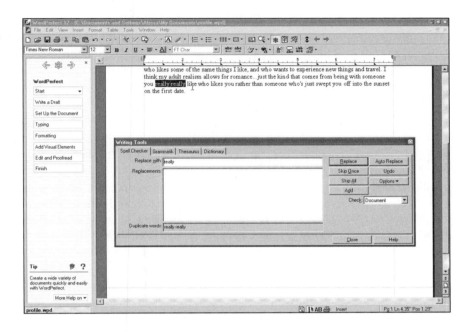

Figure 9.2
Some online dating sites, but not many, offer a built-in spellchecker in case you don't want to bother with a word processing program.

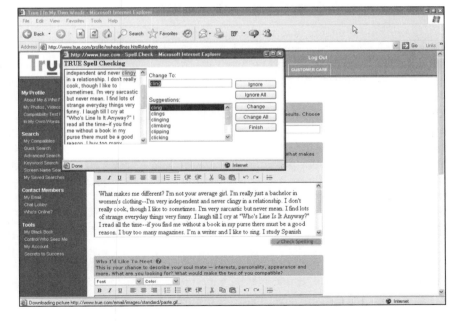

One other thing to be aware of—spellcheck won't catch everything. Yes, it seemed like we were offering you a magic fix, but you do have to expend some effort here. Spellcheck only catches words that aren't words. It doesn't tell you if you've used the wrong one. Homonyms (words that sound alike but are spelled differently and have different meanings), are the main problem. For instance, if you've used "there" instead of "their" or "butt" instead of "but" or "your" instead of "you're," then you're out of luck. You need to actually pay some attention when you're proofreading your profile to make sure you've used the right choice of homonyms.

Online Writing Rules

Most online dating sites have several big boxes they expect you to use to answer their essay questions. There's usually one that asks who you are, one that asks who you want to date, then a few more short questions that ask each site's idea of an insightful question that will reveal a lot about you. These are usually questions like "What was the last book you read?" or "What are your favorite hangouts?" and sometimes "What songs get you in the mood?" There are some key things to remember when answering all these questions.

We've all come across someone's intensely personal Web site while surfing the Internet. We've all wondered what makes someone feel so comfortable talking about things you would only put in a diary and would never want your mother to read. There's something odd about the Internet that makes people want to just spill their guts, knowing that everyone with an Internet connection could happen across it. This is an impulse we want you to avoid.

On an online dating site, you want to put your best foot forward. We've worked very hard to help you take the best picture possible of yourself. Now we want you to write the best possible profile. We want you to be honest, and we want you to show us who you really are—we just don't want you to be overexposed. Remember that this is a public site, and anything you say could be read by thousands of people.

Also, remember the audience you're playing to. These are people you want to date who you hope will want to date you. You need to be honest, but keep the big picture in mind. You know your good qualities, your bad qualities, and your quirky qualities. Stick to the good ones for now. The others will follow as your potential dates get to know you. You want to start a dialogue. No one would get anywhere if they just put everything out there from the beginning. Some things to avoid talking about in your profile are

> ▶ **Your ex.** Never start a sentence with something like, "Since my breakup…" or, "With my last girlfriend…" No one needs to know at this early stage what baggage you may still be carting around with you. Hopefully you've tossed your baggage in a dumpster and are coming to online dating with as close to a fresh slate as possible. If not, maybe you should reconsider dating for now.

> ▶ **Avoid any sort of sexual innuendo.** Don't talk about how good you are in bed. Don't talk about specific body parts that would normally remain unspoken of until a third date in the live dating world. This is neither the time nor the place.

▶ **Your bad habits.** You may imagine someone will think it's cute that you eat crackers in bed or haven't bought new clothes in two years. And someone might. But if you want to play the numbers, you're better off leaving the crackers for a later conversation.

▶ **How rich you are.** Yes, we're all looking for someone who's financially secure. We don't know anyone who would rather date someone poor than someone wealthy. It's human nature not to want to worry about money. But, while it is a selling point, you've already stated your income range in one of the multiple-choice questions. If you start talking about money here, it will look like bragging. And if you start talking about all your houses and all your cars, you'll seem materialistic. And you'll attract people who are only after one thing—your money.

So, you ask, if I can't talk about my ex, my sex, my crackers, and my Porsche, what the heck am I supposed to talk about? Well, let's hope that's not all there is to you. Here are some suggestions of things to bring up in your profile:

▶ **Anything you do that's creative.** Do you write, paint, play music of any sort, sing well at karaoke bars, act in plays? All these things give you depth. But don't lie. If you haven't played guitar since you were 12 and don't remember any of the chords, your date isn't going to think much of you when you start strumming away tunelessly.

▶ **The pleasure and enrichment you get from your job.** We know that not everyone loves his job. But everyone should. And if it's something that gets you excited and makes you want to get out of bed in the morning, your potential date is going to think it's cool, too, because you love it. They'll catch on to your passion.

▶ **For the same reason, you can talk about how much you love your child.** Especially if you're a guy, this will make women go, "Awwwww," when they read it. Just be careful about how much you elaborate. If you go on about how your child is the most important thing in your life and always will come first, you're likely to turn off anyone who doesn't want to play second fiddle. It may be true that your child will always come first, but this is something inherent in being a parent. If you don't say it, at least your potential date can pretend that they might get a leading role.

▶ **How great of a cook you are.** How good you are at choosing wine. How much you enjoy hiking. What a good surfer you are. Basically, any positive hobbies you have are worth mentioning. People love to have someone cook for them, think people who know wine are sophisticated, know that hikers and surfers are outdoorsy and at least somewhat athletic. You never want to talk about your career as a couch potato (unless it means you're a TV critic). Talk about anything fun that keeps you busy, makes you happy, and makes your life worth living.

You have a good starting place now. So don't be afraid of those big empty boxes. Just jump right in. But beware. You'll see a count of how many letters/characters you've used at the top of the box. It probably says you have 2000 characters to use. But don't think that means you *must* use 2000 characters. In fact, you're a lot better off keeping it short and sweet.

As time has passed, online journalists, and even some print journalists, have begun using shorter and shorter paragraphs in their writing. This is because the average reader scans. Readers are intimidated or bored by big blocks of text. They want sound bites in text version. They want their information quick and easy. For this reason, you need to keep things short and entertaining.

You're better off saying what you want to say in about half the space that they give you to say it. You don't have to tell your life story. Let's try that another way—**don't** tell your life story. Just hit the bullet points. There's time to tell more once you've caught someone's attention. For now you just have to come across as appealing enough to get that wink or e-mail. Figure 9.3 shows how intimidating a big block of text can be in a profile.

Figure 9.3
If you write too much in one paragraph of your profile, no one is likely to want to read it. Keep it short, and divide it into smaller paragraphs.

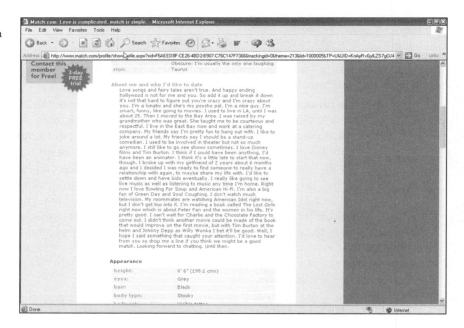

However, you don't want to say too little. You need to say enough to intrigue your potential date. If you're writing the bare minimum required by the box, usually 200 characters, you're not saying enough. You want to paint a thumbnail picture of yourself. If you don't say more than the bare minimum, your date is going to think you didn't want to put the effort into writing more. If you're not spending effort at this point, what's going to happen later in a relationship?

HOW YOU SAY IT IS JUST AS IMPORTANT AS WHAT YOU SAY

Don't use clichés. You know them when you see them—and they're abundant in online dating ads. Avoid any and all of the following phrases: Renaissance man, special someone, soulmate, spiritual journey, long walks on the beach, quiet evenings at home, girl who can go from jeans to an evening gown, someone to share my life, it's hard to describe myself in this box, and I'll try anything once.

Don't sound desperate. Try to come across as a confident person who just wants someone to enjoy things with, not someone who might slit his wrists if he can't find someone who will love him.

Don't use chat room speak. Don't use shortcuts like LOL or TTFN. Your audience may not know what you're talking about, or they might think you spend too much time in chat rooms. Either way, you're better off avoiding them. Don't use emoticons (J or L)—they just make you look silly. Don't write in ALL CAPS. On the Internet, that's considered yelling. Don't abbreviate words unless you're running out of space.

Don't use slang. It goes out of style quickly enough that you may seem out of date by the time your potential date reads your profile. You'll have plenty of time later to show how dope you are.

Security in Your Profile

Let's repeat here: An online dating site is a public site. Don't say anything in your profile that you're not comfortable having potentially thousands of people read. In all likelihood, your profile will probably only be read by a few hundred people at the most, but even so you want to keep to what you're comfortable with. And you want to be careful not to give too many clues to your personal information. Here are some things to avoid in your profile for the sake of security:

▶ **Your address.** If you live in a big city, it's probably safe to say what neighborhood you live in, as that will still probably include a pretty big area. But if you live in a smaller city or town, stick to naming the town. Don't go beyond that.

▶ **Where you work.** If you give the name of where you work, it's extremely simple for someone to find you. Businesses are listed everywhere. A simple search on the Internet and a potential date, who you'd rather not have as a potential date, could be showing up at your cubicle.

▶ **Your telephone number.** Do you really want your phone ringing constantly with who knows who on the other end of the line?

▶ **Your date of birth.** By itself, this is unlikely to be an issue. But if someone starts a conversation with you and finds out your real name, you've just given them two key parts of your identity. Can identity theft be far behind?

▶ **Your full name.** All someone needs in order to find you is your name. Wait until you've gotten to know someone before you reveal this.

▶ **A personal, traceable e-mail address.** We told you in Part I of this book how to set up an anonymous e-mail account. Use that e-mail address if you want to try to include one in your profile.

We don't want to scare you. Everything should be fine as long as you follow these rules. But we want you to be aware of what you're putting out there. Date online, but date safely.

Bad Profile/Good Profile

A bad profile is riddled with clichés, chat room speak, and security lapses. It hasn't been spellchecked, and it tells too much. Here are a couple of examples of bad profile writing:

> I'M A GOOD WOMAN WHO LIKES LONG WALKS ON THE BEACH, ROMANTIC CANDLELIT DINNERS, N QUIET EVENINGS @ HM W/THAT SPECIAL SOMEONE. ;) I BROKE UP W/MY BOYFRIEND OF 7 YRS A COUPLA MONTHS AGO N I HAD A HARD TIME GETTING OVER HIM. I RECENTLY WENT ON A SPIRITUAL JOURNEY N REALIZED U HAVE 2 LIVE LIFE 1 DAY @ A TIME. I'M LOOKING 4 MY SOULMATE TO SHARE MY LIFE, 1 DAY @ A TIME. MY PRINCE CHARMING. COULD U B HIM?
>
> I WORK @ ST. FRANCIS HOSPITAL I'M A NURSE, SO I'M A VRY CARING PERSON. ONCE I HD THIS PATIENT WHO HAD A CAR ACCDENT N I REMEMBER HE JUST LOOKED UP @ ME N TOLD ME HOW MUCH MY LOVING TOUCH HAD MEANT 2 HIM. HE WS MARRIED, SO WE NEVER WENT OUT, BUT IT MEANT SO MUCH 2 ME THAT I HAD TOUCHED HIS LIFE. I'M SURE I CN TOUCH YOURS, IF YOU JUST GIVE ME A CHANCE.
>
> Y IS IT SO HARD 2 FIND A GOOD GUY OUT THERE? I TRIED 2 DATE A COUPLE O TIMES SINCE MY BREAKUP BUT SEEMS LIKE ALL ANYONE WANTS IS SEX N 2 HAVE A GOOD TIME. I WANT MORE THAN THAT. I WANT A HUSBAND N CHILDREN. I HOPE I CN FIND SOMEONE WONDERFUL ONLINE. PLEASE E-MAIL ME @ HOTNURSE20006@AOL.COM IF YOU'RE INTERESTED. REALLY HOPING 2 HEAR FRM U.

Scary, no? Here's another…

> Hey, ladies, are you looking for a good time? I've got it for you right here. I'm a great looking guy with a smokin' body. And I realy love to shake it on the dance floor! I'll try anything— I'm a guy who lives on the edge. I got my own company and a couple of houses, one in Silicon Valley and one in LA then a condo in NY. I'm hoping to close soon on an apartment in Paris. My favorite thing is to take my Jag up into the Hollywood hills and drive the curves. Maybe you'll let me drive you're curves… My number's 415-555-9724. Give me a call sometime."

Ugh. The person who finds either of these profiles appealing is someone who should have a few years of therapy before entering the dating pool.

A good profile will be funny, smart, and honest. You want to come across as interesting and sincere. Here is an example of good profile writing:

> What makes me different? I'm not your average girl. I'm really just a bachelor in women's clothing—I'm very independent and never clingy in a relationship. I don't really cook, though I like to sometimes. I like going out and trying new places.
>
> I'm very sarcastic but never mean. I find lots of strange everyday things very funny. I laugh till I cry at *Who's Line Is It Anyway?* I read all the time—if you find me without a book in my purse, there must be a good reason. I buy too many magazines.
>
> I'm a writer, and I like to sing. I study Spanish, despite being completely incapable of speaking it except when cornered. I watch ridiculously political documentaries as well as indy films and Hollywood pics. I'd rather walk on the beach than sit and sun myself on it. It's San Francisco, so sun can be a rarity anyway.
>
> I'm not looking for a prince. Who needs the paparazzi following you everywhere? I'd just like a guy who's smart, who knows how to make a clever comeback, who really enjoys talking to me, who likes some of the same things I like, and who wants to experience new things and travel.
>
> I love the guy with a great smile and blue hair who calls himself a geek because he works with computers.
>
> And I really like the super-smart guy who talks about science and politics and who doesn't look like he'd have devilish thoughts under his wire-rimmed glasses, but does.

This profile has been carefully spellchecked and grammar checked. It uses no slang. It's not boastful and is occasionally self-deprecating. It clearly paints a quick picture of who the person is who wrote it. And it's just clever enough and intelligent enough to intrigue without being pretentious.

HEADLINES SHOULD NOT BE TAKEN LIGHTLY

Most online dating sites make you fill in a headline. This headline will show up next to your picture and user name and will be part of your potential date's first impression of you. You may think this is a throwaway decision you have to make, but it's not. A good headline starts you off on the right foot and gets a browser's attention.

The average headline is something like "Fun-loving single seeking same." Not very inspired or memorable. Your best bet is to use something clever if you can come up with it. Some of the headlines we've seen and liked were "Dances with squirrels," "My Shoes Match My Belt," "I ken raed, rite, and spehl grate," "I said 12 inch "PIANIST," and "Recommended by 4 out of 5."

If you can't come up with something inspired, we think it's okay to pick an appropriate song lyric or quote. Some dating sites suggest this isn't the best way to go, but frankly it's better than "Spiritual Warrior Looking For Spiritual Goddess." Though maybe that works for some people...

How and When to Write That First E-mail

You've written a great profile and put yourself out there. You've winked at someone whom you like, and he's read your fabulous profile and winked back at you. Now what? Now it's time to really start the conversation. Someone needs to e-mail.

Hopefully, at least one of you is a paying subscriber and can actually e-mail the other. Let's say the one who ponied up the bucks was you. So you know it's your move. This may seem more intimidating to you than writing your profile, but keep a couple of things in mind.

He likes you. He winked back at you. Just keep doing what you did in your profile, and he'll keep liking you. Plus it's just an e-mail. There's nothing big you've invested in this relationship yet. And who knows, maybe *you* won't like *him*. You just never know. And you won't know until you try.

So you're sitting at your computer. You're staring at the blank e-mail message you want to send. Before you start typing, stop and remember the basic rules you used for your profile. Keep it short and sweet. Don't say too much. And keep it clean. A basic guide for your first e-mail is as follows:

1. Say what you liked about your potential date's profile, what made you want to e-mail him. This is important, as you want him to know that you actually read his profile and connected on some level. Some profile spammers will jump on any mutual wink to write an e-mail, no matter who may have responded.

2. Continue to avoid anything of a sexual nature. It's good to say something complimentary about your potential date's photo, such as "nice eyes" or "great smile," but you don't want to go too far. "Great pecs" or "nice butt" should be saved for later.

3. Tell a little more about yourself. Elaborate about something you enjoy. Talk some more about your favorite things. Try to emphasize things you have in common with your potential date.

4. Continue to steer clear of any identifying information, such as where you work, where you live, or specific personal information. But do give him your anonymous e-mail to reply to.

5. End the e-mail with something cute and snappy. No desperate pleas for a return e-mail.

6. Read it over several times before sending. Make sure you're saying what you mean to say, use spellcheck, and make sure you didn't say anything that could be misinterpreted.

Cold E-mailing

If you're feeling particularly bold, you might want to skip the whole winking stage. This is a trickier e-mail, but often a more appealing way to contact someone for the first time. You're able to personalize your e-mail more effectively than a wink, and you might make more of an impression on the person you're hoping to impress.

When you're e-mailing through the online dating services, they automatically link the e-mail to your profile, so whomever you're e-mailing can easily click the link and check out your profile after they've seen your e-mail. There's also usually a small photo included in the e-mail so they can get a quick idea of who you are while reading your e-mail.

In a cold e-mail, it's even more important to keep it short. You're taking up someone's time whom you haven't had any encouragement from. You need to get in, say what you want to say, and get out.

1. Compliment her profile and photo, explaining what it is that caught your eye.
2. Suggest she take a look at your profile.
3. Tell her a few things the two of you have in common.
4. Politely say you hope she'll write back, and give her an e-mail address to write back to if she's not a paying member.

How and When to Respond if You're E-mailed

You're minding your own business when suddenly an e-mail pops up in your Hotmail account saying someone from a dating site has e-mailed you. No, don't panic; it's going to be okay. Just calmly click on that e-mail and check it out. We'll guide you through this.

Someone's cold e-mailed you. There are a couple of ways this could go. If he's a profile spammer, most likely his e-mail is going to look something like this:

Hi, would you like to talk sometime?

This is not an e-mail you should feel the need to respond to. Chances are this person has no idea who you are. Go ahead and trash it.

However, maybe someone has cold e-mailed you, and his e-mail looks like this:

Hi, how are you? I came across your profile today and Wow! You have gorgeous hair and I love your smile. I really like the way you express yourself. You seem really intelligent and funny.

I can't believe you love Hunter S. Thompson, too! I think his writing is great. I'm really going to miss him. Did you see the documentary about him that came out recently? Very interesting.

I'm a part-time musician who works in IT down in Palo Alto. I'm also a great cook, and I like trying out all the new restaurants. On the weekends, I usually like to go hiking up at Mt. Tam or sometimes surfing down in Pacifica.

Please take a look at my profile and e-mail me back if you think we're a good match. I'd love to hear from you.

This is a good e-mail. You know the writer has read your profile. He's complimented you, talked about a common interest, and given you a little information about himself. You will want to respond to this e-mail.

Your response is going to bear a strong resemblance to the e-mail we suggested you send before. You're going to keep it clean, keep it simple, and not say too much. But there is a slight difference.

You've got someone who's written to you out of the blue because he's really interested in you, so much so that he's put himself out there. Don't leave him dangling. Once you've checked out his profile and decided he's someone you want to get to know, write back ASAP. You can play it a bit coy, wait a day to avoid seeming like you were watching your e-mail like a hawk. But don't wait too long.

When you write your response, you can be a little bit more effusive. Tell him several things you really liked about his profile and photo. Write a little bit more about things you have in common with each other. And most importantly—ask questions. This is going to facilitate his next e-mail to you. Ask him more about what he does in IT. Ask him what kind of food he likes to cook. Ask him about the documentary he mentioned. Then likely when he responds, he'll ask you some questions. And before you know it you've got a dialogue going. Just like that.

E-mail Etiquette

Think of your first couple of e-mails with someone as your first date with that person. You've been on first dates before. You know how they work. So just relax. You don't even have to dress up for this. And there's no concern over who pays for dinner.

If you went to dinner with someone for the first time and all he did was talk about himself, what would you think? You'd think, "Check, please." The same is true in these early e-mails. You want to talk about yourself, certainly. You're getting to know one another. But you also want to seem interested in him. You want to ask questions. You want to expand on things that he's said and talk about his interests. You want to make him feel like you're interested in him and want to know more about him. Following are some examples of good questions to ask, if you're at loose ends:

> ▶ "What kind of work do you do?" If you know already, try, "What's your favorite thing about what you do?"
> ▶ "What's your family like? Any brothers or sisters?"
> ▶ "What do you like to do in your spare time?"
> ▶ "What are your favorite hangouts?"
> ▶ "What's your favorite thing to do with your best friend on a weekend?"
> ▶ "What are your favorite bands, books, movies, TV shows, etc.?"

The important thing is to keep the dialogue going. Asking questions will do that. And if, when he writes back, he doesn't ask you questions in return, just answer the ones you asked him while commenting on his answers. Then ask some more questions. Just don't go crazy with too many questions at once. Pace yourself. If things go well, there will be many e-mails in which to ask all of your questions.

How to Say No

Just as in real life, you're going to find yourself approached by someone you're just not interested in. Maybe it's her photo, maybe it's her grammar, maybe it's her political or religious views. Whatever the reason, you just don't feel you're compatible. So you're going to have to figure out how to say no.

Cold E-mail

If someone's sent you a cold e-mail, it's easy enough to say no. She has no reason to believe you'd be interested in her in the first place. So you just have to let her down easy. There's a good way and a bad way to do this.

The bad way is simple avoidance. The e-mail's sitting in your inbox—just a click of your mouse will delete it. Some think this is actually the kind way of dealing with the e-mail. If you never respond, the sender can imagine you just don't check your dating account anymore. You never read the e-mail. There's no rejection there, just a big nothing. We don't recommend this, just because it keeps the sender guessing. She might feel compelled to send a follow up e-mail, wondering if you never got the first one. She might wonder if she just didn't say the right thing and want to try again. Sometimes it's kinder just to rip the Band-Aid off rather than keep her in limbo.

The good way is a simple, "Thanks but no thanks" e-mail. Try something like, "I really appreciate your e-mail, but I just don't think we're compatible. Good luck in your search!" This kind rejection won't break her heart, unless she's a little too emotionally invested. She'll just move on, knowing she needs to try someone else. Easy-peasy.

Mutual Winks, Mutual E-mails

It's a lot harder to say no once the date has started. In the middle of the cheese plate, you suddenly realize he's not the guy for you. But you can't just disappear in the middle of dinner! What now?

Rejecting someone is never easy, but it gets harder the longer you know the person. The same is true when you're e-mailing. And once again, there's a good way and a bad way. And, unsurprisingly, the bad way is the same as with the cold e-mail.

The bad way is to end contact. He e-mails you, and you just don't e-mail back. We definitely don't approve of this method. Once you've begun to have a rapport with someone, just disappearing is cruel. He'll wonder where you went. He'll wonder if you've gone out of town. He'll wonder if you lost his e-mail address. He'll e-mail you a couple more times to try to get a response from you. Then he'll be forced to decide you just got tired of him and lacked the guts to tell him. This is sad for him, and very bad karma for you. Please don't take the easy way out.

The good way is the hard way. You need to tell him. On the plus side, you're not face to face. You don't have to sit through pleadings of "Why, but we get along so well, let's give it another try, I know we can work this out…" So just suck it up, and write the e-mail. Be kind but firm. Make it clear that there's no changing your mind. Tell him now that you know him better, you just don't think your interests/values/goals/future plans are in sync. Tell him you don't think the chemistry is there. Tell him whatever is the truth without being mean. Read your e-mail over a couple of times before you send it to make sure you've been as honest and kind as you can be.

Finally, no matter which method you choose, don't agree to a meeting after rejecting him. He may suggest that you'll change your mind if you meet in person. But this is too dangerous. You've already decided you're not compatible. You're not going to change your mind. And if you agree to meet someone in person whom you've just rejected, you're running the risk of meeting a very angry person. It's not worth the risk to you.

Everything Seems So Perfect

You've exchanged a couple of e-mails now, and you feel really excited and happy about the way things are going. You seem to click on so many levels; he thinks you're cute, you think he's cute. Everything in your profiles seems to match up perfectly. You feel the little flutters in your stomach when you see his e-mail pop up on your screen.

Good for you! But calm down a little, okay? You need to take things slow. It's easy to get overly excited when you finally meet someone who really seems to click with you. But if you get over-eager, he may not keep clicking with you much longer.

Just as you wouldn't start planning your future with him (at least out loud) after two dates, you shouldn't start doing so after two e-mails. There's a lot more to learn about each other. And if you're sticking to our advice, your e-mails have been relatively short thus far.

There's no specific rule for how long you should e-mail with someone before you start talking about meeting in person. It's all about your comfort level. But we do have a recommendation: E-mail for at least two weeks before deciding to make personal contact. Assuming each of you responds within a day or two during that period, you'll have exchanged 7-10 e-mails. That's enough to have talked about a lot of things and determined a compatibility of interests, plans for the future, and an idea of whether your personalities click.

During this time, it's unwise to get too emphatic. Make sure that he knows you like him, but don't push it too hard. Never suggest that you love him already, even if you secretly think you do.

Never start talking about your future home, future children, what your wedding would be like... all common sense, you would think. If you started talking about any of that two weeks after meeting someone for the first time in real life, you'd scare him into the next state. So take it easy. Keep your dream romance to yourself for now. You want the opportunity to meet this man of your dreams. Don't scare him away before you get that opportunity.

And don't e-mail him back multiple times before he has a chance to respond to you. You don't want to appear over-anxious. Give him time to read your e-mail and form a response. Understand he's got a life, just as you should have. Not everyone is waiting with bated breath until that new mail icon pops up on his screen. You probably want someone who has other interests, not to mention a job, which might keep him busy sometimes. And if you're sitting there waiting with bated breath for his e-mails, maybe you should go out and get some other interests and a job so that you're not quite so focused on him. Nothing's less appealing than neediness, especially in this early stage of communication.

Summary

Writing your profile can be scary at first. But if you follow some simple guidelines and let your personality come out, you'll do just fine. Be honest, interesting, and funny. Write it in a word processing program, and make sure you use spellcheck and grammar check before you submit it. Take care with headlines and make them interesting. And when you start to e-mail one another, keep it short, interesting, and ask questions.

GUY SAYS

I think the worst profiles are the ones where a woman says that's she's just online because her friends dared her to.

Wait! No, the worst profiles are the ones where the woman goes on and on about all the endless and totally unrealistic things she fully expects in a man, and then fails to say a single thing about what she has to offer in return.

Well, maybe the worst profiles are the ones that say the woman is as comfortable in an evening gown as she is in jeans.

What I am trying to say is that the worst profiles are the ones where a woman says absolutely nothing at all. The above are not only references to real profiles I've read, they are very common. When I read them, I didn't learn a thing about the person except that she was not really serious about meeting someone.

Profile text is important but so are the headlines. Many profile headlines are real turn-offs. Heads such as "Just looking for fun" or "Friends First" are surefire clues that a woman isn't really looking for fun or a real date. I kept looking for a profile with a headline that read "I'm a nice person, and I'm looking for a nice person too." They just don't seem to exist.

Okay, I wasn't afraid to come out and tug at a few heartstrings when I wrote my profile head. It said

"Looking for a whisper only I get to hear."

That's actually what I was looking for. I wanted to explain that I was looking for a sensitive person who could reach me in a way that only she could do... that I wanted to be the special person in her life.

I didn't play games, and I wasn't cute or clever. I simply described myself accurately, took the most important message in the text and used it as my headline. By accurately describing yourself in the text, you will know real fast if someone is interested in you for the right reasons. It's the only way to go.

Oh, I used MS Word and its spelling and grammar checkers. When everything sounded right, I copied and pasted it into the profile form. I figured I had one chance to impress, and I didn't want anything distracting from the pure poetic majesty of my profile text. Well, at least it wasn't in ALL CAPS.

—*Terry*

CHICK SAYS

When reading through men's profiles, there are certain things that catch my eye, for better or for worse.

The first thing I notice is the length of their answers. If they've written little, I'll read it to see if they made the most of what they've said. Most of the time, if they've written the bare minimum, there's not enough information for me to go on.

If they've written a lot, I might not read the answer at all. If it's a big block of text and they're seeming to go on and on, I might just say forget it. Who has the time? There are other profiles to get to. And I'm someone who reads a lot, all the time: novels, magazines, newspapers, online sites. And I'm daunted by some of these huge long paragraphs. These answers would be better served by being broken up into shorter paragraphs and trimmed of excessive verbiage.

The next thing that hits me is spelling and grammar. Like I said, I read a lot. If I see a lot of typos, bad grammar, or misused words, there's a pretty good chance I'm going to dismiss the writer. It may seem harsh, but I can't help thinking that if you can't write a decent sentence and can't be bothered to use spellcheck, then you're really not too bright.

The third thing I notice is whether you're saying anything new. It's astonishing to me how many profiles use the same clichés over and over again. You'd think all the men got together and sat around saying, "Ooh, let's use, 'I'm looking for that special someone'" and "Hey, I'm going to say, 'I'm looking for a woman who can go from jeans and a T-shirt during the day to an evening gown at night.' Why don't you try that, too?"

Lastly, if all of the above have been avoided, I notice the person who wrote the answer. I notice intelligence and humor, assuming there is some. I see someone interesting and clever. I see someone I would consider dating because he didn't wrap himself up in anything distracting, because he dared to be original. And that's the guy who gets my wink.

—*Alyssa*

Part III

Learning about Others You Meet Online

Chapter 10
Edited Photos: Spotting the Phonies

The bad news is that when done by a professional retoucher, you'll never be able to spot a photo that has been modified in Photoshop or other sophisticated image editing program. The good news is: The photos that have been "edited" in such programs that show up in online dating profiles are seldom done by professionals and are usually pretty easy to spot.

We aren't going to teach you how to retouch your own photographs—not in a book about telling the truth in your profile. But we will show you how to spot the photos that have undergone a bit of the old image editing magic. That will help you spot the phonies and the people who may not be telling you the whole truth about how they look.

Understanding Image Editing

Once you understand what can be done with image editing programs, such as Photoshop, you'll quickly understand why it may be temping to improve on appearances with the power they offer. In just a matter of minutes, most average computer users can actually do some major adjustments to their pictures, including such tricks as

- ▶ Removing wrinkles
- ▶ Removing shadows under the eyes and all kinds of blemishes
- ▶ Whitening teeth
- ▶ Changing the shape of a face or the whole body
- ▶ Taking away double chins and jowls
- ▶ Adding or removing hair
- ▶ Trimming waistlines, removing fat, and adding muscles
- ▶ Getting rid of tattoos

As if Photoshop was Botox or a health club in a box, someone good at using it can chisel away at the years, the features, or the pounds. When thinking about posting an online profile picture, many people don't think a nip here or a tuck there can hurt—but they're wrong.

Image editing is one of the purest forms of lying in the online dating world. You'll want to be sure that the picture you see has not been modified in any significant way. You'll want to be sure that what you see is what you get, not what the person wishes he was. Let's take a look at some of the most common forms of image editing using photos of poor Terry.

Making Old Photos Look New

One common mistake people make is using non-contemporary photos of themselves in their online profile. It can be as simple as finding an old photo and posting it, or it can be done even more deceptively by applying some image editing tricks. Let's start with an old photo (Figure 10.1) and make it look new.

Figure 10.1
This is the oldest photo Terry has of himself as an adult. Note the hairstyle, the tie, and the collar. This picture was taken during the disco daze, and Terry was pretty happy it seems.

You can't always tell if old photos are old from the quality of the actual photograph. There are older photos that can look clear and current, but most are probably before the age of digital cameras and may be pretty low-quality. In Figure 10.1, Terry's photo looks old due to the way he's wearing his hair and the clothes he's wearing.

Terry does like the fact that he's 21 again and is so happy in the picture. In fact, since it's one of his favorites and it's how he still thinks of himself, he would love to use it to show his "true self" to all the women searching for him online. Although Terry is delusional in this one area, he still is grounded enough to know that the clothes do "date" him a bit. Being pretty handy with Photoshop, he sets to work to make the old picture look somewhat like he does today, regarding style and hair.

Figure 10.2 shows the first things he chooses to do. He removes the background so he can put in his current apartment complex. Next, he gives himself a haircut and even adds an ear that was once covered by hair. This is a tricky process, and although not perfect, once viewed at a small size, the hair is good enough to pass at a quick view.

Figure 10.2
Using Photoshop, some basic changes are made to the old photo. The background is stripped out, and the hair is roughly brought to modern standards.

It may look silly at this point, but the look is becoming more contemporary. The remaining problems are the collar and the tie and the little black vest under the jacket. The jacket is a bit dated in its lapels and the fabric, but that can be forgiven. Terry lives in a small cowboy town in Northern California, and it's actually a style that's worn up there.

Undaunted by the challenge, he moves forward and adds his apartment complex. This is a very clever trick. He doesn't show any identifiers about the actual place, but he figures that he'll mention in his e-mails that he lives in the area, and the complex is pretty well known in the small town where he lives. The trees and landscaping are also common in the area. It "grounds" his old picture in the community he currently lives in to make the picture look contemporary.

Next, as shown in Figure 10.3, he blends himself into the background and makes major changes to his attire. The tie is covered over by white to match the shirt. The shape of the collar is brought under the jacket lapels, and the shirt is given a casual look overall. It may not be perfect, but reduced down to the thumbnail size of an online profile photo, except for the fact that he looks pretty dorky, it can pass for a modern-day young version of Terry.

He could keep going and make it more natural looking by changing lighting, making subtle tonal changes, and adding details. Overall, this is good enough to use online, so he stops and gives it a try.

This 50-year-old is passing himself off as a young man in an attempt to get a young date. That's not fair, is it?

Figure 10.3
The background is added, and the collar, tie, and shirt are made more contemporary. At a thumbnail size, this photo will look fine, and, aside from the silly smile, it's an old photo made new.

It's not, and it's a flat-out lie, but hey, this is the digital age, and people are doing this all the time with photos. Even our news photos have sometimes been doctored. Pictures of celebrities have been heavily retouched for decades. Tabloid publications create new realities on every page. Is it any wonder that regular people are doing this? If the celebrities and the politicians and the ad agencies lie, you can reasonably expect the average Joe to be influenced by such pervasive image manipulation.

SPOTTING OLD PHOTOS

It's not too hard to spot an older photo that has been through a makeover. Most amateur retouching has telltale signs, such as sharp edges around the person in the photo, shadows on the person that do not match the shadows in the background, a different "color temperature" for the person and the background, and an overall artificial look. The most common clue is irregular shapes on body parts or the face, indicating that areas have been manipulated.

Spotting Retouching

Although people will use older photos sometimes, most people will take somewhat current photos and attempt to make themselves look a bit better through image editing. These are simple tricks, and they are used pretty often. The most common fixes are to trim off a few pounds, whiten teeth, remove wrinkles, or take someone else out of the picture.

The figures in the following sections show how these edits often look. They are subtle, and they may not be easy to spot, so look carefully at the samples, and then think about such image editing when you're looking at pictures online to see if any of these techniques are being used by people you may be interested in.

Removing Wrinkles

Wrinkles happen to all of us, even at a young age. In our society, wrinkles are frowned upon, and wrinkle removal is a multi-billion dollar industry. An image editing program is a quick and inexpensive form of plastic surgery—unfortunately it only works on the digital image and not the actual person.

Most wrinkles can be removed by using an overall blur or image softening filter. Or you can use a Smudge or Healing tool which allows the specific wrinkles to be smudged and blended into the face. The Healing tool will actually sample the area selected, create an "average" of the area and change anything, such as a wrinkle, that is not like most of the information in the picture.

Figure 10.4 shows Terry getting a digital face lift by having his wrinkles removed. The change is subtle, and most of the time the removal of wrinkles is pretty hard to catch.

Figure 10.4
Terry with wrinkles, then without. Terry claims he did it the other way around—he had to add wrinkles for this example. Okay, whatever. And hey, what happened to that double chin?

Since wrinkle removal is pretty hard to spot, here is a simple rule to consider. Look at the age the person claims to be in the profile. Chances are, if he's past his mid-thirties, he'll have a few wrinkles. If he's in his forties or older and the photo doesn't show any wrinkles, he probably did a bit of touching up.

Making Teeth Whiter

Just as with wrinkles, another common concern that is part of the cosmetic landscape is white teeth. Actually, although it's hard and expensive to fix wrinkles in real life, it's pretty easy and cheap to get your teeth whitened in the real world. There are even home whitening kits available. Regardless, another common fix in many photos is making teeth whiter.

This fix can apply to any age and may be the only retouching in the photo. Having pearly whites is a dream most people have, and in the attempt to put their best smile in front of you, teeth can easily be whitened by using a Dodge tool found in most image editing programs that allows you to lighten specific areas of a picture. By "dodging" the teeth, they get whiter. Another technique is to manually select the teeth with a Selection tool, and then lighten them using the Contrast and Brightness controls; you can also to change the color cast from dingy yellow to pure white.

As with any image editing, it's possible to improve teeth. If one's missing, a good tooth can be copied and pasted in. This is less likely, but anything is possible. Figure 10.5 shows Terry's new smile.

Figure 10.5
Look out Hollywood—
Terry's smile is now big-
screen white. Put on
your sunglasses, or it'll
burn your corneas.

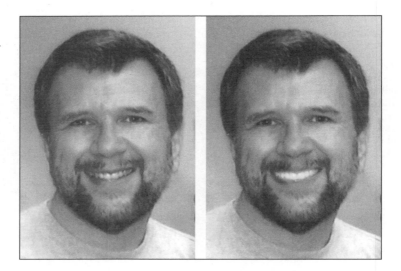

Actually, whitened teeth are pretty easy to spot. They often look too white. In color photos, there is a natural tone for even the whitest smile, and if it has been played with, it will look artificial.

Changing Hairlines and Styles

After wrinkles and teeth, the next concern many people have is their hair. For men, it's most often a lack of it; for women, it's usually the style or the color. After the trip to the Photoshop plastic surgeon and the Photoshop dentist, it's only natural (no pun, seriously) to visit the Photoshop hairstylist.

Spotting changes to hair is usually one of the easiest fixes to spot. Hair is one of the greatest challenges for any retouch artist—even the best of them. Hair has a variety of colors, tones, and tons of detail. To try to bring all of those details together in a new style is very hard to do. Programs such as Photoshop do have Cloning tools that allow you to select one area and then paint with it just as if the selected image were a brush. This works pretty well for creating edits to hair.

Figures 10.2 and 10.3 showed Terry removing lots of youthful hair, and you could see in those intentionally amateur-level retouching samples how artificial the hair change looked. Figure 10.6 shows a more current photo of Terry in which he adds a bit of hair, and this time he's letting you see a bit more of a professional retouching sample. It's pretty hard to tell that the change has been made.

Figure 10.6
Terry wasn't exactly balding in the original, but the receding hairline was just too tempting not to adjust. Here, the hair is added in a very natural way, and chances are you would never be able to tell.

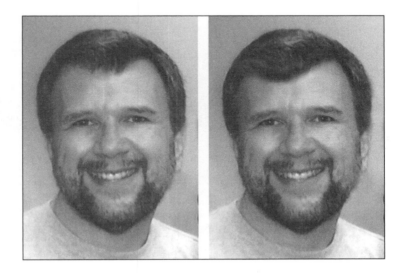

Trimming, Slimming, and Shaping Bodies

The next stop is the Photoshop gym, and Terry is going to have a quick workout to take off a few pounds. This is a common fix and is often done with mixed results. Changing body shape is pretty hard to do, and it's usually easy to spot when a body has been modified.

We've all probably seen a photo in which someone has copied her head and pasted it onto a different body. This is often done in magazine ads for diet pills, for example. It's possible that you could see such cheesy image editing tricks online, but you'll be able to see those from a mile away. The more common fix to look for is when little changes or improvements have been made, such as

▶ Taking a few bulges off of the waist or other body parts

▶ Adding larger breasts on women

▶ Adding muscles on men (and women, too)

▶ Removing cellulite ripples

Figure 10.7 shows how Terry has dealt with his love handles, although he insists they are quite useful—but only after getting to know each other a while. This bulge removal involves a number of techniques, such as copying bits of the background with a Cloning tool and pasting them over the parts that need to be removed. Mostly, when a retoucher trims a person, he's actually adding a bit of the background over the unwanted shape. That's why in previous examples in this book,

Figure 10.7
Although Terry loves his love handles, he was willing to show us what he would look like without them through the power of image editing. The things Terry has had to endure for the sake of this book!

backgrounds were removed—it makes it very easy to modify the body shape, then the background can be pasted in behind the new body shape by making the background a bit larger than it was originally.

Figure 10.7 shows how subtle a body change can be. Think of it this way: When you're about to date someone, you may say, "I should lose about five pounds if I can." It's not enough to make a big difference, but enough to make you look and feel a little better. Similarly, it's the little trim used virtually that's so tempting, and that can fool you.

Removing Someone from the Picture

It's a perfectly smart thing to cut or erase someone out of your picture of you. We've told you to do it. However, the ability to remove someone from a photo may also mean the person who has done so has the ability to do other types of image editing—like some of the other examples in this chapter. But rather than suggest anything sinister, we're going to give you the benefit of the doubt. It may be as simple as the editor wanting to follow the advice in this book and leave someone out of the picture. So just for your information, we're going to show you what happens when people are removed. Whatever trust issues may result from this knowledge are your own to deal with.

In a photo in which someone has been taken out, the background has to be filled in. Another problem is that, when pictures are taken of people together, they are often interacting with one another, so the photo may not look natural missing half the interaction. Figure 10.8 shows a very simple and innocent removal of a bit of a buddy in a picture of Terry. If you really look hard, you can tell it's been retouched because the right arm just isn't natural—not the retouching, but the position that Terry is in. He has his arm around someone who isn't there—and without the person, it doesn't look right. Blurs in clothes such as the T-shirt are also good clues the image has been worked.

Figure 10.8
Removing a person or unwanted element isn't a bad thing—actually it's a good practice. But it does indicate knowledge of how to image edit, and that means a close look at other aspects of the picture may be in order.

Reserving Judgment on Editing Photos

Since image editing can do great things, such as remove identity or location information from a photo, it really can't be said that image editing is an "evil" practice. Sometimes it's a good thing.

Simple picture touchups, such as whitening teeth, may be perfectly justified. Sometimes a photo changes the appearance of things like teeth. The shadow created by lighting or flash pictures may actually make the teeth appear darker than they do in real life, and image editing fixes the photo to appear realistic. Shadows can also exaggerate wrinkles and create harsh shadows under the eyes when you don't really look that way in everyday lighting.

And that's the problem. You can simply explain away almost every human flaw as the way the picture was taken, the way the lighting was, or that you "really don't look like that."

You probably do, but we understand. We all want to look our best, and with something as important as a profile photo, image editing really can fix up a lot of little flaws.

Our recommendation is not to image edit except to protect your identity or remove people from photos. Use proper lighting to take an honest picture to begin with. Then you can't lie to yourself and blame the photo.

Don't succumb to the temptation to improve on how you really look. As we have stressed throughout this book, it's important to be the very same person you are in your photo when you finally meet that magic person who may be the love of your life. Don't disappoint her by making yourself into a person who looks different than his profile photo. You will be liked and loved just like you are. If Terry can find the love of his life with his photos, so can you!

Summary

Image editing programs like Photoshop allow everyone to retouch their photos to improve on their looks. Old photos can be made more contemporary, and basic features, such as hair, teeth, wrinkles, and body shape can be modified to make a person look much better, or at least different, than they do in real life.

Except for removing personal information, you should avoid the temptation to edit your photos in any significant way to ensure that you don't disappoint a new love by making yourself into a better-looking person than the one she will get to see when you finally meet.

GUY SAYS

I am a genuine, whiz-bang, "I've written books on Photoshop," photo retouching artiste extraordinaire. However good I am at the art of retouching, I didn't, and wouldn't, retouch my photos for online dating services.

More than anything, I knew that when it came time to meet that special someone, if I didn't look like I did in my photos, I would be in big trouble. That type of thing is a deal-breaker. It can ruin a good thing faster than anything in this process.

As I mentioned earlier in this book, when I worked for *Playboy* a long time ago, I used to retouch the pictures of the models I was working with. I would slim a waistline, take out the natural wrinkles or a little fat in the tummy when the model was leaning over a bit, and remove all the stray hairs that fly up from the static of the lights on the set. When I was done, the photo was pristine and the woman was flawless.

Unlike the readers, I got to meet those models, and I can tell you that they looked so much better in person—with all the bumps and bruises, a little tummy fat, and hair flying here and there. They were real, not some artificial and phony image like the ones I put in the magazine.

I have yet to retouch any photo—of models, friends, family, or even myself—that improves a person or makes them look better than they do in real life.

I think it's so much better to take a good picture of yourself than to take a so-so picture and attempt to retouch it. A good un-retouched picture always looks better than a retouched picture.

Guys, you are what you are. Beer belly, balding, or dorky, you don't need to play games with the right person. The love of your life will love you just as you are. Leave the photo retouching for the art directors like I used to be at *Playboy* and enjoy their skill in that recent issue you are reading while you are waiting to meet that special love.

—*Terry*

CHICK SAYS

I'm no expert at Photoshop, but I do have it. From the first photo I took with my first digital camera and opened in Photoshop, I discovered the magic that could be done. With just a little bit of playing, you can make you into the best version of yourself. This can mean two things.

First, I've managed to take a lovely picture of myself, but I've got spinach in my teeth. Click, spinach is gone. My hair is blowing a little too much in the wind. Click, random hair is gone. There's a little red-eye from the flash. Click, red-eye is gone.

Or second, click, my uni-brow is gone. Click, my belly is gone. Click, my hair's a different color. Click, my forehead lines are gone. And yes, click, my pinkies are thin.

Scenario 1—good. Scenario 2—not me. I never take a picture of myself and post it on my Web site or send it to a friend without first doctoring it a little. It's rare that the light is perfect or the shot is perfectly framed or there's not some little thing that could use some alteration. That's okay. It's when I change who I am that it becomes a problem.

My uni-brow is part of me (or was until I had it waxed… a little physical editing is fine). My belly, sadly, is part of me. And I love my hair color most of the time, my forehead lines remain un-Botoxed, so they're still part of me, and as I mentioned before, the pinkies are what they are.

If I got rid of any of these things in a photo, it would reveal a level of insecurity about me that I'm not willing to reveal or accept. I'm in my 30s. If I haven't come to terms with myself, what I look like, and who I am at this point, then I shouldn't be putting myself out there.

I recently went out on a date with someone I met online. I'd sent him several pictures of myself. And I was pretty nervous to meet him for the first time. But what made me nervous was wondering if he would match his photos, hoping we would have enough to talk about, and whether I was wearing the right outfit. I didn't worry about him not being attracted to me or him being surprised to see what I really looked like—because I sent him honest pictures. He knew exactly what to expect. And it made a big difference to me. I was glad I'd been honest because if I'd been deceptive at all, I'm not sure I could have shown my face. And truthfully, the date went well.

—*Alyssa*

Chapter 11
Reading Photos: Clues to Age and Locations

*N*ow that you've seen a bit of what can be done with image editing, you'll be more aware of what's really going on in a profile photo when you view it. Profile photos are very important, and they play a key role in deciding if you want to contact a person or respond to an inquiry that's sent to you. If the photo looks funny or like it's been doctored a bit using the techniques covered in Chapter 10, you should probably use caution.

Most photos used in online dating services are plain old photos that have not been retouched, so we don't suggest looking at each photo as if it were a fake. In fact, this chapter covers a much more likely scenario in which the photo has not been retouched, but it's simply an old photo or a photo that doesn't really match what the person is saying about herself in her profile.

Like a detective, you can use a profile photo to learn a lot about a person—particularly her age and where she lives or hangs out. Since people often use older photos of themselves, learning to "date" a photo is a handy skill in the online dating world.

It's good to have some general rules in place for looking at a photo when viewing any profile. Here are the ones to keep in mind:

> ▶ Does the person in the photo match the general description the person has given in her physical description and the text of her profile?
>
> ▶ Does the picture make her look the age she stated?
>
> ▶ If you know where he lives, does the location in the photo seem to match where he's said he currently lives?
>
> ▶ Is the hairstyle a current one?
>
> ▶ If she wears glasses, are they a current design?
>
> ▶ Are the clothes he's wearing current fashion?
>
> ▶ If there are cars in the background, are they late model cars?
>
> ▶ Do wrinkles and age lines match the stated age?

As you can see from the above list, it is possible that an un-retouched photo can be as deceptive on issues that matter as one that has had a visit to Photoshop. One of the goals of this book is to help you find a person who is telling you the truth about himself in every possible area. In a relationship, truth is the foundation, and you want to make sure that you start off with someone whom you can trust. The photo he selects is not only about that trust, it is about how he thinks of himself and if he's comfortable inside. If he is, he'll use a recent photo.

Learning to Read Photos to Read People

It's not hard to "date" a photograph, spot locations, and see if the person in the picture really is the person posting it. By simple observation and having an objective attitude, you can either spot a fake or be totally reassured that the person you're interested in is telling you the truth through the selection of her photo.

The following items are examples of photos that are put forward as "recent." You can see why we may think that they are not.

Clothes Make the Date

While it is true that some people just dress poorly or are completely out of fashion, clothes often don't last too long—at least not long enough to look flat-out old fashioned. When you consider what a person says about himself, such as, "I love to get dressed up for a fun date," you may assume that he cares about how he looks and dresses.

What you need to decide in terms of clothing when viewing a photo is the following: Is he old-fashioned, is he wearing old clothes, or is it simply an old photo and those old-fashioned clothes were really fashionable when the photo was taken?

Figure 11.1 shows Terry again, and he claims that it's a recent photo. What do you think?

Figure 11.1
Terry claims that checkered jackets are the latest craze and that this isn't an old photo—it's a picture of a genuine trend-setter.

Old photos usually show old clothing styles. In today's world, where a wide variety of fashions are in play and retro is often chic, it's getting harder to determine what clothing is new—but as Figure 11.1 demonstrates, you can spot a photo that's from the '70s.

Older photos will also look old—Figure 11.1 is low resolution and soft in focus. This looks just like what it is: a Polaroid snapshot. Those haven't been used much lately, so that may be a clue as well.

With women, it can be a little easier to tell from the fashion what era the photo may be coming from. While some modern women do replicate an era's fashions to a T, it's a lot more common for them to add modern twists or for them to simply take certain aspects of the era's fashion and blend it into a new, updated look. While there's a certain nostalgia for the era of Alyssa's youth right now—the '80s—few women would think of dressing exactly like Olivia Newton-John in her "Physical" days, for instance.

However, Alyssa thinks Figure 11.2 looks so sweet with the big pink bow that she posts it and says it's her, taken at a recent '80s-themed party. But could she have put together an outfit so authentic without going over the top? And would that outfit include a 16 year-old baby face when she's admitted to being 34? The school desk is a bit of a giveaway as well.

Figure 11.2
Alyssa may swear this is a current picture of her, but aside from the fact that she's not Hispanic, she could never get her hair that big. Besides, this girl is so perky she must be a cheerleader. Alyssa doesn't do perky or cheers.

Another clear signal for "dating" a woman's picture fashion-wise is the prom dress. Men's formal looks tend to be limited to the tuxedo. And while the tuxedo has some variations, it tends to stay pretty standard, which thus makes it harder to date and harder to figure out what the formal occasion might be. The picture could be from a wedding last weekend just as easily as it could be from Junior Prom. The same is not true of women's formal wear.

There are specific sorts of dresses women wear on certain occasions. Women may dress up for a variety of occasions—big dates, church, holiday parties—but their dress on such occasions is something they might wear a dozen or more times in their lifetime. There is another kind of formal dress—that gets one wearing only. That's the prom dress. This dress is usually satin, ruffly, shiny, lacy, and/or strapless. It might have a bow on it somewhere. You can usually safely assume that if you see this dress, the photo is from high school. Figure 11.3 shows a lovely example of just such a dress. Alyssa is claiming that she's a size 8 and that this is from her sister's wedding

Figure 11.3
Alyssa doesn't want you to know that not only isn't this a recent photo nor a dress that would be worn at a wedding, but due to her rebel status in high school, she wouldn't even have worn this dress, since she didn't go to her prom.

last week. However, this dress is neither modern nor a color generally chosen by brides for their attendants.

It's also rare for a woman to willingly use a photo of herself in a bridesmaid's dress, as they are almost universally unflattering. Also, there's a certain pose used in a prom photo: either standing alone in what is clearly her parents' house or standing with her hand through the crook of her date's arm, in what is clearly her parents' house. In this case, the date has been cropped out, but you can still see the crook of his arm. A corsage is also a telling sign, but in this case our prom-goer is corsage-less.

You can also take a fashion cue from films of a period. Often films of an era inspire certain fashion trends, or the trends help inspire the movies. Here in Figure 11.4 Alyssa seems to think this picture looks smart and professional, shoulder pads and big hair included. She neglects to see the resemblance to *Working Girl*, an '80s film about women with big hair and big shoulder pads who make it big in the business world.

Figure 11.4
Our working girl is motion picture perfect in her big-shouldered blazer, shirt collar pointing up, gold hoops, and big hair. Would you trust this woman with your big account?

Similarly, keep an eye out for sweatshirts hanging off one shoulder, leg warmers, pastel-colored exercise gear, and satin dresses pulled down off both shoulders. If her look reminds you of someone you saw in an old movie, chances are she was imitating someone from that movie when the movie was popular.

Hairing the Real Story

After checking for any fashion clues, you can learn a lot about the age of a photo by hairstyles. Except perhaps for the crew cut, hairstyles do change with the times. You may think that's true just for women, but it's not. Men's hairstyles have changed, too. If you see a guy with a mullet, spiked hair, or hair slicked down with gel, and he claims to be 40, chances are he may be using an old photo.

Sometimes hairstyles can be regional. If a woman tells you she's lived in Chicago for the past 20 years and the photo shows her in a classic Texas (brassy blonde, big do!) style, she may have taken that photo when she was in school at Texas A&M. Regional styles, styles that come and go—they all may provide a bit of a clue as to when the photo was taken.

In general, women's hairstyles will pin them down to an era. With the exception of the few women who choose a basic, natural look, women's hairstyles reflect the time. The '60s had the flip and the bob. The '70s had the shag, Farrah feathers, and long, straight Cher hair. The '80s had big, hairsprayed hair and odd angled cuts. The '90s had the "Rachel," inspired by the TV show *Friends*. Most women's hair in these periods reflected those influences. Figure 11.5 again suggests Alyssa's belief that big hair is all a girl needs to catch a man.

Figure 11.5
Possibly AquaNet's best customer, currently being investigated as a likely instigator of global warming. Alyssa's not fooling anyone. She'd be laughed at walking down the streets of San Francisco in this do.

Men's hairstyles, though not quite as telling, do provide clues to a general time period. Male hairstyles have gone through similar cycles. The '60s had long hair and beards. The '70s had sideburns and shoulder-length looks. The '80s had Duran Duran highlighted tall hair and Flock of Seagulls-type strangely pointed styles. The '90s had the Caesar, also known as the Clooney, for George Clooney who sported it on the TV show *ER*.

Terry has again assured us that the photo in Figure 11.6 was taken about the same time as the one at the beginning of the chapter. He claims he has always had that 70's rock band hairstyle.

Figure 11.6
Terry loves groups like Foreigner and Toto so much, he pays tribute to them with his hair in this photo, which was taken last week. It's his dog whose hairstyle is dated—who has longhaired dogs anymore?

Looking for Little Clues

In addition to the hairstyle and the clothes, if it's an older photo, you can usually find little clues that give it away if you can see some of the background.

In Figures 11.1, 11.3, and 11.6, you can look carefully at the backgrounds to get a clue as to the date the picture was taken.

The wallpaper in the photos of Terry looks very '70s, as does the coloring of the carpet, walls, and the wood posts in the prom photo. The furniture isn't contemporary. The lamps are older styles. The paintings are right from a garage sale today. There are so many hints that these photos are vintage that you shouldn't have much of a problem finding the clues.

Figure 11.7 is another photo that Terry said was taken within the last month. The problem, beyond the sweater vest and the white walls, which are pretty out of style for the new house he claims to live in, is that there is a Christmas wreath showing, and he's posting his pictures in August!

In Figure 11.8, the shape of the photo itself is what's telling. Aside from the big hair and the blue eyeshadow, Alyssa's profile photo is a wallet-sized photo with cropped, rounded corners. It could not be more obviously a senior class photo. If you could flip it over, you would undoubtedly see it signed, "High school is over! Have a great summer. BFF, Tina." Alyssa swears it just came that way from her recent studio shoot.

Figure 11.7
Sometimes little clues such as a Christmas wreath in a photo that was supposedly taken in August will help suggest that the person in the picture may not be the age he claims, since the photo is suspect. Or he's really bad about taking down decorations.

Figure 11.8
The cropped, rounded corners give away the fake Alyssa's high school status. And surely a girl with skin that smooth is already dating the quarterback, not needing Match.com.

Figure 11.9
It wouldn't be hard to figure out from the car, the trees, the name of the ranch, and even how Terry is dressed that this photo is not only old, it's from when he lived somewhere else.

Looking at the Environment

Since many people include body shots, usually taken from a snapshot in a social setting or outdoors, you can learn a bit about the age of the photo—and also where the picture was taken.

Figure 11.9 shows another of Terry's wild claims. He's claiming that this recent picture was taken in Northern California where he lives. Well, it's outdoors. That's good. He looks pretty goofy, but he had a goofy profile, so what can you do with that? The car? Well, it seems to be pretty old. And the ranch house doesn't really look like the ones around the area. The trees are small, and they are not like the ones that should be there. And that sign—after doing a quick search on the Internet, the only Pine Valley is in the Midwest, and the only Pine Valley Ranch phone listing is there too. If we could, we'd check out the license plates, but they are too small to see.

So, after a quick e-mail to Terry, he assures us that he was visiting a friend a few weeks ago and that car is some clunker his buddy let him drive while he was eating hot dishes and going to bake sales at the Methodist church. He'll send us a picture that he loves of him in his office.

So the e-mail arrives, and there's a nice picture of Terry in his "office," as shown in Figure 11.10. Well, maybe he has a job, so that's good. But he lives up in the mountains of Northern California, and he seems to be in a high rise office building. Look out the window—there's a big tall building out there, and it's made of stone. There's nothing like that anywhere near where he lives.

And what is that he's doing? He claims to be a writer, but he's working at a drawing board like an artist. There's no computer there either! And on the wall, hey, that's a little bunny logo. Wait a minute… that's a picture of him in his office at *Playboy*, so that picture has to be at least 20 years old and that's Chicago. Even worse, he has ferns and feathers in his office. What a girl! And what a nerve to send this photo and say it's recent.

Figure 11.10
Terry is a writer, but there's no computer in his office, and that's a drawing board. There's a high rise in the background, and there are none where he lives. All are good clues that this is an old photo.

Summary

Now and then, people have pictures of themselves they really like, and they use them even if they are old—not to deceive you, but because they feel good about the way they look in those shots. Once in a while, someone will use a photo that is deceptive, but most of the time the pictures are just bad choices. Regardless of what the intention was, it's good to pay attention to hair, clothes, locations, and little details just to make sure that what you're being told matches what is being shown to you. If everything tallies up just right, it will help you have some confidence that the other things the person is telling you are accurate, too.

GUY SAYS

I know for sure that I've seen lots of online profile photos along the way that were pretty old. The hair and the clothes are always a giveaway. It was a concern, but I understood to a certain degree that it's hard to find a good photo to use.

I know one thing: It's not fun to meet someone and find that she isn't what you expected. I definitely never responded to profiles with photos that I thought might be relics—because the women in them were not playing it straight.

If the headshot and most of the photos look recent, then a fun older photo from a trip to Europe or from high school can actually be helpful. I think that when you look at a bunch of photos with that type of range, you can tell they are put there to show life experiences, and it is nice to see a bit more about the person than profile text can share.

Basically, it's common sense. If a woman said she was 25 and the photo of her looked 40, I knew it was trouble. If the woman said she was 40 and in the picture she looked 25, it was even more trouble. If the basics don't match, and something isn't right, it's got to be a hint that other items may be stories too.

Most of my experiences were that women put up photos of themselves where they were young primarily because they were thinner. When you meet, they are just way heavier than the photos. That's not to say that they aren't attractive, and that's what is so silly: Being skinny isn't the only quality a guy looks for. A great look, nice hair, wonderful eyes and smile, and a sense of style add up to more than a size 8 ever could.

Don't try to fool us guys with old photos. We use recent photos that show our hairy chests and beer bellies, but damn it, we're proud of them!

—*Terry*

CHICK SAYS

First of all, please don't show your hairy chests, no matter what Terry says. Button up that shirt, please.

So I've seen photos that I've suspected were old pics. Often they're pictures of men in tuxedos in which they look about 18. I always suspect they're from prom rather than a wedding, but it's tough to tell. Unlike Terry, I'm not an expert at spotting inconsistencies, though my instinct serves me well enough. But I actually think men are less likely to try this trick.

More often, the photo tricks that I see men trying are theoretically less deceptive than posting an old photo of oneself. I'm far more likely to see a man posting a blurry photo, a low-resolution photo, or a photo of himself dressed from head to toe in a ski suit. Maybe men are aware that women tend to be more attuned to fashion and hairstyles and are more likely to notice those inconsistencies. So they try to hide their less appealing traits behind blurs and goggles.

I think men are also a little more likely to be stuck in a bygone fashion era. Especially as they get older, some men stick with a fashion they felt worked for them in the prime of their life. For instance, my father dresses very classically in jeans or slacks and button-down shirts. It's a look that works for him, admittedly. And it's been working for him for about 25 years. A photo of him from the age of 35 and a photo of him now will look virtually the same, fashion-wise. Now, if 25 years ago he'd thought he looked good in pink shirts and white blazers a la "Miami Vice," there's a pretty good chance he would still be wearing that same look. Thank goodness that's not the case, but if it were, you wouldn't know if the photo was current or not. There's the rub. And men call **us** hard to figure out.

So there's a lot of common sense needed in figuring out vintage pictures of men. Look at the age he's given in his profile. Men don't tend to lie about their age, though they'll make a point of saying, "a young looking 53!" or "45 but living the life of a 25 year-old." Compare the age given with the face you're looking at. Take in the other cues of fashion and background, but aside from the post-plastic surgery patients, you should be able to tell approximately what age the face you're looking at is.

Ultimately it's the eyes that tell the truth. Look at those youthful pictures of Terry, and then flip to the more recent ones in earlier chapters. Those young pics show an eagerness and excitement in his eyes that gives way to the wisdom and life experience you see in them now. And that's not something plastic surgery can take away. Nor would you want it to.

—*Alyssa*

Chapter 12
How You Write Should Reflect Who You Say You Are

*I*t's an imperfect science, but you can tell a lot about people by the way they write. It's not just what they say, it's how they say it. If you pay attention to the clues, you can determine whether the essays in a profile match the answers given in a person's multiple choice questions. For instance a college graduate shouldn't write like a 4th grade drop out, and, in our opinion, a self-described professional shouldn't write like he's been watching too much MTV. Unless he works for MTV.

Assess the Overall Writing Style

People usually try to describe themselves in the most flattering way. They want to appear smart, funny, clever, attractive, optimistic, caring, sensitive, hip, romantic, successful, and affluent. While this package does exist, chances are the writer is taking some license with her character if she describes herself as all of the above. Or she may genuinely believe she is all of the above. But once you get to know her, her actual package will become clear, and there are likely to be some objects broken during shipping or some that just didn't make it into the box. But sometimes you can determine this before opening the box. Sometimes you can tell by looking at the packaging whether what's inside matches what the box has stamped on it.

You come across a profile in which a person says all the right things. He says how smart and successful and funny and fantastic he is. And you want to believe that to be true because he's cute in his photo. But there are some things that make you start to wonder. For instance, he says how smart he is—but his grammar is atrocious. He says how funny he is—but his profile is the driest thing you've ever read, worse than that computer installation manual. He's tying himself up as a perfect package in a big pink bow, but you suspect there's just a pair of sweatsocks inside—when you were hoping for a diamond ring.

It's not always so obvious. But you can get an impression from the way someone writes. It's like listening to someone speak. If they're confident and straightforward, they don't use slang, and they make sense, then you're likely to trust them and think positively about them. If they use "um" a lot, use a lot of slang, don't seem to ever make their point or don't seem to have a point to make, or are just talking to hear themselves speak, then you're likely to get a negative impression and not want to spend time listening to them. The same is true in writing. People tend to write somewhat how they speak. It's unusual to find someone who speaks like the person in the first example but writes like the person in the second example. Unfortunately, the opposite can be true—someone can speak badly but write well. That's someone to whom you're going to have to talk on the phone later in the get-to-know-you phase to see what the truth is.

Some things to look for when getting these first impressions:

- ▶ **Slang.** You may be dealing with someone who's genuinely hip and knows all the slang, but chances are it's someone who thinks he's really cool and uses the slang to prove it.

- ▶ **Meandering.** Does the writer use a lot of words without really saying anything?

- ▶ **Short, simple sentences.** Either the writer can't write better and longer, or she didn't want to take the time.

- ▶ **Excessive descriptions.** If the writer uses all the space available to explain how great he is, chances are he's not or he's much too aware that he is.

- ▶ **Dullness.** If the writer can't make her profile even vaguely interesting, what do you think she'll be like in real life?

- ▶ **Too many demands.** If the writer spends most of the profile describing the person he's looking for, he's probably too picky and demanding.

Aside from how well they say what they're saying, you can also get an idea of their personality from the way they write and what they choose to write about. A happy person will come across as, well, happy. He'll be positive and warm and excited to be writing his profile. A sad or depressed person will be trying to sound upbeat, but you'll be able to read the desperation, unhappiness, and negativity in their profile. For example, which of these profiles would you be more likely to respond to?

Hey, welcome to my profile! Let's see, describe myself. I'm a young-looking 42, good-looking my female friends say. I work at a great non-profit that makes me excited to get out of bed every morning. I really feel like I make a difference every day. In my spare time I like to hike, read, see movies, go to art and music shows, go to coffee shops, walk on the beach. I watch some TV—I love *The Simpsons* and Jon Stewart. I like to travel. One of these days I'm going to go to Machu Pichu; that's a goal for me. I'm looking for someone who would like to go with me, who likes adventure, and would want to share the search for new things with me. I know a lot of people who've met their mates online, and I'm looking forward to doing the same. I know you're out there!

Or...

> I'm 38 years old. I'm smart and clever. I like a good laugh. I work in the stock market. I make a good living. But I get tired of going home to an empty house. I want someone to be part of my life. I've gone to all the places you're supposed to go to. I've been to bars and coffee shops and joined clubs. But it seems like there are no interesting single people out there for me. So I thought I'd try online dating. I figured, what the heck, I've tried everything else. I hope you liked my profile and will respond to me. Thanks.

While there's nothing inherently wrong with that second profile, is there anything really right about it? In the first one, the writer is energetic, talking about things the writer likes, and sharing some interests. The writer talks about finding someone to share things with and sounds optimistic about the search for love online. In the second profile, the writer claims to be smart and clever but doesn't show any evidence of that in the way the profile is written. The writer doesn't really tell you anything about the writer's interests or life beyond the basics. The writer simply sounds lonely and tired of looking for a partner. The writer does not sound optimistic about finding anyone online. And, frankly, the fact that the writer has tried so hard to find someone but hasn't found anyone makes you think there must be something really wrong with this person.

You can usually tell a serious person from a funny person in these early essays, too. Anyone who's got a decent sense of humor will find some way to inject it into the profile. It would be more of a struggle not to do so. Little jokes or self-deprecating humor are common in profiles. If there's nothing funny in a profile, chances are there's nothing funny in the writer, which can be fine. Seriousness is a quality some look for. You just have to know what you want and keep your eye out for it.

Education and Writing Skills

We're not going to be prejudiced here against those without a higher education. We know that some of our best authors never went to college, or they even dropped out of high school or grade school. This happens, we know. And we're not putting college on a pedestal. But the fact remains that, generally speaking, those with a higher education write better than those without. Not because of a higher level of intelligence, but because they've been forced to write about a thousand papers in the course of getting that 4-year degree. When you're forced to do something a lot, you get better at it. It's just the way it works.

That said, you can often tell a level of education from the way someone writes. The more simplistic the writing, the less likely it is that the writer went to college. Someone who knows how to form good sentences, someone who uses a broader vocabulary, someone who uses words correctly and grammatically—all are signs of a well-educated person.

The problem comes when someone has claimed to have a college education but can't seem to put two words together properly. What is likely to blame for this? Sure, it's possible that this person never has to write for his job and has forgotten how. It could be that he didn't spend much time writing the profile and didn't proofread it before posting it. But it's more likely that the writer is lying about his education.

On the other hand, if the writer reads a lot or writes a lot for a job, the writer could be a high school dropout and still write a nice profile. Intelligence and education don't go hand in hand. This is one reason why, back when you were thinking about your selections in the multiple-choice section of your profile, you might have wanted to keep the education options open. You might find a high school dropout who's more successful and smarter than that post-doc whom you had your eyes on. Life experience has a big impact on what goes into someone's writing.

Life Experience

What a person chooses to write about and how she writes about it reflects her life experience. Again, with talking to someone in person, you can quickly glean this information from a simple conversation. The same is true of reading a profile.

For instance, the writer has indicated in the multiple-choice questions that he's in sales. And guess what—in his profile he really sells himself. It's his job. He knows what to say to make himself look good. He probably does a lot of talking and writing in his job, and he can easily handle the essay questions.

Or say the writer has traveled extensively. She's likely to talk a lot about travel because it's something she's passionate about. She'll also likely express herself well because she's used to talking to a lot of people on her travels and telling her life story.

If the writer is a parent, it would be unusual for him not to mention his child. Having children is such an important, life-altering event that it becomes part of your identity. So to describe yourself and not mention your child or children would be out of character for most parents. Keep this in mind when looking at the multiple-choice questions—if someone has marked that he has children but later does not mention them in his profile, there might be something odd going on there.

Politics is another big one. Not mentioning politics shouldn't raise any alerts. But if someone mentions in her profile her political views, makes a comment on the last election, or talks about her feelings about a certain current president, then you can assume she's pretty political. And you might want to make sure your views are somewhat compatible, unless you're looking for a combative relationship.

An interesting example is money talk. Once again, if the writer doesn't talk about money, it shouldn't raise any red flags. But if the writer does talk about money, it's a pretty strong indication of both lifestyle and character. There are a couple of ways this could go. The writer could say something like, "I work at a coffee shop while I'm writing my novel/trying to get an art show/working on getting my band a contract. I don't make much money right now, but it's enough to live on while I'm doing something I love." In this case you know you're going to be with someone for whom money is not really that important and who doesn't have much. Or the writer could say something like, "I'm a successful, high-level executive in a Fortune 500 company. I make a six-figure salary and want for nothing. I have several houses around the country and own more cars than my garage will hold." In this case you know you're going to be with someone who puts a high level of importance on money and possessions. And if that's okay with you, he'll probably buy you a lot of stuff. It won't always be quite so clear cut, but you get the idea.

And you should be able to tell whether things have gone well for the writer in life. It's hard to hide certain things in your writing style. If you've had a hard life that's worn you down, it will show up in your profile. You might be trying to be upbeat but end up saying something like, "I feel like I really deserve to find someone wonderful because I've gone through a lot to end up in a place where I can be happy with someone else in my life." It's easy to see the underlying pain and neediness in that sentence. Sometimes the hard life and unhappiness will be even clearer, and you'll wonder how the writer was even hopeful enough to post their profile. On the other hand, if the writer is hopeful and hasn't been beaten down by life, you can tell that, too. What if the same writer wrote, "I'm really at a point in my life where I'm enjoying every day as a blessing and I'd love to find someone to spend all those days with me."? If so, you might suspect that this writer's life hasn't always been this happy and blessed but that the writer has taken everything in stride and is looking at the future through rose-colored glasses (in a good way).

Does Their Picture Match What They Say?

The tone of a potential date's writing should match what she's said in her profile. And in the same way, the tone of her photo should match the tone of her profile. As Alyssa mentioned earlier in this book, when she was only sort of looking for someone and still slightly wary of the online dating scene, both her profile and her photo had a hesitancy to them, a wariness in word and look. Then when she started to think she might like to date after all, she changed her profile and photo to match her newfound optimism. The fun flirtiness of her profile, the twinkle in her eye, and sly smile in her photo matched both each other and her outlook on dating. This is the kind of consistency you should look for when browsing profiles.

Aside from matching your potential date's feelings about dating, the profile and photo should also tell you the same story about the personality and characteristics of the person in them. It's not uncommon to find a person's photo telling a whole different version of the truth than his profile.

There are happy people and sad people. There are serious people and silly people. There's nothing wrong with any of this. However, if a happy person posts a sad photo of herself, she's sending out the wrong message. And you're getting that wrong message. And if you don't like sad people, you're going to take one look at that photo and pay no attention to the written profile, if you even bother to glance at it. Because the picture your potential date chose to post was a sad one, that says something about her. Maybe we should repeat it yet again—a picture really is worth a thousand words, especially when someone's far more likely to spend three seconds looking at a picture than they are reading that one thousand words.

SMILE FOR THE CAMERA
A lot of people don't like getting their picture taken. That's a given. But if every photo you have of yourself has you rolling your eyes and scowling at the camera, that's not a good shot to post. If you've posted this photo of yourself and then tried to describe yourself as a happy, easy-going person, no one is going to believe you. That's why it's important to go back a few chapters and take another look at Chapter 6. It's not just the photos you've taken; what matters is the photo you've chosen to put up on your profile as representative of who you are and how you look at life. People will be scrutinizing you just as you're about to scrutinize them.

Let's say you've found Terry's profile. He's written the long, sad story of his life. He's abandoned at the age of six and left on the doorstep of an orphanage. Raised by a long succession of foster parents, he becomes a delinquent living on the streets by age 15. He's finally mentored by a man at a boy's club who teaches him to read and write and helps him go back to school and apply to colleges. When he gets out of college, he picks up a serious coke habit and spends the next nine years back on the streets. Eventually, he checks himself into rehab and cleans up his life. He's now a model citizen, but can't quite get over his past. He wants to find a woman who can help him take back control of happiness in his life. Figure 12.1 shows the profile photo Terry chose to post.

Figure 12.1
Terry looks awfully happy and carefree— could he really have had such a past?

Yes, it could be that Terry is trying to put a good face on it. But it's hard to imagine that someone who is still haunted by his past could look so cheery. The best case scenario is that this is an old photo from a (brief) happy time, maybe when he was in college. The worst case scenario is that he's either lying about his sob story or using someone else's photo. The photo and story are just too divergent.

Example 2—you've found Alyssa's profile, and you like it. She claims to be serious and studious. She spends 60 hours at work per week and is trying to go back to school for a Master's in philosophy. She cries at the news because of the inhumanity of man. She's angry at the political situation in the country. She's reading Tolstoy for fun. She's a vegan and a big contributor to PETA. She volunteers at a battered women's shelter on the weekends. And Figure 12.2 shows the profile photo she chose to post.

Figure 12.2
Alyssa also says she's a church-goer and reads to the blind.

What is to be believed here? Sure, it's obviously a Halloween costume (at least you hope so). And even though she said she has red hair, you suspect this is a wig, so that doesn't worry you. But what is she saying about herself? There seems to be no correlation between the photo and the profile. Surely someone serious and studious wouldn't pick this photo to post, even if it was the only one she had. You suspect you're being led on, that there's some joke involved. And you're probably right. It looks to us like Alyssa has a sense of humor, admittedly strange, and probably is not a church-goer—at least not in this outfit.

Not all examples will be quite so obvious. You might get someone who claims to be shy who posts a photo of herself in a bikini. You might get someone who claims to be playful but posts a picture of himself in a business suit. You might get someone who claims to be a starving artist but has a couple of gold teeth. Again it's not just the photo, it's that they've chosen that particular photo to post. The photo you choose is the photo you think represents who you are. If the photo doesn't match the profile, there's something wrong with the writer's perception of himself, or he's not telling the truth.

Matching Up the Photo with the Profile

So take a good, hard look at the profile you're judging. Make sure everything has come together properly. Each piece of the profile is a piece of a puzzle. The pieces all have to fit together properly for you to trust your potential date.

Most importantly, you need to make sure the message and impression you're getting from the profile is the one you want to be getting. It's hard to get past a pretty face or a charming turn of phrase. But take in the big picture. Is the person in the photo smiling at you with hope and excitement for the future? Or is he smiling at his new Mercedes and the camera just managed to catch that glint in his eyes. Read the profile, and it should tell you.

The bottom line is that the writer of the profile probably is not lying to you. Most daters want to find someone who really is compatible and, therefore, will try to be honest, inasmuch as they feel comfortable doing so. But you want to be as certain as possible about someone before sticking your neck out and contacting her. So take the time to do your detective work.

Summary

It's pretty easy to pay attention to little clues left by a profile writer to determine his truthfulness and personality traits. If you have in mind what things to pick up on, you can feel more confident about the person you're thinking about dating. Make sure the writing style and the writer's education and life experience match. Make sure the subtle clues in what the writer says match up with the kind of person you want to date. And make sure the photo the writer has posted is an accurate reflection of the kind of person he's described himself as in his profile.

GUY SAYS

Whenever I look at an online profile, I do a bit of simple detective work. I try to put all of the clues together and see if all of the pieces fit. If something is amiss, then a flag goes up real fast.

As much as we would all like to think of ourselves as a "mystery" waiting to be solved by some new love, the truth is more like "you're pretty easy to figure out!" At least when it comes to your online profile.

First I read the profile heading, then the profile text. Then I look at the picture. They should all fit nicely together and complement each other. After that I go through all the check boxes and see the preferences and background information. If the person is telling the truth, again, it should support the photo and the message in the profile text.

I've read a lot of profiles from women who have checked off items that indicate they have a college degree and are in an executive or teaching position, yet their profile text doesn't reflect that in any way. Some had bad typos, improper word usage, and bad grammar. I'm not talking about writing badly; I'm talking about not knowing how to write. When I see a profile like that, I instantly shy away. It isn't right.

I get the same heebie-jeebies when I see a woman's picture and she is dressed in an extremely provocative style, with piercings and tattoos, and she says she is a homebody who likes church and quiet evenings at home. That may be true, but I know that there is probably more there that she is not telling me, and at a minimum the message is so confusing that I would shy away again.

Just as you can lie in your photo by using old pictures or ones that don't really look like you, you can lie in your profile text, too, without even knowing it. Leaving out important information, glossing over key flaws, painting an idealized rather than realistic version of yourself—these are all little lies that are as damaging as a retouched photo, where you take out the wrinkles or the extra pounds.

In addition to matching the pieces together, men tend to be direct, and they are often proud of things that most women laugh at. Overall, I don't think most women—at this point—need to hear all about your Corvette, your yearly hunting trip, how much you love beer, how you and your buddies are just a bunch of good ol' boys, and how sexy you are with the ladies wherever you go.

Wait, I take that back. If you are all of the above, please put that first in your profile so that you save most women a whole lot of time by passing you up.

Take your manly Clint Eastwood-like quality of using few words and simple metaphors and use them to accurately describe what you are like.

I'm pretty sure that when the ladies read that you are "a quiet, strong, and caring man who seeks a warm, gentle women who loves the outdoors, fun rides with the top down, cocktails in front of the fireplace, and the excitement of simply being together wherever you go," she'll get the right message.

Provided that's what you are really like.

—*Terry*

CHICK SAYS

As a writer, I tend to be extra judgmental about other people's writing. I'm not forgiving of typos, spelling errors, bad grammar, and flat out bad writing when I find it in print media.

However, when reading profiles posted on an online dating site, I have to make myself remember that the writers are not professionals. They're not even pretending to be professionals. And unless they've indicated their profession as "writer," I need to cut them some slack.

That being said, there are some things I let myself be judgmental about. A typo here and there I can deal with. But bad grammar to the point at which I know the guy probably speaks just as badly is a little hard for me.

A meandering profile that goes nowhere and tells me nothing real about the guy writing it is another automatic dismissal. If you can't be focused for a length of under 2000 characters, then when am I going to be able to have a real conversation with you?

Slang drives me crazy. I can take a word here and there, as I know some guys genuinely have certain words as part of their vocabulary and don't even think twice about using them. But if there are more than a few slang words in a profile, I'm out of there. I don't want to hear it out of his mouth; I don't want to hear it in his profile.

Arrogance. You can practically taste it when you read it. And it's sour and unpleasant. Of course you're going to hype yourself up in your profile. But there's a limit. There's a level of praising yourself that makes you sound like a pompous ass. And when you hit that level—never use the words *brilliant, gorgeous, stunning, make you roar with laughter, fantastic body, six-pack abs, knight in shining armor,* or *sex machine*—that's when I get off the elevator. I don't care if you really *are* just that great. I don't want to have to hear about it from you or deal with your better-than-thou attitude for the length of a date, much less a relationship.

Just be yourself. Try to write interestingly. Try to use some humor, but don't aim for making me bust my gut. Be brilliant and gorgeous and a knight in the way you write, but don't tell me you think you are those things. Be honest. Tell me you're a geek. Tell me you always plan to work out three times a week, but the last time you went to the gym was January 2nd. Tell me you love heavy metal, but you can't explain why and won't foist it on me. Tell me things that give you character. Write in an intelligent way so I know you're intelligent. And post a great picture so I know you're stunning, even if it's in your own geeky way.

—*Alyssa*

Chapter 13
Finding Out More about Your Potential Date

*Y*ou've found someone you like—you think. All you've got is the profile to go by. But you've examined all the clues in the way he writes. You've looked for discrepancies in his photo. You've scrutinized his check boxes to learn who he is and who he's looking for. He seems really compatible, and you winked at him. He's winked back. You've started a conversation with him. But how do you find out who he really is? How do you ask the important questions and, for that matter, what are the important questions?

Things You Should Always Ask a Potential Date

Sometimes it's hard to know what is harder—asking the questions or answering them. But things are always a little awkward in this early stage of getting to know your potential date. And no matter how awkward it may be, you need to take the time to ask all the important questions. Even if it feels weird or you have to screw up your courage to do it. Some questions you should always ask are

- Where does he live?
- Did she live anywhere else before?
- Is he married?
- What was her last relationship like?
- How did it end, and why?
- What kind of a relationship is he looking for?

Let's take these one at a time.

Where Does He Live?

Your potential date probably already has indicated this in his profile. However, you'll want to confirm this and get some specifics. You shouldn't ask for a specific address, just a general location. If you're looking for someone local and he's indicated he lives in your city, you should clarify that he really lives in your city. We've seen profiles that claimed the person lived in San

Jose, CA, when really he was just visiting on an extended business trip and in fact lived in England. If the person insists he's local but you're suspicious, you can always ask him what neighborhood he lives in, then ask some questions about restaurants, stores, and so on, in that area.

If you're going to try to have a relationship with someone, it's vital to know where he lives. Starting a relationship by e-mail with someone whom you think is local but turns out to be thousands of miles away is simply a waste of time if you're not interested in a long-distance relationship. And while it may feel awkward to seemingly doubt his honesty by asking him specifics about his neighborhood and permanence in the city, he'll likely think nothing of it. He'll think you're just comparing notes about places you like and wondering what his future plans might be.

Did She Live Anywhere Else Before?

There are a couple of reasons to ask this. Where someone is from tells a lot about her. If someone is from New York City, you might surmise that she's hip and stylish. If someone is from the South, you might suspect she will be earthy and a good storyteller with a really cute accent (or an accent you'll find grating if you don't like southern accents—also good to know). If someone is from the Midwest, you could assume that she'd be hearty, hard working, and honest. If someone is from California, you could guess she'd be a little new-age-y and liberal. Mind you, all of these are stereotypes. But stereotypes are usually based in some truth.

You might also want to know if English is a second language for her. Communication is important. If she's from Argentina and never learned English until she moved to America last year, then there could be some problems in communicating. On the other hand, if she's been studying English for 10 years but comes from Brazil, she's going to have a very sexy little accent and will probably make herself understood easily enough.

This information will also come in useful later if you decide to run a background check on her. We'll talk about this in a later chapter.

Is He Married?

Theoretically, someone who's married will not be prowling an online dating site. And if we stay in the theoretical, you don't have to worry. But the fact is, there are a lot of married people out there on the sites, and they won't necessarily say it in their profiles. Some will, surprisingly. Someone who does might be part of a swinger couple. He could be part of a polyamorous relationship, and he's looking to add another spouse to the mix. He could just have an open relationship with his wife.

However, most married prowlers won't state this up front. There are a variety of non-single lurkers on the online dating sites. Some are looking to have an affair. Some are looking for a one-night stand while their spouse is out of town. And some are just looking—wondering if there might be someone else out there for them: someone more compatible, someone sexier, someone new and interesting.

Whatever their reason for lurking, you're going to want to know that they are and know why they are. And if you want to have a relationship with someone who doesn't already have one going on, you're going to want to say good-bye once you know the truth.

But how do you get to the truth, you ask? Always a pickle. You just have to ask and see what he says. The bottom line is, you won't know it if he lies to you. You just have to hope for the best—and maybe run a background check.

What Was Her Last Relationship Like?

This can be tricky even with someone you've met and dated a few times. But, while you want your potential date to avoid talking about exes in her profile, when it comes to getting to know her and deciding whether to date her, you should ask this question. There are a couple of reasons.

If her last relationship was short and barely the definition of a relationship, then you should ask about the relationship before that. If you keep going back and none of her relationships lasted through a change in the seasons, then you may have a serial dater on your hands. She may be someone who is always looking for something better, so she doesn't stick around long enough to really get involved.

If her last relationship was 10 years ago, that's something important to know as well. Why hasn't she been involved with anyone since then? Was the relationship so painful it turned her off men? Was the relationship so significant that she's still in love with her ex and will never be able to love another?

What if her last relationship lasted 10 years? To be with someone that long requires a fairly long recovery period during which you would probably be considered a rebound. And why did they break up after 10 years? You'll want to know what kind of wounds she might be licking.

What if her last relationship was with a woman? Knowing your potential date's sexuality is generally considered essential. Asking about her last relationship might open a can of worms, but it's better to see them than just hope they don't exist.

How Did the Relationship End, and Why?

Knowing how your potential date's last relationship ended will tell you her state of mind when you eventually meet her. Was her last relationship violent? Was it dull and she's looking for excitement? Was it wild and she's just looking to settle down? Did her ex die and his spirit will always be with her—in that urn on the mantle she'll never part with?

How a relationship ends will usually shape how the next relationship forms. If your potential date came out of an amicable breakup, she's far more likely to be open to whatever may come in her relationship with you. If she came out of a bad breakup, she may be gun-shy and nervous, hesitant to really get in too deep with you.

Then there are the ex issues. Is she still best friends with her ex, and you'll be expected to have friendly brunches with him regularly? Did she break her ex's heart, and he's out there wanting her back? Did she have to move to another zip code to get away from her ex, and he's still out there stalking her? These are all very important things to know. And you'll never know unless you ask.

What Kind of Relationship Is He Looking For?

People come to online dating looking for a wide range of things. Not everyone on the site is there for the same reason you are, whatever reason that may be. And it's good to know going in what kind of relationship he's looking for to make sure it matches your hopes for the future. People generally come to online dating looking for one of these things:

▶ **Love.** The most common reason to be online dating. Who doesn't want love? It makes the world go round. It's all you need. It's a drug. It's a many splendored thing. And it seems to be ingrained in the human psyche to search for it. Love is everywhere around us, in movies, in music, in books, and in that horrible couple on the bus who keep making gooey noises at each other. We want the gooey noises. We want to be that horrible couple. And if you're looking for love online, you're in the majority.

▶ **Friendship.** Yes, there really are people at online dating sites looking for just friendship. However, this is the least common thing people are looking for. Often, even if someone says he's looking for friendship, he's just looking to get to know someone under that safe platonic blanket before moving it into another kind of relationship. However, if you're looking for someone to smooch and coo with, you'd best not get your hopes up. Ask him first if he's really only looking for friendship, and if the answer is yes, move on.

▶ **Just dating.** While we suspect most of those who claim they just want to date and have a good time are really looking for one of the other things in this list, there are plenty of daters who do claim that's what they want. And it may be true in some cases. But if all they want is dating, it's best to know up front because the relationship won't likely go beyond that stage.

▶ **Sex.** Ah, yes, the sex-seekers. They are pretty common, even on the mainstream dating sites. And they'll usually make it clear in their profiles. But if not, it usually comes out early on in their communication with you, even if you don't ask. But you should ask. It's best to know this up front. If all they want is sex and you're looking for something serious, it's not going to work out unless one of you changes your mind. And as much as you'd like it to be he who changes his mind, it's unlikely that's what will happen. If you get involved with a sex-seeker, don't expect anything beyond that.

▶ **One-night stand.** Just a variant of the sex-seeker, but even less of a committed dater. You're likely to find out in your very first communication with him that this is what he's looking for. After all, if you're just looking for one night, why would you spend weeks e-mailing someone, getting to know her?

▶ **Marriage.** Probably the second most common reason to be online dating. In many daters' minds, if they're looking for love, they're looking for marriage. The two go hand in hand—most of the time. But it's a good idea to find out if he's looking to give his hand or not. Not everyone believes in marriage. And not everyone is ready for that level of commitment. There are certain Web sites that cater specifically to those wanting to get married precisely because it's so important that you have the same goals for online dating, that you're looking for the same thing. If you didn't meet on one of the marriage Web sites, ask him if he's open to the prospect—without making it seem like you're proposing.

TIP FOR ASKING QUESTIONS

Asking some questions can be tough. Consider making a fun little questionnaire. Ask lots of silly questions as well as the difficult ones. Ask your potential date to fill out the questionnaire and send it back. As long as you make it fun, asking enough goofy questions like, "What's your favorite song to sing along with in an elevator?" then your potential date might not mind it as much when you ask, "Have you ever been arrested?" In fact, as long as she hasn't ever been arrested, she'll just think it's another jokey question to answer.

Things We Suggest You Ask a Potential Date

During the get-to-know-you stage of your e-mailing a potential date, you'll find you get into a pattern. You may spend all your time talking about your day-to-day life, writing to each other about things that happened that day. Or you may find you just keep exchanging favorite things— movies, books, music, and so on. Or you may keep asking each other silly but somehow meaningful questions, trying to come up with ever more intriguing things that will reveal something about the other person. Or you may end up giving each other your whole history, talking about your family and past and fears and hopes, as if you were talking to a therapist instead of a date. Your interactions with your potential date will be specific to who you are and who she is.

But there are some subjects we suggest you go into, as they'll tell you some important things about the person you're looking to date. These are

▶ Family
▶ Kids, their living situation, and his relationship with them
▶ Job
▶ Living situation
▶ Friends
▶ Hobbies
▶ TV viewing

Again, let's take these one at a time.

Ask about Her Family

Family is a huge part of many people's lives. Family can be good or bad, but either way it shapes someone. Asking about her family will result in an answer that will reveal something about her. Either she'll give a terse answer like, "Two brothers, one sister, parents divorced," or it might be longer, a full description of them and her closeness with them, some anecdotes about her past with them. While she might not want to go into a lot of detail about them before she knows you well, she'll probably expand on them a little if she likes them. If there's something unpleasant in her past regarding her family, you'll probably be able to pick up on that.

For instance, Alyssa's response to this question in these early e-mails is, "I have great parents who are still together after almost 40 years. I have an older sister whom I love and a French brother-in-law. I have a lovely grandfather who still lives back home in the Midwest whom I go visit a few times a year. I have a college-aged cousin who's part of my extended family and who's really cool." She doesn't reveal too much in this answer but reveals enough to let you know her family is important to her and that it's a close family. She's not a child of divorce, and her sister is married, so her view of marriage may be positive. It's also likely she doesn't believe in divorce, or at least would treat it as a last resort. If she wants kids, since she has a sibling she's close to, she might likely want to have more than one child. She mentions extended family, not just parents and siblings, so she believes in a broader definition of family.

The feeling would have been different if her response had been the following: "I've lived away from home since I was 18. I see my family usually once a year at Christmas. I have a sister and a brother. My parents divorced when I was 10. They both remarried, and I have various half-siblings." What can we glean from this? Though she doesn't intentionally put any emotion into these statements, they're brimming with subtext. She left home as soon as she legally could. She rarely sees her family, so they're not close. She mentions her full siblings only briefly, so she's probably not close with them any more than she is to her divorced parents. She doesn't even bother to mention what gender her half-siblings are or how many there are, so it seems likely there's some jealousy or bitterness in regard to them. There's no mention of her parents' new spouses, so it's clear that there are issues there as well. You can assume there will be no happy family dinners in your future if you date her, at least not with *her* family.

Ask if He Has Kids, Ask about Their Living Situation and His Relationship with Them

Like the family he grew up with, the family he has created also has a huge effect on who he is. It will also have an effect on your relationship with him in the future, if that develops. So make sure to ask these questions.

If his kids are living with him, then naturally he has a close relationship with them, or at least as close as they'll let him have. If he has them part-time, you'll know he probably really loves them and tries to see them when he can, but he has to share custody. If he doesn't see them very often or at all, you might want to ask some serious questions about why. There could be a bad situation with the kids' mother, or your potential date may not want anything to do with his kids. In all of these cases, you'll want to do some serious thinking.

If the kids live with him, he's probably a pretty caring person. He takes care of his kids and is good with responsibility. But if you're dating someone with kids living at home, you're dating him *and* his kids. If you fall in love with him, and especially if you marry him, you're marrying a whole existing family. This can be a wonderful experience, but you need to be prepared for it and comfortable doing so.

If he has them part-time, then most of the above is still true. You're still in a relationship with him and his kids; you just won't see the kids as much. But again, if you marry him, you will be part of his kids' lives, and they'll be part of yours.

If he doesn't see them often or at all, you need to ask some tough questions, both of him and of yourself. Why doesn't he see the kids? If it's a bad situation with the kids' mother, do you want to find yourself in the middle of that? Chances are that trouble won't just go away. Or if it's your potential date who has chosen not to see his children, that's a can of worms you might not want to open. Sure, there may be legitimate reasons he's chosen that path, but generally speaking a parent wants to see his kids. If he doesn't, you want to tread lightly. And if you want to have kids yourself, you'll have to realize that he's probably not going to be a good choice as a partner for you.

Ask about Her Job

Someone's job can tell you everything or nothing about her. But even if it's telling you nothing, it's telling you something. Let's clarify that.

Sometimes we choose a job; sometimes a job chooses us. Some people go to college, get a job in their field right after graduation, and then work at that job or in that field for the rest of their lives. This happens. And if it happens, you'll know that is who this person is. A couple of examples are a doctor or a lawyer. A doctor had to know from pre-med that she wanted to be a doctor. She went through years and years of study, became a doctor, and it's unlikely she'll ever be anything else. To do what a doctor does, dealing with the sick, dealing with the dying, dealing with the intricacies of the human body—it's a level of dedication few people just give up. The same is true in a different way of being a lawyer. To be a lawyer, she's gone through law school, she's sweated through the bar exam, and she's chosen a usually lucrative career that it's unlikely she'll want to give up. Both of these careers involve long hours and a lot of stress. The fact that she's chosen one of them means she's passionate about what she does, and it's probably a huge part of who she is.

And sometimes the job chooses us. This is more common. We may have certain passions, especially artists of various sorts, which don't always do us any good in living day by day. Or we may not know what our passions are, but still have to work. So we take a job in the short term to get by, to pay our rent, to put food in our mouths. It may not feed us mentally or emotionally, it may not tell anyone who we are, but it gets us through life. And if we're good at it, it does become part of who we are. We're good at our job, we're good at the creative thinking necessary to do it well, we're good at the multi-tasking it requires, we're good at dealing with co-workers or customers. So even though that job at Starbucks chose her, because it was a job she could get that allowed her to keep working on her novel, she's still great at making foam for the cappuccinos and the customers love her. So it becomes part of her identity, whether she likes it or not. And that will tell you a lot about who she is—not "oh, she's a coffee shop worker," but rather, "oh, she works in a coffee shop and takes pride in her work, even though it's a grunt job. And she's working on a novel, too, so she's probably smart enough to have a better job but chooses to do this for the sake of her future happiness." So while the nature of the job tells you nothing about her, the story of her job tells you a lot.

Ask about His Living Situation

Aside from being a covert way of asking if he's married or involved with someone, which it can be, finding out about his living situation will give you information about his maturity, sociability, and character. He'll probably have indicated in his profile whether he lives alone or with roommates. But there's more to be discovered about this.

Yes, asking about his living situation is a great way to subtly ask if he's married or living with someone. But of course, it's easy enough for him to lie about this, so don't expect to get a revelatory response. However, it is an easy opening for him to tell you—if he chooses to. And if it turns out he's married or living with someone, then you can decide if that's the kind of relationship you want and take it from there.

If he's living alone, it usually demonstrates a couple of things. Usually it means he's making enough money to afford to live without roommates. It can mean he's secure and happy enough with himself that he doesn't mind being alone. And it could mean that he's reached an age where he thinks it's not really appropriate to live with roommates.

If he's living with roommates, you can assume one of two things. Either he can't afford to live alone, or he really likes having people around him, making him a very social person. If it's the latter, you might want to find out if there's a reason he feels the need to have people around him all the time. There's nothing wrong with being social, but you should also be comfortable enough with yourself to be able to be alone some of the time.

Then there's the dreaded "living at home with his parents." There's not much to be said about this except the unacceptability of this increases with each year he passes beyond 18. If he's reached the age of 30 and is still living with his parents, there better be a damned good reason. It just denotes a lack of maturity, responsibility, and independence.

Ask about Her Friends

The main intention of this is to make sure she has some. She doesn't have to have a lot, just some. Even if she's recently moved to a new town, she has friends back home—or should.

The problem arises if someone doesn't have any friends. Most people are happy to mention a few friends, usually cheerfully saying how great they are. As long as this is true, you're fine. But if she can't come up with anyone, then she may not be a very likeable person. Or she might be so painfully shy that she can't make friends. In which case your first date with her might be incredibly awkward. Or she might have had a huge falling out with all of her friends, in which case again there's probably a personality issue.

Normal people have friends. It's a good idea to ask. And if she has them, she'll think you're just really interested in her life.

Ask about His Hobbies

Again, part of the reason to ask this is to make sure he has some—aside from watching TV. Hobbies make someone interesting. They make someone happier. And they're a normal part of most people's lives. And if someone doesn't have any hobbies, you might end up sitting around the house a lot if you date him.

Hobbies can be something active like hiking, swimming, surfing, playing sports, sailing, jogging, or working out. Or they can be something like reading, seeing movies, going to live music shows, collecting stamps, painting, writing, playing the guitar, and so on. They don't have to be anything big and exciting; they just need to be something, anything, that he enjoys and make him happy. If he has hobbies, he's got something interesting in his life aside from you. You never want to be all someone has to do in his spare time. Otherwise, you'll never have any spare time for the things you like to do.

Also, hobbies make a person interesting. If all he does is go to work and come home to watch TV, then what's he going to talk about? He's going to talk about work and TV. If he talks at all. Dullsville.

Ask about Her TV Viewing

This relates back to the hobbies issue. People watch way too much television these days. And as much as we may enjoy it, it's an inactive thing we do that doesn't involve too much thinking and results in virtually no interaction. Yes, it keeps you up to date on pop culture, but is that all there is to life? And is that what you're looking for in your date, someone well versed about which star is dating which star and what's up on *Survivor*?

Everyone underestimates how much TV they watch. If you watch a lot of TV and you add up the hours you spend doing it, it will scare the hell out of you. What could I have done with those hours? So no one likes to know or admit how much time she spends on the couch with the remote. So if you ask how much TV she watches and she says a couple of hours a night, you can safely assume the TV is on from the moment she gets home until she goes to bed. If she says a couple of hours a week, then it's possible she does do some other things when she's home. This is all relevant because you may want to do something other than watch TV with your date. You may want to go out. And if she won't leave the house for fear of missing her shows, you'll have a problem. And considering how easy it is to fall into a rut in a relationship, if what you do when you're together is watch TV, that's probably what you'll continue doing for the rest of your time together.

Occasionally, you'll find someone who's gone to the other extreme and will tell you, "I don't own a TV." There's really nothing wrong with this person—probably. In fact, some of the most interesting people are those who have chosen to live outside of the world of television. There's a pretty good chance she's an intellectual. She might be a hippie. And she probably has a lot of interesting thoughts to share with you. But you'll have to leave her apartment if you ever want to watch a ball game or a presidential address.

We think too much TV is bad for you. But we both own TVs, and Terry even has his own TV station. So while it's important not to go overboard, we also don't think you need to be intellectually pure and TV-free. And that's usually the view most people hold. So ask how much TV she watches, double it, and see if you can live with that. Chances are you watch some TV yourself, so you're probably not too different.

PROBING TECHNIQUES, OPEN-ENDED AND CLOSED-ENDED QUESTIONS, AND SUPPORTING ANSWERS

People who ask questions for a living, such as investigators, doctors, and sales people all use simple techniques to help them get at the truth. You can use some of these techniques yourself.

Probing

When you probe, you're looking for information by using a series of questions. It's a situation in which you're the one doing the questioning and leading the conversion. If you want to learn if a person has been married, you can use a variety of probing questions, such as a direct question (Have you ever been married?) or a more subtle technique of using an indirect question (Would you ever consider getting married?). The secret is to keep probing until you get an answer.

Open-Ended Questions

In probing, you can ask a mix of open-ended and closed-ended questions. An open-ended question is one in which you ask a question that can have a variety of answers or initiate a dialogue. Examples of open-ended questions are the following: Tell me a bit about the type of person you like? What do you find attractive in someone? What's a fun date to you?

Closed-Ended Questions

Where open-ended questions allow for a number of different answers and opinions, closed-ended questions are intended for specific information, most often a yes or a no. Examples of closed-ended questions are as follows: Have you ever been married? Do you like serious people? Do you like long hair? Do you like bars?

By probing with a nice mix of open- and closed-ended questions, you can find out a lot about a person very quickly. The open-ended questions will give him room to explain complex issues, and the closed-ended questions will allow you to get specific answers.

Supporting Answers

Finally, it's important to "support" a person's answers. When he answers an open-ended question, you can support what he says with a comment ("Wow, we have the same views on marriage. That's great!") or simply follow up with another open or closed-ended question ("That's interesting. Tell me more."). Use closed-ended questions to support a complex answer or to settle something that you were not sure of ("So, you were married two times then?").

In probing to learn about the other person, be sure to support his answers and opinions and express your interest in a nice way. Creating an open exchange will also mean that you should be prepared to answer the same types of questions in return.

Asking the Tough Questions

We've taken it easy on you so far. The last few questions are the most awkward to ask. But they're worth asking. However, you may want to play it by ear to see if they're all really necessary to ask. Sometimes in the course of getting to know someone, the answers become clear.

▶ Is he currently involved with or dating anyone?

▶ What are her religious beliefs?

▶ Does he have a criminal record?

▶ Does she do drugs?

One at a time…

Is He Currently Involved with or Dating Anyone?

Yeah, we know, we've already covered married and living with someone. But if he passed both those tests, you only need to hand him one more. You'll want to know what competition you might have.

He might be dating someone but still looking. If the relationship he's in hasn't progressed beyond a certain point, he may think it's perfectly okay to keep his options open and still date around. And while some people may have a problem dating someone who's dating someone else, others just think it's fair play. If you don't have a commitment, is there really anything wrong with playing the field?

And it's not uncommon when corresponding with someone prior to an actual date that he might be corresponding with others at the same time. And he might go out with someone else before you if their correspondence began before yours. When you start writing to someone online, it's rarely clear from the beginning whether he'll be the one, or even the right one for right now. No reason to limit your options if there are multiple people you're interested in. But it's also fair to know if you're one of many. Go ahead and ask if you feel you really want to know.

What Are Her Religious Beliefs?

This is a question usually answered in the multiple-choice questions in her profile. However, not everyone chooses to answer. And sometimes you might like some elaboration. Especially if she's chosen the ambiguous response, "Spiritual, but not religious."

This question is most important to ask if your religion and hers are not the same. For instance, if you're Jewish and she's Catholic, and you feel you need to marry someone Jewish, it's probably not going to work out between you. Or if you're Protestant and she's a Scientologist, and you think Scientology is crap, again it's probably not going to work out between you. In fact, no matter your religion, if you think your date's religion is crap, dating that person is generally not a good idea.

It's also a good idea to ask this question if one of you classifies yourself as non-religious or atheist. If one of you is religious and the other is not, you need to know how serious of an impact this could make on your relationship and possible life together. If it's as simple as she goes to church on Sunday and you stay home, that's fine. But if she constantly talks about God when you're with her, and you don't believe in God, you're going to get tired of her pretty fast. And vice versa.

Now as for the "Spiritual, but not religious" answer, it'll need clarifying. Does she meditate every morning? Does she worship Satan? Does she dream of a day when trees will be freed from the oppression of evil roots and set free upon the world? We think it's a good idea you know what she means by "spiritual," as there are a wide variety of answers. In all likelihood, it means something less extreme, such as she believes in some sort of higher power but doesn't believe any of the major religions has gotten things quite right. But ask, and then you'll know.

Does He Have a Criminal Record?

In a perfect world, you wouldn't have to ask this. In a perfect world, there wouldn't be people in prisons. But unfortunately, this world is not perfect. We're not suggesting you ask this of everyone you meet online. But if, as you communicate, there are little things that make you wonder, go ahead and ask. Better to know than not to know.

It's unlikely that anyone who's actually in prison is going to contact you online, as access to the Internet is limited in jail. However, it's not out of the realm of possibilities. Though most prisoners are not currently allowed access to the Internet, and those who are are not allowed unmonitored access to the Internet, there are ways around it. Since prisoners are still able to send regular mail, it's possible that they could send information to an outside source who then posts the information online. The one good thing in this situation is that, if he is in prison, chances are that when you suggest a meeting after a few weeks, it won't ever happen. Unless he convinces you to drive to San Quentin.

So it's pretty safe to assume you're not being propositioned by someone doing 25 to life. But that doesn't mean he's never done time. If you have any doubt or worry in your mind about the person you're thinking about meeting, go ahead and ask him if he's ever done time. Chances are the answer will be no, and you two can laugh about it. If the answer is yes, you'll be glad you asked.

Does She Do Drugs?

How you want to approach this one is up to you. But first you need to decide how important it is to you. Chances are you'd want to know if she did something hard, like cocaine or heroin. But do you care if she smokes pot? Do you care if she does Ecstacy on the weekends occasionally? Figure out what you're willing to accept before you ask. Then ask. This is a question they don't often touch on the mainstream sites. And it's unlikely that someone will volunteer it in her profile. So it's a fair question to ask. Just be willing to reciprocate with your own answer.

Summary

Just as with getting to know someone in any other kind of context, getting to know someone you've met online involves a lot of questioning and answering. Be strong and ask the questions you think it's important to have answered. And make sure you ask the questions that will really tell you who you're going to be going out with. The more you know about your potential date *before* your date, the more comfortable you will be meeting in person. And the happier you'll be if you find out something that doesn't sit well prior to your first meeting. It's a lot easier to break up with someone you've never met.

GUY SAYS

One thing that really helped me find the love of my life—and for her to understand that I was that man she was looking for—was my willingness to ask important questions and to answer all of hers.

The last thing anyone wants—and this applies to both men and women—is surprises later on. If you meet someone great, only to find out at a later date that she used to be something that you dread (like being married 18 times), that could be a show-stopper. It's better to find out now, and do the same in return for her.

After some pleasant talks or e-mails, it's really not that hard to start "probing" a bit, and I don't mean in the sack!

I like to start probing early in the process, asking very nice, easy questions such as "What's your favorite type of movie?" or "Do you like wine?" Those may seem simple, but it's more the process of being able to ask questions in an open and supportive way that will set the stage for the more complex questions that will follow.

I know it's hard to ask questions like, "How many people have you slept with?" but they need to be asked—and the sooner the better. A good way to handle such a question is to go "open-ended" where you ask, "Tell me about your first love?" That gets the conversation started. After the first, you can ask, "So what happened after he stole your credit cards and left you stranded in Morocco?" You'll be surprised how a genuine interest and an understanding nature gets people to open up.

Guys, women are just as interested in finding out about your history and background as you are about theirs. If you are having a hard time getting her to talk, you can always say, "Hey, I'm so interested in you that I want to know everything about you!" and that pretty much covers all the bases. On tricky subjects, such as past relationships or sex, you can preface it with, "I know this is a hard subject, but I really want to know, and I will share my experiences with you if that will help."

It's the willingness to give information about yourself that will get the other person to open up.

The last little tip is the most important one: What matters most is where things are going. Everyone has a past, and everyone has baggage. If you react badly to the past experiences, you can shut down all communication pretty fast. So, if that special person has some history that is upsetting, maybe the best questions to ask are, "Is that where you are now, or something you would do again?"

It's where you are both going together that really matters. Find out where that is.

—*Terry*

CHICK SAYS

It's one of my great talents to imagine the worst in any situation. If I'm on an airplane, there's no chance I won't spend a minute imagining it crashing. If I'm driving down the coast, I'll inevitably imagine the car plummeting over the side of a cliff. If I think I've left the oven on, I'll spend most of the time I'm out of the house imagining the house burning down. And if I find someone I like online who seems to like me, I'll spend part of every communication wondering what's wrong with him and what horrible thing could possibly happen to me if I meet him.

I'm not a pessimist, surprisingly. And I'm not a defeatist. But I have a very active imagination. This ability to imagine everything that could possibly go wrong is actually a great benefit in the world of online dating. If you prepare for the worst, you can only end up with an improvement on your expectations.

It's hard to ask the tough questions. This I know. And you can choose to bypass them and take your chances. But it's better if you ask. And *do* take the time to read everything carefully. Look for subtext. Ask as many questions as you feel comfortable asking, and pay real attention to his answers as well as the way he answers. If it's not a simple question, you shouldn't expect a simple answer. If it's a simple question and you get a long, involved answer and explanation, there's probably a reason for that, too.

Remember that you're hoping to build a great, honest, serious, solid relationship with this person. Ask the questions that are weighing on you instead of leaving them to linger in your imagination where you can dwell on them incessantly. You'll feel relieved—like going back to see if you really left the oven on.

—Alyssa

Chapter 14
Background Checks: Additional Peace of Mind

*A*s you're learning, meeting someone online is often tricky because you can't be sure about anyone until you get to know him well through direct contact. In a world full of horror stories about nice normal people who go on rampages, people saying they're single but they're really married, or simply the fear of getting involved with someone you met on a dating site, it may help to get a little additional peace of mind.

Just as the Internet has made online dating possible, it's also a great tool for finding out background information on just about anyone. Better yet, there are a lot of free services and databases to find out about someone's background; and when you really want to dig deep, for a fee well under $50, you can find the most private information possible. It's a new world where we actually can't hide from prying eyes of information gatherers, so you can use that to your advantage when you want to confirm what someone tells you about her life or background.

Most people worry about the following background items when they meet someone online:

- ▶ Marital status
- ▶ Age
- ▶ Job and employment history
- ▶ Income
- ▶ Residence

When you meet someone online, you will generally learn through his profile, or initial contact, whether he is married or not, his age, if he is working and what he does, roughly how much money he makes, and where the lives. Those are all things that are good to know, which help you understand the person and how he's living.

As you get to know the person, you may find that, although he's told you all of the above, some of it may not "fit" right. He may say he isn't married, but he's vague about where he lives or where he works. If that happens, it's reasonable to assume that he's keeping where he lives or works from you because he may be married and doesn't want you to show up where he lives or call his work. Or he may say he makes over $100,000 per year, but he avoids saying where he works, or he lives in a poor part of town and drives a beater.

When certain key facts don't align or make sense, it may simply be that the person doesn't fit the standard profile of most people, or it may be that he's not telling the whole truth. What are you to do? If you confront him and express some doubt, you may hurt his feelings or sound mistrustful. It's always a tricky time.

As you learned in Chapter 13, it's good to probe and ask as many tough questions as possible. When the answers don't jibe, then it's time to do a little background checking.

Checking the Facts

There are a number of online resources that can help you find out about someone quickly, easily, and often for free. After an hour or two online, you should be able to confirm a lot of what someone has told you and move forward, assured that she's telling you the truth, or leave her in the dust if she's lied.

To begin any type of background checking, you will need to know some very basic information:

- ▶ First and last name
- ▶ Age
- ▶ Current address

With the name, age, and address, you can begin your background check. If your date won't provide that information, you may not be far enough along in your contact, and it may be that she doesn't want to reveal her identity or location yet. If that's the case, keep trying, and eventually (and certainly prior to ever meeting directly) you should have enough information to work with.

Finding Phone Numbers

Begin by visiting any "white pages" online telephone directory, such as www.smartpages.com from SBC or Yahoo!'s phone directory. Enter the first and last names to see if his telephone number is listed, as shown in Figure 14.1.

Using online white pages is a no-brainer, but it's just a start. A better way to look up a person is to start with his phone number and find out if he's the person listed as the owner of the phone line. If you're looking up a man, and a woman's name comes up, you've got problems. If he's told you his name and number, and you do a "reverse" lookup of his number and a different name comes up and he doesn't have a roommate, again, you may have some serious questions to ask.

Figure 14.2 shows a reverse lookup where you enter the phone number to see who is listed on that phone line.

Phone lookups are a good start but may not always bring results. Private listings and cell phone numbers are not ones you can look up, so it's good to ask for a home phone number if he has one. Common names in simple lookups are also tricky. Everyday names, such as Jones or Garcia, may bring up so many listings that you can't be sure if the person is one of the listed—or even a relative.

turned out my name was listed on my sister's Web site because I was in her wedding photos. I'd also posted something to another Web site using my own name, and that had come up. I think the third listing was from my employer. I realized suddenly that I was findable online, which can be a little disturbing when it first happens to you. Now, like Terry, there are a lot of listings for me due to my own Web site and books and whatnot. And if you type your name in online, you'll likely turn up more listings than you thought would appear, just as will probably happen if you type in your potential date's name. But here's the tricky tightrope-y part. We tell you not to give your potential date your full name until after you've met. And I stand by that. And unlike Terry, I think you'd be nuts to give him your date of birth. I think men are less skittish about these things, as it's usually the woman who's more vulnerable. So it's tricky. How can you get his full name and date of birth without giving him yours? Sometimes you don't have to ask. A lot of guys, more than women I think, use their actual names in their e-mail addresses. So if you're e-mailing outside of the online dating site, there's a decent chance you've got his full name. And there are other clues you can pick up on as well. For instance, I saw a profile of a guy the other day who had used an unusual name for his user name. I noticed that in one of his photos he was wearing a T-shirt with the same name on it. I Googled the name on his shirt from his user name. And I found him, with the same photo from his profile on the Web site. He had written a book by the name I had Googled. I've managed to do this several times with different guys. One had posted some poetry he'd written and signed it with his pen name, which came up in a Yahoo! search. Just use your best judgment. Don't meet someone in person until you feel comfortable doing so. And if you need to do a background search to feel comfortable, then do it. The most important thing is for you to be open and confident when you meet him. And you should do whatever you have to do to be in your comfort zone on that first date.

—*Alyssa*

Part IV

Power Dating:

Getting the Word Out

Chapter 15
Creating Template E-mails Using Your Word Processor

*A*t this point you've been through the process of creating the message you wish to send to prospective dates in the form of the profile you write, the pictures you choose, and, as covered in Chapter 9, the e-mail message you'll be sending. Now it's time to think about how to spot the people you'd like to contact and send them that "wink" or e-mail.

One of the first things you'll notice when you use an online dating site is that there are lots of people you want to contact. There's nothing wrong with admitting it's a numbers game—one in which you contact everyone who looks interesting with the hope that a few people will get back to you. You'll quickly find that not everyone you contact will respond and that e-mails work better than winks or icebreakers.

The steps most people use to initiate contact are

1. Identifying a potential date
2. Winking or icebreaking
3. Waiting for a wink, icebreaker, or e-mail in response to your wink or icebreaker
4. Waiting some more
5. Sending an e-mail either in response to their wink, icebreaker, or e-mail responding to you
6. Sending an e-mail saying you sent a wink or icebreaker and you're sad you haven't heard back.

Whether you start with a wink or start with an e-mail, if you get any sort of reply, you will need to e-mail the person to get the party started. That means one thing:

You will need to write a lot of e-mails.

With a long list of people you're interested in, you'll need to have a few tools to help you with the process or else you're going to spend a lot of time writing custom e-mails for each person.

Since it's a bit of a numbers game, once you start writing to lots of people, you'll be sending out enough e-mails that you will quickly face the following challenges:

▶ Customizing a basic letter for each person based on their profile

▶ Keeping a record of when you sent it and what you said in the letter

▶ Tracking the response, or lack of response, so you don't e-mail them again and again

This chapter, along with Chapters 16, 17, and 18, will help you create and manage your e-mails when you're in touch with a large number of people.

Writing Template Letters

Even though each person you send an e-mail to is unique and her profile has special interests you'll want to respond to, the basic "hello" message you send for the first e-mail will be pretty much the same for most people. It's a letter that says "Hey, I'm interested in getting to know you!"

It's entirely possible to write and send e-mails directly from the mail feature within the online dating service. But as suggested in Chapter 9, it's always best to write your e-mails in a word processing program, such as Microsoft Word. This will help with spelling and grammar. Once you write your e-mail in Word, you can easily copy and paste it into the e-mail feature of the online dating service.

WORD ROCKS!
Always start by writing your e-mails in a word processing program. The spelling and grammar checks are important features to take advantage of—you'll be a step ahead of most of your fellow daters if you just spell and write correctly.

Figure 15.1 shows a typical first letter being written in Microsoft Word.

The letter shown in Figure 15.1 is pretty typical of many first e-mails. It's very short, very simple, and, well, not very good. It expresses interest, but it doesn't indicate in any way that you even looked at your potential date's profile text. This letter could be sent to anyone, and it reads that way.

It's better to write an e-mail that at least expresses some personality or interest that may apply to the person you're contacting. The problem is, in a first e-mail you don't want to go into a lot of detail—or spend too much time—since you have no idea if she will get back to you. A good solution is to create a series of e-mails that apply to a variety of profile types and have them handy to use as "templates" for a semi-custom letter.

Figure 15.1
Everything starts somewhere. When you write e-mails, start with your word processing program—then copy the letter into the e-mail form of the online dating service.

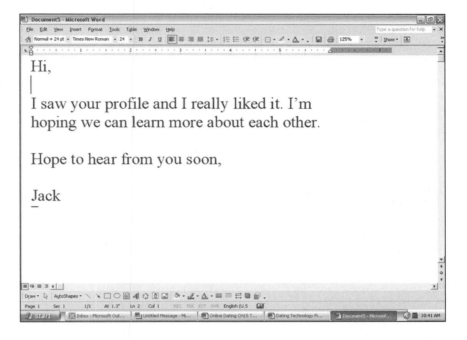

Examples of template letter subjects would be

▶ I'd like to learn more about you.

▶ I love your profile, and I'm wondering if you have a picture you can send me?

▶ After you look at my profile, I'd like to hear from you. If you aren't a paid member who can e-mail, just wink at me, and I'll send an e-mail suggesting ways to contact each other.

▶ I think we have so much in common—check out my profile and see if you agree!

Figure 15.2 shows the basic e-mail, only this time it has been written to indicate that you at least looked at her profile and are not a profile "spammer" who is just e-mailing everyone on the service with the same e-mail.

Figure 15.2 is an example of a basic "template" letter that you can use over and over. Even better, you can create several template letters and modify them easily without harming the original version using the Template feature of your word processing program. The samples shown here use Microsoft Word's Template feature, but if you use a different word processing program, it should have a similar feature.

Making a Template Letter

Using Microsoft Word, go to the File menu and select New to create a new document, as shown in Figure 15.3. You'll be creating a basic document that you can use as-is or customize at a later time.

Figure 15.2
Even a general message
will help get a response.
This e-mail implies that
you have at least read
her profile and you're
not just a profile
spammer.

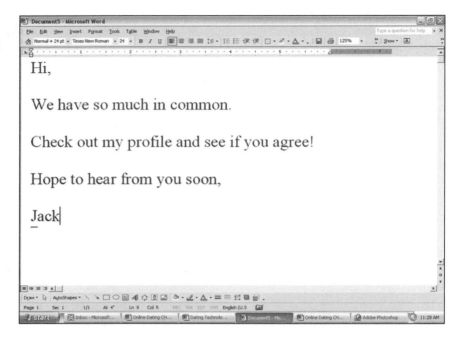

Figure 15.3
To make a template
letter, start by creating a
new document from the
File menu.

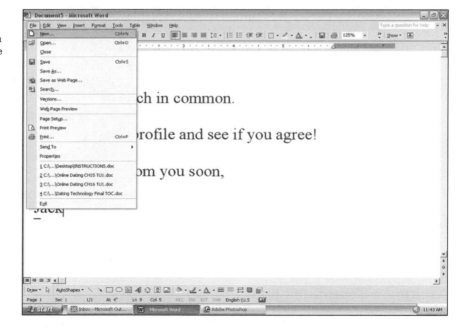

Next, create your template text. As shown in Figure 15.2, it can be any basic letter that you plan to use for a large number of e-mails in the future. Be sure to check your spelling and grammar, and also make sure that you've written the e-mail in a manner that can work for anyone who gets it, making sure it's not too specific.

After writing your basic template letter, you create the actual Template document by going to the File menu, and choosing Save As (see Figure 15.4). At the bottom of the Save As dialog box is a drop-down menu from which you can choose a file type. Be sure to save the document you created as a .DOT, or document template document. This document will be stored in the Templates folder that Word uses for templates.

Figure 15.4
Select a name for your Template document and save it as a .DOT, or document template file.

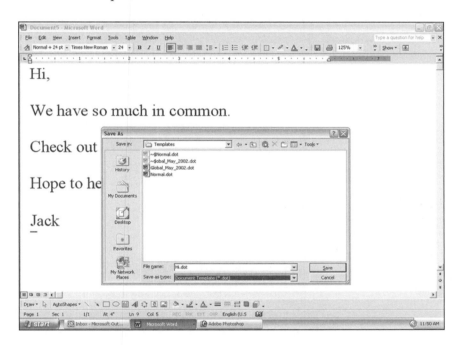

You can repeat this process for a number of template letters, being sure to label each in a way that will help you choose the right letter when you're in the midst of e-mailing prospective dates. Once you have a number of template documents created, you can start working with them.

The advantage of having the template letters are many, and include the following:

▶ You don't have to write a new letter each time you e-mail someone.

▶ Even though you can modify the letter while working with it, unless you save the changes back to the template document, you won't accidentally change or erase the original.

▶ Templates help you organize a series of letters by subject.

▶ Template letters will help when you begin to create custom e-mails for each person.

Working with Template Letters

Once you've created a series of online dating template letters, you're ready to start sending some e-mails. When you find a person you're interested in, you can open a template letter and use it as-is, or you can tweak it a bit if you have the time.

To open a template, go to the File menu and choose Open. You'll see the New Document ask pane (or the Open dialog box, depending on your version of Word) where you can select to open an existing document, a new document, or a template document. Select General Templates in the New From Template section of the task pane, as shown in Figure 15.5.

Figure 15.5
Choose General
Templates from the New
Document task pane.

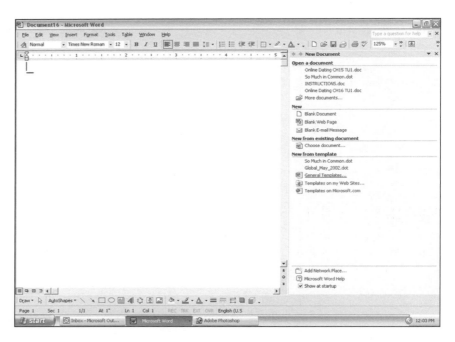

Once you have chosen General Templates, you'll be presented with the Templates dialog box, as shown in Figure 15.6. From the General tab, you'll find the template documents you created. Click on the template you want to work with, and it will open it as a new Word document. Your original template document is never touched, and you can freely edit the new document without altering the template letter.

By using templates, you'll have a nice library of letters to work from, and you can change or modify letters without changing the templates. You could simply use the Save and Save As features time and time again with a basic document; but as you move forward, in the next chapters, you'll create customized, and even mail merge letters, so it's good to get to know how to create a template document.

Figure 15.6
Choose the Template letter you created. It will open as a new Word document that you can edit, and the original template letter will not be altered.

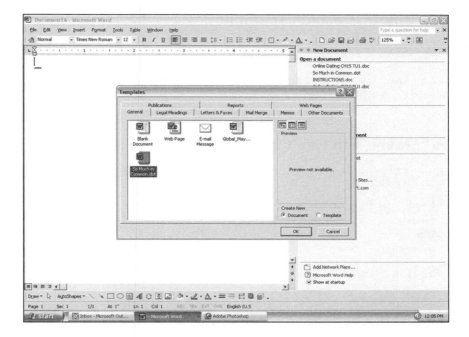

Writing Templates That Work

Now that you know how to create a template letter, it's good to create a few basic templates that work well for most situations. The following are examples of some letter types that any self-respecting online dater should have in her Template folder!

A good introduction letter should do the following:

> ► Express an interest based on reading his profile.
> ► Invite him to respond.

If you're taking the trouble to send an e-mail, be sure it's one that will get a response. Make it fun to read, short and sweet, and include a "call to action" that says, "Get back to me!" With that in mind, here are some basic e-mails that are good to have—but be sure to write them in your own style and using your own words. Remember, this is a book about truth, and you'd better be sure that you speak like you write when you eventually talk or meet.

You should have templates for when you make first contact, when you don't get a response, when you want to say a bit about yourself to someone who is a good match, and finally one for when you need to shut down inquiries from someone who has been e-mailing you but in whom you're not interested.

An "I'm Interested" Template

Hi,

I just saw your profile, and I am interested in learning more about you. After you have checked my profile, let's talk.

A "Maybe You Can't E-mail" Follow-Up Template

Hello Again,

I sent you an e-mail a few days ago because I think we may be a good match, but I haven't heard from you. Maybe you're not a paid subscriber. If you wink at me to let me know you're interested, too, I'll e-mail you with some ways we can get in touch without your having to subscribe.

Till I hear from you,

The "All About Me" Template

Hi,

I saw your profile and wanted to get in touch, since I think you are amazing. A quick note about me if you haven't had a chance to view my profile yet. I'm your age, live in the same town, have been single for about a year, and I have many of the same interests as you. As I went down the list of what you're looking for, I couldn't help but say to myself, "That's me!" So, here I am.

I hope to hear from you soon,

A "No Thank You" Template

Hello,

I got your winks and e-mails, and I appreciate your interest. I don't think there's a good match here, but good luck in your search!

Regards,

Summary

Template letters are documents you create to use as-is or to create new letters from. Since they can't be permanently changed (unless you do this intentionally), you can play with them over and over without accidentally changing the original. By writing short, simple e-mails that express an interest with a call to action, you'll be able to quickly and easily send a lot of e-mails to a variety of prospective dates. Just make sure you don't abuse this power by spamming everyone on a dating site.

GUY SAYS

One of the first things I learned in online dating is that it's a lot of work!

Winks, e-mails, adding people to "favorites" lists, and then keeping track of who you said what to is quite a challenge.

I started to create a number of documents to work from in Word, but I found that I kept modifying them a bit. Then in the midst of copying and pasting into the online dating e-mail form, I was saving the documents with the changes. Pretty soon I had a bunch of documents that were very different than when I started. Even worse, as I tweaked them along the way and saved those tweaks by mistake, I started sending letters with the wrong messages, such as "I love your eyes" to someone who was wearing sunglasses in her picture. Oh, bother.

Then I learned how to create templates in Word. They were as easy to create as any other document, but I found that by using a template, I couldn't accidentally save to the template the changes I had made in the regular document. That solved the problem perfectly because the template remained untouched.

What I liked was that in creating templates, I started to build a little library of messages that were all in one place (the Word Template folder). Finding documents, for me, is the hard part, and this problem was solved too.

By seeing the same e-mail over and over, I started to think about how important the first e-mails were. My early ones were so off-track. They were just "Hey, how are you?" things, and they didn't work well. After a while, I started saying what I was interested in and asking them to write back. It worked much better.

Take a few minutes to get organized, and you will be rewarded. Try templates and see how they work for you.

—*Terry*

CHICK SAYS

I can't tell you how many crappy first e-mails I've gotten. It's actually ridiculous what men will expect to get a response to. And I don't mean this unkindly to the men who actually try to write something specific to me. But they're in the minority.

Of all the e-mails I've gotten, I'd bet 75 percent are unaltered templates from clear profile spammers. This is not what we're suggesting you send to people. A template from a profile spammer goes something like this:

"Hi, would you like to chat sometime?"

Scintillating reading. Why would I want to chat with him? Who is he? Why is he writing to me? If this is all I get, I won't even look at his profile. What's the point? He clearly didn't look at mine.

But I've got no problem with using a template. I think for those who see a lot of people online who are appealing and fit what they're looking for, then it's a great device. Just make sure you don't send the template as is.

Take the "template" (and I use the term loosely) above. Try adding the following:

"Hi, would you like to chat sometime? I read your profile; you seem really cool, and you've got a great smile. I think we're a lot alike. Check out my profile, and if you think we're compatible, wink or e-mail back to me."

What a difference three extra sentences make. Write your template with everything except the "smile" part, and you can replace it with whatever body part caught your eye (within reason). You're still not putting yourself too far out there, but you've given me reason to believe you actually read my profile. That goes a long way toward getting a response from me. Chicks, don't dismiss someone just because you think he's used a template. As long as he's spent a little time making it specific to you, you know he's read your profile and you know he's actually interested in you. If you show him that you're interested, then he'll likely write an e-mail just for you next time. Then you can take it from there.

Guys, if you write us a template that says nothing, that's what you'll get from us—nothing. And chicks, that's true for the template users among you as well. Just as you customize the smile you send to the guy you see across the bar, so you should customize your e-mail to tell him it's just for him.

—*Alyssa*

Chapter 16
Creating Custom Letters for Outstanding Results

*I*f you plan on sending e-mail to a lot of people over time, you'll need to create a way to write all of those e-mails without having to write each one from scratch. When you think about it, most of the time you'll be saying the same things to each person but with a bit about them added. Chapter 15 showed you how to create template letters, and with that knowledge you can learn how to customize each one for outstanding results.

There are lots of little tricks we'll share that will make it easy to get the message right—and not send the wrong message to the right person. The goal is to create a letter from a template document that looks and feels like you wrote it just for the person you're interested in. Remember, you did write it for that special someone——you just may have more than one special someone you're interested in.

Making Small, Quick Changes to Template Letters

Now that you're an expert at creating template letters, as shown in Chapter 15, you'll be able to open up a template and customize it to your heart's delight. By customizing, you can add detailed information that you gathered from a prospective date's profile or picture. With the right customization, you can make your template letters look like original documents without all of the rewriting.

To start, think about what information you can gather from almost any online profile that would work well in a letter suggesting to the person that you've read her profile and like it. The following list shows key fields that are present in most online dating profiles.

- ▶ Age
- ▶ Body type
- ▶ Location
- ▶ Astrological sign
- ▶ Occupation

▶ Single, separated, never married

▶ Turn-ons and turn-offs

▶ Hobbies or interests

▶ Religion

▶ Ideal date

▶ Ideal match qualities

In addition to the list of fields above, you'll also be able to read the profile heading and text to gather lots of information that may be a bit harder to classify for each letter, but which can still be used as part of your customized letter. Items to look for in profile text include

▶ Special interests, such as home ownership, gardening, kids, or religion

▶ Personal qualities or personal description

▶ What he values in life

▶ What she is looking for in a mate or a date

Profile text can include anything and everything about a person, and it often provides your best clue as to what will reach her. A good idea is to have a little scratch pad handy to jot down a few notes while reading her profile, or you can certainly use your PC's Notepad or a blank Word document for the same purpose.

Look for things that are special about her, as well as have value to you, and take simple notes about them. For example, if she loves to cuddle up by a warm fire and you do, too, then jot down that she loves fireplaces. Simple notes work best—remember this is a first letter, and you don't want to try too hard or go too deeply into her interests until you have had a chance to hear back from her and start a conversation going.

Next, take a look at a template letter. Figure 16.1 shows a simple one being created. Note that the basic letter is there, but there are no "hooks" for customization.

The letter is very simple, and in truth it could be sent to anyone. The person getting it may feel that's exactly what it is: a template letter.

Next, as you create the template document, think about how to build hooks into the same message for customization. Figure 16.2 shows areas where hooks can be added by highlighting the appropriate areas. The letter has been modified to allow for the hooks, and you can see how the document is being transformed into a much more personal letter.

Two areas have been defined as hooks. The first is a reference to what you read in the profile, and it can be just about anything that peaks your interest, such as "that you're a Christian" or "that you want to get to know someone as a friend first." Next, a place for listing values or interests has been added.

Figure 16.1
As you write the template document, think about how to build in "hooks" for customization.

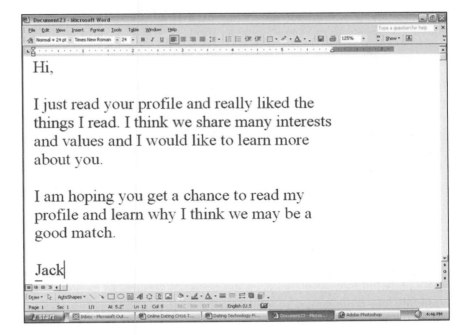

Figure 16.2
"Hooks" for customization have been added to the base template letter.

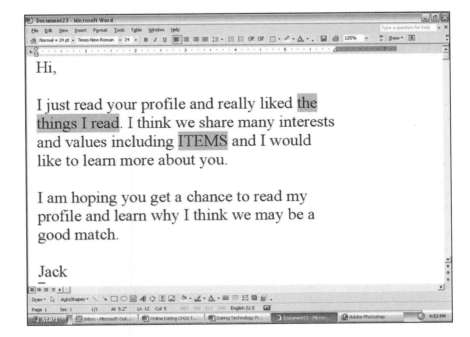

It's possible to create a template letter with lots of hooks, but one or two will add the personal touch, showing that you really took the time to ponder her profile. It shows that you've considered what she's said and that you share some of the same values or interests—that goes a long way toward getting someone to write back to you to find out more.

It's a good idea to highlight the hooks, as shown in Figure 16.2. When you open the document for your mini-customization, the highlights will be in place, and you'll know exactly where to make changes. Use a bright color, such as yellow or light blue, so that you don't miss them. Since you'll be copying the letter into the online dating service's e-mail form, the formatting and highlights won't translate to the Web form used, and you won't have to worry about deleting the highlighting.

Figure 16.3 shows a sample of the template letter fully customized with information from a prospective date's profile. Note how much different the customized version is from the base letter.

Figure 16.4 shows the same letter used for a different potential date. It shows how one letter can be used to create very different messages. Don't be shy about mixing and matching references. You can reference her photo or the way she looks or pull items from the profile text or any of the descriptive fields. Figure 16.4 used the photo and the list of turn-ons, such as tattoos, to send the right message.

Figure 16.3
The base letter has been customized by adding information found in the prospective date's profile.

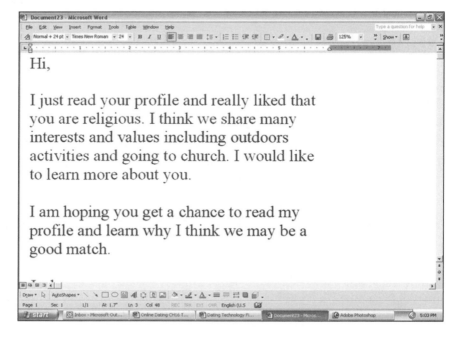

Figure 16.4
The base letter had been customized for a very different type of person than the one in Figure 16.3.

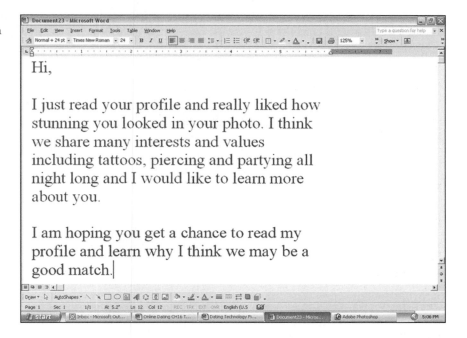

Adding More Detailed Hooks

Fast, simple changes are great, but when you find a really great candidate, you may wish to go a bit deeper into his profile and find things that are points of interest to both of you. This more extreme form of personalizing a template letter takes more time, but it will be worth the effort.

By adding a simple hook that allows for a whole sentence (see Figure 16.5), you can add a very effective message to the template letter.

Examples of whole sentence hooks include

- ▶ I love the fact that you put your family first. So do I.
- ▶ We both love sailing, so I had to get in touch.
- ▶ You look so happy in your picture, but your profile sounds so sad. I know how that feels.
- ▶ Hey, I'm just looking to have fun, too. It's nice to hear someone admit it!

Figure 16.6 shows the template letter with the whole sentence hook filled in. The addition of the one sentence doesn't take much more work to create, but the result is super. You can really bring a template letter to a fully customized, written-from-scratch feel with this process.

Figure 16.5
Adding a whole
sentence hook pumps
up the personal message
to the best level
possible.

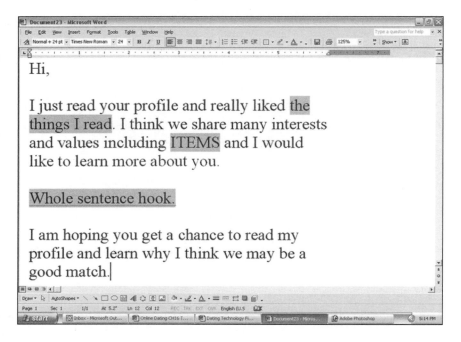

Figure 16.6
Whole sentence
customization has been
added to create a
"written-from-scratch"
feel.

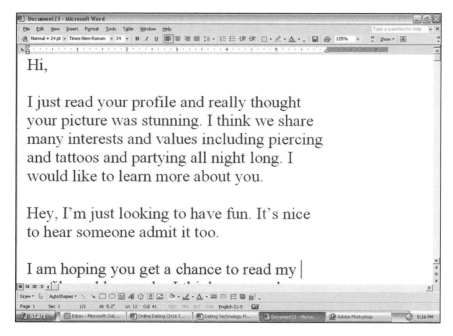

Creating More Complex Template Letters

Once you master the creation of template documents and learn how to do on-the-fly customization, you should begin to rethink how you structure your template documents. Templates created for general "hello" or "no thank you" letters may not be best for customization templates.

Keeping in mind that you don't want to be doing a whole lot of cutting and pasting work on a first letter, you should write a template letter that contains hooks that would be present in most online profiles. If you're comfortable with the process, you can simply make the templates more complex and have them contain more hooks. That's up to you and depends on how much work you want to do with each letter.

Let's take a look at two basic letters that use more complex customization.

Writing the "First" Letter

One great technique is to flatter someone and talk all about him and his interests. At the same time it's good to point out that you're just the type of person (physically or with shared interests) he's looking for. Yes, flattery will get you everywhere, and all the best daters know that you talk more about your date than yourself.

The sample template letter in Figure 16.7 does just that. It takes references that could come from any profile and fills in the blanks to make it look like a virtual ode to the person you're writing to. This is over-the-top to be sure, but it shows how much customization is possible using the technique detailed in this chapter.

Figure 16.7
Flattery runs amok in this very complex template document. The hooks create a totally custom letter.

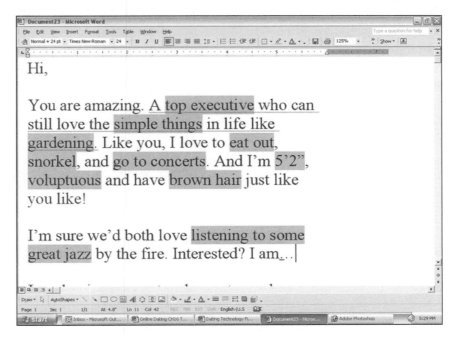

Figure 16.8 shows the same letter with a very different set of fields. The beauty of template letters is that they take the shape and form of the person you're writing to—and that will help communicate what you like about him and tell him what interests you share.

Figure 16.8
The same letter from Figure 16.7 but with different data creates a very different letter.

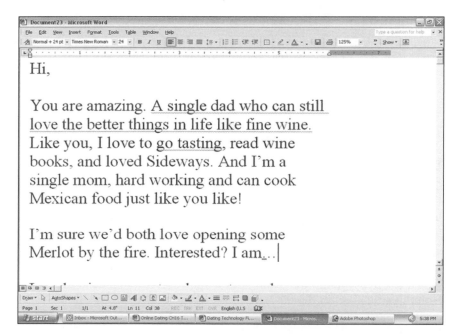

Writing an "All about Me" Letter

Sometimes someone just doesn't have that much to say in her profile. You may love her photo and the few items she did include, but there simply isn't much to work with. What to do?

In that case, you can check to see what she's looking for in a date and tell her all about yourself. It's always best to talk about her, and you actually are in a way, since you're talking about how you are what she's seeking and how you fit her wish list.

Figure 16.9 shows a template letter with lots of hooks about you in reference to what she's looking for. Why not simply have a template letter all about you without the need for hooks? You can, but each person may stress different qualities she seeks. Some people will say that they like long hair (and you have it) while others may say they love to travel (you do, too!), so customization still works best here.

Figure 16.9
Talking about yourself isn't talking about yourself when it's in response to their "wish list" date qualities.

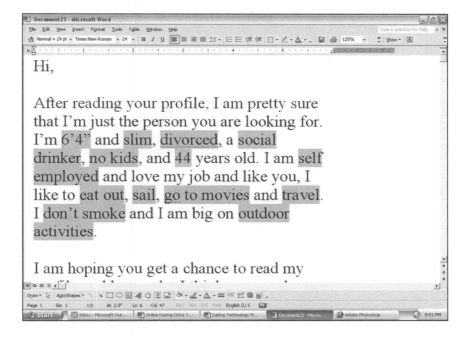

Summary

After mastering the creation of template documents, you can begin to add "hooks" to your template, which will allow you to customize each letter you send in a simple and efficient manner. The hooks can be few or many and allow you to control the amount of time and effort you put into each letter you send from a template document. A template can be a great device for a quick e-mail when you add customization hooks and use them well.

GUY SAYS

I learned to customize template letters pretty easily. In fact, it was the structure and format of the template that made my letters pretty good. Before using a template and customization, I would leave lots of important things out. The template showed me what to include and made it easy to do. I think that when it's done right, you can't tell a customized template letter from an original letter. I'd have been pretty embarrassed if anyone ever knew I was writing from a template, but truthfully, after I customized them, they were the same as original letters. The template just helped me go through the process. The best thing that template letters did was make me really read profiles. It's amazing how easy it is to read a profile and think you *really* read it, even when nothing sunk in. When you go into the profile and look for all the hooks you will use, you end up spending some quality time with the profile and learn a lot about the person you are e-mailing. That's a good thing on every level. Sometimes a template letter just didn't sum it all up, so I would write one from scratch, but the process of using templates and hooks helped structure my original letters, too. I am sure you can do without templates, hooks, and customization, but you may find yourself better organized and effective if you use them.

—Terry

CHICK SAYS

I'm not a fan of the template letter. The problem with the template letter is, if I realize it is one, I suspect the guy who's e-mailed me has probably e-mailed enough women to fill a ballroom, if not a stadium. If he hasn't bothered to customize it, he's not taking the time to get to know who I am. That means he's not terribly discerning. But if I don't realize it's a template, then what does it matter? What harm has been done? And that's the point of this chapter—use a template, but make it seem like you didn't. It's as simple as that. If I don't know you used a template on me, I will go on thinking I'm special. I will go on thinking you spent a lot of time deciding what to write to me. I will be flattered by your attention, and if you're appealing to me, I'll respond to you. While I suppose I should be upset by that—by thinking I'm special, that you spent a lot of time, that you're giving me your attention when none of it is really as true as I think—the fact remains that if you used the template correctly, I'll never know that it's not completely true. I will still be flattered. And I will still like you, if I'm inclined to. The template isn't a lie—it just gives you a fast, easy way to get your e-mails out there. And considering you're paying to be on online dating sites, time is of the essence. You've got to get your information out there, appeal to as many people as possible who appeal to you, in the time you have. And I understand that. I'm no romantic fool. And most chicks aren't either. We can be as practical as the next guy—even more so. So guys, do as you will. And we'll do as we will. And don't be surprised if it turns out that chick you like just sent you a customized template. And don't be offended. She's just being practical. And if she read this book, you probably couldn't even tell.

—*Alyssa*

Chapter 17
Taking Advantage of Free Trial Periods

*N*ow that you're fully prepared to take pictures, write your profile, and begin winking and e-mailing potential dates, you're faced with the fact that, for the most part, it actually costs a bit of change to subscribe to online dating services.

So many dating sites—so little cash.

Sure, you could spend a lifetime as a guest and view every profile, but you will learn all too quickly that in order to actually make contact—to e-mail someone—you will need to pony up and purchase a subscription. But it's worth the money. When you think about it, subscribing for a month isn't too much more than the dry cleaning bill for your best clothes for a date. For that amount, you get access to a virtually unlimited universe of love and friendship. Isn't it worth $25 for that?

Hell, yeah!

Whoa—calm down, Tiger. Since you may be trying the online dating world for the first time, you may want to experiment a bit. There are quite a few services, and it's hard to tell which one will work best for you and which will get you the most interactions with members. When you try a few of them at once, the first month's tab can reach well over a $100—and then you're faced with next month. You should be a bit cautious before shelling out the bucks.

Online dating services have a crafty method to get you to subscribe. First, they make it so you can almost taste the action by allowing you to browse and wink for free. Then, when you finally decide you need to e-mail and have to subscribe, they hit you with the $25 for one month or $75 for six months offer options.

So you've said to yourself that you're just going to try the service for one month, then try another service the next month. But suddenly the idea of paying $25 for what could be had for about $10 per month if you sign up for longer makes that a hard decision.

The good news is that most services offer a free trial period to help you with this dilemma. They allow you to sign up with a credit card, but don't charge you until the three-day trial is over. If you don't like the service in the first three days, you can cancel your subscription and your card won't be charged. If you fail to cancel, they will charge your card for whatever subscription period you selected, and then you can't cancel or get a refund.

So, the following question arises: *How can I meet the love of my life in three days?*

Getting the Most from the Free Trial Period

Although free trial periods are offered to allow you to sample the service, if you're a hard worker you can use some very clever methods to contact as many people as you can and give them ways to get in touch with you after your free trial period ends.

It's tacky, but so is asking you to pay $25 bucks for something that you could also get for $10 bucks.

WHERE THE TRIAL PERIODS ARE

Many of the larger services have begun to offer seven-day free trial periods. These offers come and go, but shop around and try different points of entry. For example, if you enter Yahoo! Personals through My Yahoo! or your DSL portal, the seven-day offer is present— but it isn't always offered if you simply go there directly.

Free trial offers are fantastic, but there are some things you need to know before you take advantage of them. As you will learn, they are limited, and you should create a strategy before trying one.

Benefits of the Free Trial Offer:

> ▶ Three to seven days of unlimited member benefits, including sending e-mails to any member on the service.

> ▶ You may cancel the subscription within the trial period, and your credit card will not be charged.

> ▶ You gain access to all member-only features, such as seeing user names, photos, videos, and audio profiles.

As good as all that sounds, there is a downside. Consider the following:

Limits of the Free Trial Offer:

> ▶ After the trial offer has finished, if you don't continue your subscription you will no longer be able to e-mail anyone—even the people who are responding to e-mails you sent them during your trial period.

> ▶ The trial offer is ONE TIME ONLY. If you try to be smart and decide to sign up, cancel after the trial, then try to sign up for the free trial offer again, it generally won't work. The services are pretty smart about this. One trick that many people

use is to create more than one profile, and then attempt to use a free trial offer under different profile names. That fails, since the service is basing the free trial on the credit card number you're using—not the profile name. When you attempt to take a free trial under another profile name using the same credit card, you will be told the offer is not available to you. If you have multiple credit cards, you can get around this for awhile—but you may find that one day your profile is shut down and you can't get back on. If that's the case, they're on to you for abusing the service. Your credit cards have your name and address, and they'll catch you with that in time, too.

▶ If you fail to cancel sometime during the trial period, your credit card will automatically be charged. It's your responsibility to cancel.

Figure 17.1 shows a typical free trial offer. If you're not a paid subscriber, the little promotion for it will be visible most often from your sign-on page. It's a good idea to click the button and read the fine print associated with the offer on the service you're using.

Figure 17.1
Many large services, such as Yahoo! Personals, offer seven–day free trial periods.

Regardless of which service you're interested in, check to see if they offer a free trial period or simply if they allow you to cancel a subscription within a specific period of time, such as within three days of subscribing, without being charged. You shouldn't subscribe to a service without first trying it for free if you can.

Preparing for a Free Trial Experience

After checking out the free trial offers and settling on a service you'd like to try, you should do some heavy lifting before actually signing up for the offer.

If you do some strategic planning and window shopping, you can make the most of your free trial period. Following are some things you should do before signing up for the free trial:

> ▶ **Create Your Profile.** Sign on to the service by creating your own profile. Go through the entire profile creation process, including uploading your photo, writing your profile text, and filling in all of the check boxes. Your profile must be created—and approved by the service (which can take a day or two)—before it will be visible to anyone you contact during the free trial offer. Wait for the e-mail saying your profile is approved and active before you sign up for the trial.

> ▶ **Shop 'Til You Drop.** Do some searches and find as many people as you can whom you're interested in. You can add the profiles you like to a Favorites list, or you can simply write down the profile names, although that's much harder to manage once you start your free trial period.

> ▶ **Categorize Your Favorites.** Since you may have found different types of members you want to contact and will want to send custom messages to them, identify which members will get which letter.

> ▶ **Write Your E-mails in Advance.** Don't use the time during the free trial to write letters. If you get responses, you will be very busy replying, so do as much letter writing in advance as you can.

> ▶ **Create an E-mail Account.** Since you will be removed as a subscriber in a very short period of time, you will want to create a free e-mail address on a service such as Hotmail to tell people how to get in touch with you after the free trial period. It is not a good idea to use your regular e-mail address for this purpose, so get this step taken care of prior to the free trial period.

Using the steps above, you'll enter the free trial period fully prepared to send out e-mails and to have the people you're contacting view your profile. Then you can use your time wisely, either responding to their replies or finding new members to contact in case many of the first batch don't reply.

Creating a Free E-mail Account

One of the best things you can do is create a safe place for other members to e-mail you. As you will learn, since you will be contacting people and they may not be paid subscribers either, you will want to "sneak" an e-mail address in your e-mails to them so they can contact you directly outside of the service.

If you create an anonymous e-mail account with a service such as Hotmail, you have the same level of privacy as you do with the e-mail system of the online dating service you're trialing. Be sure to use a very abstract or general name for your e-mail account (all the good names were taken years ago anyway) that doesn't give away your identity.

Figure 17.2 shows the sign-up page for Hotmail, although you can create an anonymous e-mail account from your current ISP such as AOL if they allow multiple screen names or e-mail accounts.

Figure 17.2
Free e-mail accounts from services such as Hotmail are a great way to contact people and remain anonymous.

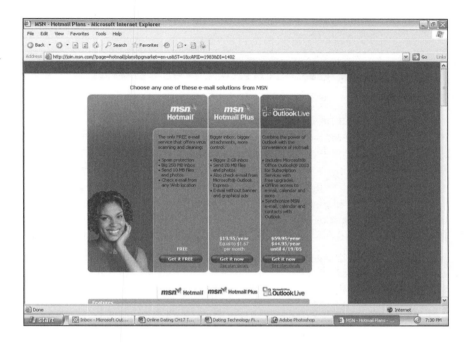

Devising Your Strategy

Finally, you should create a strategy to use during your free trial period. Yes, you could simply send one basic e-mail to everyone on the service, but then you would be one of those dreaded profile spammers. People can spot that in a second, so it's not a very good strategy, unless you're one of the moron guys who goes to a bar and thinks that if he asks every woman he sees to have sex with him, sooner or later one will say yes. If that's the case, get offline and go to a bar.

Profile spamming is just plain rude, and you won't get quality results. As covered in previous chapters, you can create customized e-mails for each person you're contacting, and they should be really good e-mails that show you've read their profile and really like what you learned. Those will get you responses.

After you build your Favorites list during the shopping phase of your planning, it's a good idea to go back and take another look. Whittle down that list to a manageable amount. The number may be 10, or it can be as many as you think you can handle responding to. Bear in mind that not everyone you contact will respond. The free trial period should be more than a numbers game—it should be a time when you find the people you would like to meet most, e-mail them, and see if their impression of you is as strong as yours is of them.

Create an "A" list, then a "B," and even a "C" list. The strategy is simple. Day one, mail to your A list. If you get some responses, you'll be pretty busy, and pretty happy. If the A list isn't coming through, e-mail to your B list on day two. Finally, if you're batting 0, use the C list on day three. You could send all of them at one time, and that's up to you if you think you can handle keeping track of who is who.

Crafting Your "Contact Me" E-mail

Now for the tricky part.

Assuming that you plan to sign-up for a free trial period and then cancel and not pay for a subscription (at least not yet), you need to hide your free e-mail address in your e-mail somehow. This will allow people to contact you directly after the trial period ends and you can no longer e-mail them back.

Why go through this step? Primarily because many members may not be paid subscribers and will have no way of e-mailing you, but more so because when you get e-mails back, you won't be able to contact them or reply once you're off the trial. Providing an e-mail address in your first letter takes you out of the paid subscriber world and into direct contact.

Now, a few more things. The people you contact may not be comfortable using their own e-mail accounts to contact you, so that knocks out a few people. Some may not understand why you simply don't pay for a subscription, so that adds a few more no-takers.

But you're saving $25 bucks, right?

More than anything, using the trial period should help you find out about the site and its members, helping to make a decision about whether the service is the right one for you, so going through this process is actually okay if you can manage it. In fact, the basis of your e-mail can be built around the fact that you're trying out the service and you're just there for awhile.

Telling the Truth

There is no harm in writing an e-mail in which you come right out and say you're using a free trial, you aren't sure whether you want to subscribe yet, and that you're checking out the site. The people you're e-mailing have been through the same decisions and will understand.

The secret is to say that while you were checking things out, you were amazed to run across her profile, and you're starting to think the service may be the best thing since apple pie. It's her profile that's making you a believer. If someone like her can be on the service, you're impressed. You can explain that you're only on the service for a short time, but since you are, it would be great if she could get in touch with you at your regular e-mail—or if that's not okay just wink and, hey, you'll subscribe just to talk to her!

Either way is good—you're giving her a choice.

With all of that in mind, you need to write your free trial, how-to-contact-me template letter.

Using a Great Template Letter

If you have a great template letter, you will get replies to your e-mail. The secret is to follow all of the advice in this book thus far, with the following items being key for this particular letter:

▶ Be warm, honest, and flattering.

▶ Make it clear that you've read his profile.

▶ Come right out and say you're on the trial subscription.

▶ Suggest an alternative way to contact you, particularly your anonymous e-mail address.

▶ Suggest if she can't e-mail you back that she send a wink and you'll subscribe and e-mail her again.

With the above items in your letter, you cover a lot of bases and give the people you're e-mailing a good chance to view your profile and get back in touch with you. The next step—write the letter.

Sample Free Trial "Contact Me" E-mail

Hello,

I just signed on using the free trial offer to see how this service works, and I was totally amazed to find your profile. I loved that you're into (HOOK) and (HOOK), and I really can relate to your love of (HOOK)—I love it too!

After you read this, I hope you check out my profile. I think we could be a great match—we have a lot in common, even (HOOK).

If you're not a subscriber, feel free to e-mail me at my regular e-mail address. I know they strip out e-mail addresses on the service, but let's try to slip it past. I am sure if you put the following together as a standard e-mail address it will get to me fine. Slyone then the AT symbol followed by h o t ma i l and then the dot com!

Or, I'm happy with a wink or an e-mail here on this service. I'll subscribe to get back to you. I hope we can connect.

Warmest regards,

(YOUR FIRST NAME and YOUR PROFILE NAME)

Although it's a bit long, it gets all the important facts across. You can make a shorter version, but this is a sample of an online dating power letter—it says everything and assumes you have one shot at getting that special someone's attention. Note that the "hooks" are ones you cull from her profile, as covered in Chapter 16.

After you craft your letter, you can put the whole process into play. Sign up for the free trial offer, and begin customizing and sending your e-mails to the Favorites list you created prior to signing up. If you have time, you can always add a few more to the list and do a new search of your area to see if anyone new has signed up since you created your Favorites list.

With all that activity, a really important part of your success will be keeping track of who you sent an e-mail to—and what you said.

Tracking Your E-mails

The free trial period will be a flurry of sending e-mails, and you will want to make a list of who you sent them to, what you said to them, and if they responded.

If you've identified people who are potentially good matches, and you said the right things in your first e-mail, you will start to get some responses. Even a few responses will send you into a state of excitement. The fun that awaits, the anticipation of communicating and someday getting together—that's the whole point of online dating. At the same time, all the names, photos, profiles, and messages you sent out will be a blur in your mind.

Keeping track of your list, keeping a record of what you said, and being able to quickly find someone's profile are all essential skills for online daters. When you get a wink back, an e-mail, or even more demanding—an IM in real time which will catch you off guard—you need to be prepared.

If you've been successful in identifying a way for people to contact you via your anonymous e-mail account, you may find that you get an e-mail from "Chris," but she failed to mention her profile name so you have no idea who Chris is!

Using a Spreadsheet, Database, or Word Processor

You could simply use a note pad and a pen to write down all the people you e-mailed, but notes are sometimes quirky, and it's hard to put all the information, such as the text of your e-mail, into a note. Since you're on your computer, you have some great programs that will help you track all of your activity.

Chances are you have a spreadsheet program, such as Excel, or even a database program, such as Access. If you don't have either type of program, even your word processing program can do the job of keeping track of your e-mails, messages, and responses.

Each program allows you to enter text and search for it quickly. A word processing program can be used to list the day e-mails were sent, which e-mails you sent to which profile name, and a copy of the e-mail. The document will be long, but it will serve the purpose. If you get a response from Chris2Good2BTrue, simply go to the Find command and enter that profile name. When the entry is found, you will see which day you sent your e-mail and even a copy of it, if you set things up that way. Once there, add a line that says that you got a response.

Regardless of which type of program you decide to use (spreadsheet, database, or word processor), be sure to create fields or text columns for the following items:

▶ Profile Name E-mailed To

▶ Date E-mailed

▶ Date Responded

▶ Date You Replied to Response

▶ Copy of Customized Letter Sent

▶ Copy of Photo from Dating Site

▶ Copy of Profile from Dating Site

It is possible to copy and paste an entire profile, complete with photo, from the online dating site directly into your spreadsheet, database, or word processing program. Although this may seem like hard work, it's a good practice. Sometimes the people who are getting back to you temporarily remove their profile from public view. If you get a response from someone and his profile is down for revision or photo approval, you'll find yourself having to reply to someone without having access to the profile you saw. By copying and pasting it into your tracking document, you will always have a reference.

Figure 17.3 shows the use of a spreadsheet program to keep track of profile mailings. You can construct your own system for keeping track of your e-mails and responses. There's no one way that's best.

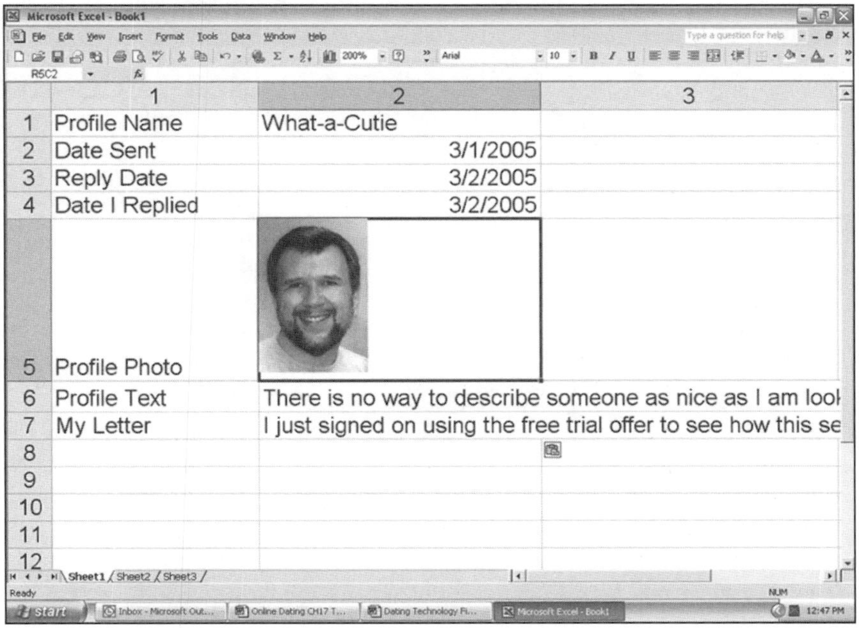

Figure 17.3
Microsoft Excel, a spreadsheet program, being used to track profile e-mail activity.

Using Calendars

Another handy computer tool that can help in the e-mailing process is using a calendar or scheduling program to create appointments for when to cancel or renew your subscription, when to follow-up with e-mails, and even to keep a record of when you were contacted by another member.

Programs such as Microsoft Outlook have robust calendars that serve as schedulers and also as record keeping tools, keeping track of what you did on a certain day. Using a program such as Outlook, you could use the calendar to make "appointments" for each of the people you contacted on the day you contacted them.

To create a record or appointment containing all of the fields described above, simply go into the calendar program and create an appointment for the day you're sending an e-mail. Name the appointment with a profile name. In the Notes field you can copy and paste the letter you sent and even the member profile and photo.

When you wish to find the profile name, simply open your calendar or use Find to search the calendar. You will be able to find all of the critical information quickly and easily using this type of program.

Figure 17.4 shows Microsoft Outlook's calendar being used to track e-mails to members.

Figure 17.4

Microsoft Outlook's calendar being used to track profile e-mail activity.

Evaluating the Free Trial Period

Once you've been through the process of building your list, crafting your e-mail, and sending your e-mails, you will need to evaluate the success of your efforts. You need to decide whether you wish to continue on the service as a paid member, or cancel your subscription before you're billed.

There's a difference between getting responses and getting dates. Once you get a response, you need to do quite a bit more to move things from a wink or e-mail to phone calls, meetings, and dates. Dates start as responses, so the quantity and quality of the replies will be a huge factor in actually dating someone.

The free trial period will be a barometer of both the online dating service—and the type of people it attracts. If the number of responses is good, and the responses have a promising tone, you will probably want to move to paid status and let your free trial roll over to a paid subscription. If you don't get any replies, it may be the service or its members—or it may be your profile text or even the message you sent in your e-mail.

You should use the free trial period as a time to evaluate not only the service, but also your own profile and e-mails. If you get responses, you will quickly learn if your profile is doing its job of communicating who you are to prospective dates. If it isn't working, keep refining it to better reflect who you are to the people you're interested in.

Summary

Free trial periods are offered by online dating services to allow you to preview what it will be like as a paid member who can e-mail other members. The short periods offered (usually three to seven days) are not long enough to create a meaningful exchange leading to a date. Using good planning, you can contact a large number of members to help gauge response, and you can even create and sneak in an anonymous e-mail address that will allow members to get in touch even if you choose not to purchase a subscription. Keeping track of whom you contact and what you say is also important in evaluating the quality of the online dating service.

GUY SAYS

I was kicked off of Match.com for abusing the free trial period. They killed my profile and told me to contact customer service. When I called them, they said that I had taken advantage of the free trial by using it, canceling, then using a different profile to use the free trial again.

And they were right. Because I used the same credit card on the two different profiles, they caught me!

I wasn't trying to abuse the service—I had simply forgotten my profile name after moving to a new computer where my auto-login no longer worked. So I created a new profile with essentially the same text and photo. I had tried the free trial when I had first found the service just to see what would happen. The second time I was actually trying to figure out if I wanted to pay to be a member. That's when they kicked me off and blocked my second profile name.

It's a good thing I didn't give up. I called them to explain things and said I would be happy to pay for a subscription, so they put me back on. Not long after that I met my sweetie online, and the rest is online dating history. I met her soon after paying for a six-month subscription, but I knew that she was the one, so I pulled my profile down and cancelled my membership for good.

And Match.com got full payment for a six-month subscription for a membership that I only used for a few weeks. That's the way it goes. I wish it were the case that when you succeeded, you could cancel and get the unused portion of your subscription refunded, but it doesn't work that way.

But, do you hear me complaining? I met the love of my life online. That free trial convinced me to subscribe because I had e-mailed her and she winked back. That subscription changed my life forever.

—*Terry*

CHICK SAYS

I'm easily lured in by the free trial subscriptions. And I tend to sign up on a whim, usually when someone interesting contacts me. One of the more frustrating things for a non-paying online dater is receiving a wink, winking back, then getting an e-mail from the person who initiated the wink who's clearly a paying subscriber—but having no way of replying back.

Most sites let you wink only once. After that, it's up to you to figure out how to contact each other. So I have to ask myself—is it worth paying just to see if this guy's as interesting as he seems? Or even worse, is it worth possibly wasting my one shot at the free trial period to see if this guy's as interesting as he seems?

It sounds terrible. As Terry keeps saying, what's $25 next to finding the guy of your dreams? But hey, it's $25. And what's the chance that this guy is the guy of my dreams? The thing is, the chances are just as good that he isn't. But I'll never know if I don't give it a shot.

If I'm lucky, the paying subscriber guy who contacts me is aware of my little dilemma and, like the chivalrous fellow he is, he puts his e-mail address in the e-mail he sends me back. Then suddenly there's no dilemma. I can contact him free and not worry about the money issues that might otherwise make me reconsider.

But yes, I have paid to join a site when the paying subscriber guy didn't consider my dilemma. If he didn't include his e-mail address in his response to me and he didn't respond within my free trial time, I gave him the benefit of the doubt and hoped he would be as interesting as he seemed.

And as it turned out, I became a fan of being a paying member on the online dating sites. It's fun to be able to e-mail someone instead of just winking at him. You'd be surprised how much better the response to an e-mail can be. And it's fun to use the tests and other parts of the site that are only available to the paying daters. You'll find it's rather addicting during your trial period. And you may conveniently forget, as I have, to cancel before your credit card gets charged.

Darn, I had to pay for the whole month. Well, hmm, guess I'd better take advantage of it since I paid for it. Let's see, what about that guy I saw last week, and oh, look at this new matching tool, and hey, he's cute…

—*Alyssa*

Part V

Finding the

Real Deal

Chapter 18
The Real Thing?–Spotting the Truth and Making It Yours

*I*t's human nature, at least for most of the glass-half-full people in the world, to want to believe the best. When it comes to dating, there are a lot of bests we want to believe. We want to believe we deserve the best. We want to believe the best is out there waiting for us. And we want to believe our potential date when he tells us he's the best. Unfortunately, all these bests aren't necessarily so.

The "best" that is always true is this: you deserve the best. So don't let yourself down and settle for someone whom you're not sure is really who he says he is. We'll show you in this chapter how to identify the best from the rest.

If Someone Sounds Too Good to Be True...

If you spend even a little time on an online dating site, you're going to come across the "too good to be true" profile. It's as inevitable as taxes. You'll be searching around absently, then suddenly there's the guy who looks like Brad Pitt, says he's independently wealthy, looking for someone with a soft heart, and that looks aren't important. Or you do a search for perfect matches for you and up comes the woman straight out of a Victoria's Secret catalog who says she loves bald men and sitting around watching sports on a Sunday. And for a moment, you can't believe your luck. Let that moment pass.

... There's a Good Chance He or She Is...

Most of the time if someone sounds too good to be true, she probably is. Take a good look at her profile before you start planning the wedding.

Start with looking closely at her picture. We told you before how to spot a photo from a magazine. Does she look too glossy? Is the photo too posed? Is there something fake-looking about her environment? Is her make-up too perfect or hair much too smooth? For men, is his suit too perfect? Is he bare-chested? Is his hair too perfectly highlighted? Does it look like he's wearing lip gloss?

Now read the profile closely. Does he say everything you think a woman wants to hear? Is he both rich and humble? Is he both sensitive and macho? Is he just a little too clever? Is he a little too romantic and interested in committing? Does she talk a lot about being sexually adventurous? Does she talk about her time as a model? Does she talk about how much she loves to cook and how good she is at it?

The signs can be subtler, but the message is usually the same. "I'm the perfect man/ woman, and I'll accept you exactly as you are. You should want to date me." But the perfect man/woman doesn't exist. And if you end up meeting this person, you're likely to come face to face with that fact.

... But Maybe He or She Isn't

Just because he sounds great, that doesn't mean he's not great. There are a lot of great people out there, and if they're being truthful, as we've told them to be so often in this book, then they'll come across as great people. And you shouldn't dismiss anyone just because he sounds great. That would be ridiculous.

It's the kind of great that you want to pay attention to. If it doesn't come across as exaggerated, then it might well be real. Take the following two profiles for instance.

Profile 1:

I'm a 37 year-old guy looking for my dream girl. I cashed out during the dot com years and no longer have to work. I spend my time between my house in Carmel and an apartment in New York. I love to travel and spend as much time touring Europe as possible. I speak three different languages and am thinking of picking up a fourth. I have a great life, but it's missing something. Someone to share all the great things in my life with. Someone to travel with, someone to buy things for, someone to hold onto me on the back of my motorcycle, someone to share a sunset with. I'd love to walk down to the gourmet food shop in the mornings and pick up fresh ingredients to make you special breakfasts every day. I'd love to take you shopping in Paris. We could have a wonderful life together. I'm looking for a woman who would enjoy all these things. I think a person's inner beauty is more important than the shell we walk around in. If you think you could be the woman for me, please get in touch.

Profile 2:

I'm a 37 year-old guy looking for that one woman who wants to share my life. I did pretty well in the dot com years so I have a good life. I have a place in Carmel, and I can't tell you how happy it makes me to wake up every morning and look out on the tremendous natural beauty of that area. I also have a little place in New York. I love that urban feeling sometimes, and it's nice that I can go and reconnect. I love to travel and do it whenever I can. I've been all over Europe but my hope is to go to Thailand next. I've heard great things about it. I've picked up a few different languages in my travels and, while I'm far from fluent, I can get around. I'd love to learn a little Thai before I go. I thought I'd try out online dating because, as happy as I am right now, I think I'd be happier if I had someone to come along on my adventures and share the good things in my life with me. I hope to find someone who would enjoy the same things I do. I'd like someone smart and funny and caring. And while I think looks are important, it's more about finding someone who appeals to you and someone whose personality shines through. If you think we'd be a good match, contact me and let's talk.

This is the same guy. The facts are the same. But the way they're presented is both subtly and vastly different.

Profile 1 comes across as definitely too good to be true. He's blatant in stating he's got a lot of money and a lot of stuff. He makes it clear that he's a man of leisure and nothing else. He promises to make you a lady of leisure if you date him. And he makes it clear that you don't have to be gorgeous to date him. As unfortunately true as it is, if this man is telling the truth about himself, he could date anyone he wants. He's unlikely to be on an online dating site, and he's unlikely to want to date someone who's not ravishingly beautiful, since that is definitely an option for him. If he was telling the truth, he'd also likely be too full of himself to date anyone who wasn't perfect.

Profile 2 comes across as a down to earth kind of guy who happens to have a lot of great stuff and lives a good life. He's not arrogant about what he has, but he puts it out there. He wants to show that he's a good catch. And he actually mentions some qualities he's looking for in a woman aside from someone who would enjoy all the things he could do for her. He's a little self-deprecating, a little humble. He knows he's a good catch, so he doesn't have to dress things up; he just states them. And all the things he talks about having, he explains how much joy he gets out of them. He's not just giving us a laundry list of what he's got. He comes across as real.

Use Your Best Judgment

Spending time at online dating sites looking through the profiles is the best way to get a good feel for what's real and what's not. The more profiles you read, the more you'll get a feel for what the average person sounds like. While certain people stick out, most profiles have a similar sound to them and cover similar ground. The more you read, the more you'll be able to notice the ones that stick out as unusual—then you can determine whether they seem truthful or not.

As we've said before, chances are good that the person writing the profile really is who he says he is. The majority of people at online dating sites are being themselves—the best version of themselves but themselves nonetheless. That's why you shouldn't let the possibility of coming across someone who's not truthful keep you from using the sites. Just don't let yourself get swept away by someone who sounds unbelievably great. Make sure you trust your instincts.

How to Tell if They're Truthful When E-mailing

You've picked someone out who you think could be great. You've looked over her profile with a fine-toothed comb and feel pretty confident that she's what she says she is. So you're ready to start e-mailing with her. Don't tell her how much you love her yet. It's easy for her to come across as honest in her profile when she's had a lot of time to revise it and make it perfect. It's harder to be both honest and perfect in e-mails which tend to be more spontaneous and more conversational.

Start Slowly and Examine Closely

As we've suggested in previous chapters, when you begin communicating with your potential date, take it slow. Keep your e-mails short and simple. You don't want to overload her, and frankly it's best if she doesn't overload you. And those short e-mails will be a lot easier to examine. While she's less likely to slip up and tell an untruth in a short e-mail, you're also less likely to miss some clue to her (dis)honesty.

Another reason to take it slow and short is, the more time you spend corresponding, the less likely she is to keep up a charade. As time passes, she's more likely to take one of the following routes if she's started off dishonest:

> ▶ She'll lose interest in the game and stop e-mailing you. It's sad, but you'll know it wasn't meant to be.

> ▶ She'll push her luck and make a mistake, either exaggerating to the extreme or just forgetting what lie she's already told you. Then you'll finally know the truth.

> ▶ She'll decide she really likes you and get real.

No matter which direction your communication takes, you'll soon know the truth. And it's better to know, even if it doesn't go the way you'd hoped.

Draw Him Out

After the short and sweet e-mails at the beginning of your communication, you can start delving into the deeper truths. You can start asking the tough questions. Refer to Chapter 13 for most of these. The point is to get to the bottom of things. And it's a good idea to come back to subjects brought up in previous e-mails. You want to check the facts you're given against the same ones you were given before. This may sound like interrogation tactics, and they are to a certain extent. But if you play it right, he'll never know he's being interrogated. And if he figures it out, he's only going to be scared off if he has something to hide.

A trick during this get-to-know-you (the real you) phase is to ask basic facts that should not change during the course of your correspondence, such as

> ▶ What college did he go to?

> ▶ How many brothers and sisters does he have?

▶ How old was he when he fell in love for the first time or had his first kiss?

▶ Where is he from originally, and how long has he lived in his current city?

▶ How long has he worked in his current job?

▶ What was the name of his first pet?

Then come back to these facts in later e-mails: "How many sisters did you say you have?"

Next, ask more specific questions about answers he's given. For example,

▶ If he's said he majored in English at the University of Berkeley, go on Berkeley's Web site and find out the names of the professors in the English Department. Either ask him who his favorite was and see if the name matches one on the list or come up with a random name and ask him if he had that professor. You can say so-and-so, a friend of yours, majored in English there.

▶ If he's said his favorite singer is Annie Lennox, ask what his favorite song is on *In The Garden* (the first album from Eurythmics, her band before she went solo). If he's really a fan, he'll have an answer.

▶ If he's said his favorite movie is *The Princess Bride*, tell him your favorite quote from the film but use a quote from a different film, like *The Princess Diaries*. He should correct you or ignore the comment, but if he agrees with you, you'll know he's not telling the truth.

▶ If he's said what neighborhood he lives in, ask something like, "Oh, there's a great Mexican place right around there that specializes in plantain burritos—what's the name of it?" Just know the answer yourself so you know if he's giving you the right answer.

He could certainly look up the correct answers to these questions as easily as you can. But if he's just playing with you on a lark, he's not going to bother.

Use information he's given you to draw him out on subjects he claims to be knowledgeable about. For instance,

▶ If he claims to have majored in physics, ask him about Chaos theory. He should be eager to give you a crash course.

▶ If he says he's a guitarist, ask him his favorite guitar licks. We guarantee you, if he's really a guitarist, he'll have an answer to this question.

▶ If he says he's a lawyer, ask his opinion about a recent court decision. You can easily come up with something controversial on a Google or Yahoo! news site to ask him about. And if he's really a lawyer, he'll sound like it when he discusses his opinions.

Again, yes, you are interrogating him a bit. But you're also just expressing interest. The answers to all these questions will tell you something about him in addition to giving you clues to his truthfulness. If the interrogation doesn't result in an arrest, it'll result in a deeper understanding of your potential date.

Reading Between the Lines

Before you even started communicating, your potential date indicated what kind of relationship she was looking for when she submitted her profile. The choices, you may recall, were probably something like the following:

- ▶ Friendship
- ▶ Play
- ▶ Dating
- ▶ Serious relationship
- ▶ Marriage

And while your potential date may have picked something serious when writing her profile, like marriage, that doesn't necessarily mean that's what she's looking for. This will become clear when you begin communication.

A lot of online daters are honest about their interest in something casual or something sexual. However, when being honest about their particular needs, they tend to eliminate a lot of potential partners. They're aware if they write that they're looking for play, that really cute guy who wants marriage is not going to be interested. So the temptation is to lie.

Sometimes a potential date's real intentions become clear quickly. If during your first e-mail exchange she tries to get you to meet up, chances are she's not really trying to get to know you. Likewise, she might start with sexual innuendoes right away. While sexual innuendoes are not strictly forbidden during your e-mail communication, they are frowned upon during the early get-to-know you part if you're actually trying to get to know one another. And the earlier they start, the less seriously you should take the person you're communicating with.

Someone who is looking for dating, friendship, or play will keep things light. She'll talk about the future vaguely and probably will try to keep from talking about anything beyond your first meeting. She'll stay away from saying anything terribly romantic or poetic, anything that might suggest love or anything more permanent. She won't want to delve too deeply into her past, steering clear of discussing past relationships and too many details about her family. She is probably not going to want to talk too much about the details of her daily life—where she works, what she does, where she likes to hang out—which would take it further than she would need to for security's sake. She may be more concerned about you tracking her down after she's stopped returning your calls after your one night together.

The Need Behind the Need

While it's more common to find someone claiming he's looking for marriage when he's really looking for play, it does go the other way. It does happen that someone may claim to be looking just to date or have fun, when really he's desperately seeking a soul mate.

As with those looking for sex, it usually becomes clear quickly that your potential date wants more. He may try to keep things light, but he will soon start fishing for more intimate clues as to who you are. He'll ask more about your family than you would expect. He'll ask a lot of questions about your life, your personality, things you like and dislike, and so forth. He'll be asking all the questions you're supposed to ask if you're really trying to find someone compatible in the long-term. The only thing he's doing wrong is asking them of someone who doesn't want the same kind of relationship he does.

It's always possible that this person isn't actually lying. He may think he wants something casual, but he actually does want marriage—he's not lying to you, he's just lying to himself. Unfortunately, it's almost impossible to tell the difference between someone who's lying to you about what he wants and someone who's lying to himself about what he wants. You're better off steering clear if you come across him. Even if he's just lying to himself, you're better off leaving him to figure that out on his own.

Seeing the Truth

Even if you've read and integrated everything we've told you in this book, ultimately humans are feeling beasts. We want to go with our hearts. We want to trust someone who seems really wonderful. We want to believe the best—so much so that we allow ourselves to overlook things we know we shouldn't. We ignore our instincts and believe what we want to believe. Sometimes we're the dishonest ones because we're not being honest with ourselves.

Be Honest with Yourself

You've been e-mailing with someone for awhile, and it's going really great. She seems perfect in so many ways. You have a lot in common. She seems to be on the same page romantically as you are. And she wants the same things you do for the future. You're so happy.

It's just…

You're sure she said something about growing up in New Jersey in an e-mail early on, and the other day she just said something about her childhood in Philadelphia. And she said she worked a regular office job, but the other day she said something about getting out of work around 3 A.M. after last call. But you're sure there's a reasonable explanation. You don't want to bring it up with her and have her think you're calling her a liar.

Be honest with yourself. Something's not right here. And you have two choices. Ask her about the discrepancies, and see if she comes up with something plausible to explain them. Or you can let it go and risk dating someone you can't trust. We don't recommend the latter. You deserve better.

You have to wonder why she lied about such basic facts of her life. She's given you wrong information about where she grew up. Is she hiding something in her past by not telling you where she really is from? Could it be that she's got a family in New Jersey, meaning a husband and kids? Could she be hiding a criminal record? And what about lying about her job? Was she just embarrassed to say she works in a bar, or is it something more sinister?

Consider the person who has told a couple of small lies to you at this early stage in your relationship. What is this person likely to be like as your relationship progresses? What else might she lie about? Are you willing to date someone who might lie about money, her health, or other men? Are you willing to bet your life that she won't continue to lie in the future? Because if one of the things she lies about is her HIV status or STDs, that could be exactly what you're betting.

Don't Settle

You deserve the best, you deserve honesty, and you deserve to find the person you're looking for. And we made you think about what you wanted when you were filling out your profile. Don't compromise now.

When you filled out your profile, you chose the qualities you wanted in a potential date. You thought long and hard on what was really important to you. We asked you to be as flexible as you were comfortable being, and you hopefully did the appropriate soul searching. So why would you change your mind now that someone is interested in you who's not quite right?

It's tempting when you first start communicating with someone to let a few things slide. He winked at you, and you looked at his profile. His photo was cute, the basics all seemed to line up with what you wanted, and he seemed really smart and interesting. But you're looking for a non-smoker—you have really bad lungs and just can't be around a smoker. Plus you think kissing a smoker is like licking an ashtray. And yet this great-seeming guy tells you after a couple of e-mails that he lied in his profile and he smokes. He says he's tried to quit but has never been able to follow through. He says he'll try to quit for you if you meet and all goes well. And you waver.

First, there's the lying. Again, what does it mean when someone has lied to you so early in the game—in fact before you've even met? Is this someone to be trusted? At least he admitted it before you actually met. Still, he couldn't have kept it hidden forever, so how much credit should he really get for that?

Second is the fact of the smoking. Just because you're getting along well, should you let go of something you were so adamant about? What about your lungs? What about the ashtray? He's tried to quit before and failed; is there any reason to believe he'll do it for you before your wheezing starts?

The combination of the lie and the smoking should tell you something. Move on. There are other fish in the sea, non-smoking fish even. Don't sell yourself short, and don't settle for someone less than who you're looking for. Don't get impatient and go for the first person who appeals to you, regardless of your criteria. You deserve the best.

Summary

It's human nature to want to find the best person to share your life with. And it's human nature to believe the best about someone who likes you and to whom you're attracted. But defy your nature, and keep your eyes open. Read e-mails carefully to get clues to your potential date's truthfulness. Ask probing questions to check his or her details. Make sure your potential date is really looking for the same kind of relationship you are. And don't settle for less than what you've stated you're looking for in a potential date. The right person for you is out there—he's telling you the truth, and she's looking for everything you are.

GUY SAYS

I was very lucky. I met someone online who actually told the truth. We're together now, and I can say from the experience of getting to know her very well that she did a great job telling the truth about herself—including the parts that were not so flattering.

Even better, I did the same in my profile. When we met, it was wonderful. Everything we said was right there, and the very fact that we told the truth in our profiles established a deeper trust once we learned that fact. We couldn't be happier.

But as I said, I was lucky. In fact, she was one of the only people who contacted me who I felt was telling the truth and not glossing over the facts or painting a rosier picture than it actually was.

When I got a wink from a woman who said she was "average" in body build and her picture quickly revealed she was overweight, I clicked away. Do I have a problem with someone who is heavier? No. I do have a problem with someone who isn't being honest with me or with herself. I would get pictures from women who said they were in their early 30s and again, the pictures told a very different story. I clicked away.

It's those little embellishments that got to me. I was pretty open to different types of people. I wanted to meet someone nice and someone I could feel good about. That doesn't happen when you read a profile that is one thing and the person is another when you actually meet. It made me wonder "why?"

And I know men make even dumber mistakes of truth. They say they work out, but their pictures show a beer belly. They say they are looking for love, and they talk sex in the first e-mail. It's so stupid. Does anyone expect to go past one date when they flat-out lie?

I know that it's hard to tell the truth when you have a few flaws. I was overweight and had just hit the 50 mark when I was online and dating. I could have said I was average in build and tweaked my age to be in my mid-40s. I'm glad I didn't. My sweetie wouldn't have found me. I was just what she was looking for, and I know now she wouldn't change a thing about me.

If I can tell the truth and meet one of the most attractive and amazing women ever online, just imagine what can happen to you—I'm sure you are better looking and a better catch than me.

Honestly!

—*Terry*

CHICK SAYS

I'll admit it. I've been tempted by a pretty face or a clever headline. I am only human, after all.

I've considered compromising what I'm looking for in a guy after receiving a wink from somebody who made my eyes bulge. And I've considered winking at someone who was clearly a mismatch just because he seemed so impossibly clever that I'd be a fool not to contact him.

And there would be nothing wrong with doing so if I had been looking for a casual relationship. You can compromise if you're not looking for something more. If only I was a little more casual. But there's the rub. I actually hope to find someone I might want to have a relationship with. That means sticking to my guns.

Even if I choose to slip my standards a bit, it's one thing to choose to compromise. It's another thing to compromise without realizing it because someone's lied to you.

I've found someone who I thought was the bee's knees, only to have it turn out he was married. Or he had kids. Or he smoked. Or he bit the heads off kittens. Okay, not that last one. Though there were one or two who I wondered about.

There are things I don't compromise on. I don't date married men. I don't date men with kids. And I don't date smokers. The kittens go without saying. So to have my potential date hide these facts or lie about them was enough for me to cut him off at his bee's knees.

I've also had someone contact me when his perfect match as described in his profile didn't resemble me in the slightest. I wondered what made him say I was a good match for him when he was looking for a slender, petite, blond woman—which I am not. I wondered, which was the lie—the profile or the wink?

I've had guys tell me they were single when they were not. To get the truth from them, it's often as simple as asking flat out if they're married. I've had men tell me they're in a better job than they're really in. And I even had a guy tell me one name, only to sign off an e-mail with a different name later.

Sometimes there's a reasonable explanation for the lies. You'd be surprised what people will say rather than tell you something embarrassing. It's never okay to lie or be lied to—but as in the rest of life, things are rarely black and white. Sometimes it's reasonable to consider some shades of gray. But you have to ask about the lie if you suspect something's amiss. You want to know what you're really getting into.

Faced with a straightforward request for an explanation for a lie, most guys will come clean. And sometimes there's no good explanation, and you have to cut him loose. But sometimes you'll be surprised. I would have been sorry to miss the double-named guy, who turned out to have a good explanation. I was glad I'd asked.

—*Alyssa*

Chapter 19
Making Contact: Take It Safe

*S*afety first. It's what Momma and your Driver's Ed instructor always told you. It's the most important thing. And with online dating, it's vital. You might feel like you know your potential date inside and out, but the bottom line is you've never met him. And there's a lot that can only be known once you've seen and talked to someone in person. Someone could seem completely sane and normal online, then really surprise you once you meet him. We're not trying to scare you in this chapter—we're just trying to keep you alert and aware and suggest some smart precautions to take. Online dating can be every bit as safe as real-life dating or even safer. You just have to follow some simple rules.

Take Security Precautions at Each Stage of Contact

There are some basic guidelines for each stage of contact you go through with your potential date. These stages are

▶ Posting your profile

▶ E-mailing

▶ Instant messaging or talking on the phone

▶ Meeting

▶ Dating

Let's start with the electronic stages of contact.

Posting Your Profile

When you're posting your profile, you want to be honest and present a good picture of who you really are. You want to talk about all your good points and reveal some interesting things about yourself. What you don't want to do is reveal so much that you've opened yourself up for every stalker who may be roaming the Internet. The trick with your online profile is to reveal just enough to grab someone's attention without revealing anything specific at all. There are hard and fast rules about what not to say in your profile. Avoid the following:

▶ Your full name. Sometimes, if you're very Google-able (you are mentioned a lot in news or Web sites or you're well known in your profession) you might even want to avoid your first name.

233

> ▶ Your address.

> ▶ Your phone number.

> ▶ Your date of birth.

> ▶ Your social security number. (Why would anyone post this in a profile anyway? Just don't do it.)

> ▶ Your specific place of work.

> ▶ Your family members' names, especially your children's names.

> ▶ Anything that suggests where you will be at a certain date and time. ("I love going to Ella's Café for brunch every Sunday morning!")

It's most important to remember that everyone and his brother can see your profile. Anyone browsing the Internet can, free of charge, look at what you've posted. So don't say anything you don't want everyone to know.

E-mailing

This is when it starts getting harder to be careful with your personal information. You're starting to communicate with someone and getting to know him. You start feeling bad about not being completely open. You don't want to seem like you don't trust him. Maybe he's shared some things with you, and you feel like you need to reciprocate in kind. But, issues of trust aside, it's important to keep focused on your primary responsibility—staying safe. You still don't know this person you're communicating with. You haven't heard his voice, looked him in the eye, seen if what he's told you about himself is even true. So take a step back and remember the rules. For this stage of communication, we think you should continue to follow all the same rules you followed in your profile for security. There's nothing in that list that needs to be told prior to meeting your potential date, except maybe your first name if you held it back.

It's true, you're not broadcasting the information in your e-mails to the whole world. But the person you are broadcasting it to is still an enigma. It's always best to imagine the worst-case scenario. What if he's an identity thief? If he gets enough information from you, he can steal your identity, get credit cards in your name, and put you into debt. What if he's a stalker? If he gets enough information, he can follow you everywhere and terrorize you. What if he's a killer or a rapist? If you tell him where you live or where you work, do you think you'll be safe?

Again, we're not trying to scare you. But be aware and be safe. If he gives you a hard time about not telling him something, let him know it's nothing personal. You're just being careful with your information until you meet, until you see that he's a wonderful guy and there's nothing to worry about. If he's a wonderful guy, he'll understand.

Instant Messaging or Talking on the Phone

We've combined these two because they're quite similar in the level of immediacy and casualness. And you can't take something back that you've just said once you've said it or pressed the Enter key. For many people these days, instant messaging (IMing) is as quick as talking.

All the rules for profiles and e-mailing still apply, except for one—if you're talking on the phone, you'll have to give her your phone number (though we recommend using a cell phone, which is harder to trace). So if all the same rules apply, how does this stage of contact vary from e-mailing?

When you're talking on the phone or IMing, you're a lot more likely to say things without thinking about them. You're just having a casual conversation. You're enjoying yourself and enjoying the back and forth that comes from having an actual conversation rather than an e-mail conversation, which involves long wait times for responses. You're talking about the places you like to go, where you work, and your neighborhood. And even though you know the rules, it's easy to break the rules without even realizing you have. But nothing's changed.

You still don't know this person. Yes, you've heard her voice if you're talking on the phone, which really does tell a lot about a person. You're having a conversation, which suggests that she's probably pretty normal, able to sustain a train of thought, able to respond to you appropriately. However, you still haven't met her in person. You still don't know if she's telling the truth about who she is. So be careful about what you say.

If she asks you specific questions about where you work, where you live, or where you hang out, don't be evasive. She's more likely to think you're the one hiding something or being dishonest. But be clear about why you don't want to answer. Tell her you read this book, and they said not to talk about those things until after you've met. Blame it on us. We'd rather take the blame for telling you to be cautious than have something bad happen to you.

Meeting Live and In Person

After spending a few weeks e-mailing, talking on the phone, or chatting on IM, you may start to think you're ready to meet your potential date. It's a big decision when you to decide to meet. And there are a lot of things to consider.

When to Meet

The most important question to ask yourself when deciding whether to meet your potential date in person is this: "How do I feel?" We've taught you all the tricks we can to help you identify the truth, but we can't teach you this. It's completely up to you. After e-mailing with someone for awhile, you'll develop feelings of some sort about him. He may be funny, but you wonder if you really have anything in common. He may be smart but has no sense of humor. Or he could be really cute but just not that interesting. Or he may seem perfect. There's really no reason not to meet all of these guys to see if your impressions are correct and see if there's any chemistry. But only if it feels right.

Some potential dates may push to meet when you feel it's still too early. There's no set rule about when to meet someone. You may feel comfortable after only a few e-mails. Or it may take you months, and you're still not sure. And ultimately that's your decision. You should never let someone else bully you into meeting if you're not ready. Generally speaking, a few weeks is a reasonable amount of time to e-mail with someone before you make the decision to meet. You should know each other pretty well by then but not have too much invested yet.

It's Best Not to Meet Too Early

It's best not to meet too early, if only for security. You want to be sure you have a good feeling about someone before you agree to meet him. You want to have exchanged enough information to feel fairly certain that this is a normal person with a normal life. You don't need to know exactly where he works to have him tell you that he does work and a little bit about his job. You don't need to know exactly where he lives to have him tell you if he lives alone or with roommates, whether he lives in an apartment or a house, or if he's got pets. And you don't need to know the names of his family members to know he's got some siblings, his parents live in Ohio, and he has a great relationship with his nieces and nephews. He doesn't have to reveal anything we've told you not to reveal in order to give you a fleshed out idea of who he is and what his life is like. And those are the things that are going make you comfortable meeting him for the first time. You know he has a background and job that he's willing to tell you about. It makes you feel like he's grounded and not some elusive online mystery. You want to feel that level of knowledge and comfort before meeting—which is why it's not a good idea to meet someone only an e-mail or two into your relationship.

Don't Wait Too Long

If you wait too long to meet, like a few months, you're more likely to have an awkward meeting. If you've known each other that long solely by e-mail and phone, when you meet it may seem very strange. It may be hard to reconcile the person you're looking at with the person you've been talking to. You may also have become very attached to someone you've been communicating with for months. A lot of people fall in love online. If you wait too long, you're falling in love with someone you've never seen in person who could leave you completely cold when you meet him. Chemistry is very important. If you're in love with someone who you turn out to have no chemistry with, where does that leave you?

What to Do Once You Decide to Meet

Once you've decided you're ready to meet your potential date, we suggest you check some items off our "to do" list. These are things that will make it easier when you do finally meet in person. Some are meant to make you feel more secure, some to make you more comfortable, some to make sure you recognize each other.

▶ **Talk on the phone.** Knowing the sound of her voice and knowing she can hold a conversation like a normal person will take a level of strangeness and uncertainty out of that first meeting.

▶ **Send each other a few more photos.** Ideally, take a picture a day or two before the date and send it to him. That way it will be as recent as possible. Make it a body shot if you can, so he knows exactly what to expect. Ask him to do the same.

▶ **Reveal anything about yourself you haven't yet revealed** that you think is relevant. For instance, you walk with a limp. Or you wear a wig (that's obviously a wig). You wear glasses, even though you weren't wearing them in your picture. You wear nothing but orange. Again, you want her to know exactly what to expect. If she likes you, she probably will not let something minor that you reveal at this point keep her from meeting you. Except maybe the orange....

▶ **Exchange cell phone numbers**, assuming you both have cell phones.

▶ **Send his online profile to a friend and get a second opinion.** Tell her about him, and make sure she gets the same impression of him that you do.

▶ **Decide what you're going to wear.**

Setting Up the Date–Safety Strategies

Once you've agreed to meet, you have some important decisions to make. As you ponder your choices, keep our key phrase "safety first" in mind. Everything's probably going to go fine, but if it doesn't, we want to make sure you're protected.

Where Should You Meet?

When deciding where to meet, you should pick a place with the following qualities:

▶ **Well lit.** No dark bars, please.

▶ **Busy.** You want a place with a lot of people going in and out so you never feel alone and intimidated.

▶ **In a well-trafficked area.** You don't want to be leaving a place with your date only to find yourself alone with him moments later on the street. Well, you might want to be alone with him, but it's safer if you're not... yet.

▶ **Non-alcoholic.** It's best to stay away from bars or places where you'll likely be drinking. While alcohol may grease the wheels a bit, it also lowers inhibitions and might make you do or say something you hadn't intended to.

▶ **Close to public transportation or with good parking.** You want to be able to make a speedy getaway if the date goes badly. The parking should be well-lit, too.

Your best and least exciting choice for a first meeting is a coffee shop. Coffee shops are well lit and usually fairly busy. No one will be drinking alcohol, and they're usually in well-trafficked areas. For instance, no matter what your feelings are about Starbucks, can you think of a safer place to hang out for a few hours? Aside from the regular customers who will surround you, the perky counter staff will likely keep an eye on you as well.

The nice thing about a coffee shop is its flexibility. Many people sit in coffee shops for hours, drinking one cup after another, reading, studying, working on their laptops, talking to friends. No one hassles you as long as you're a customer. You can stay as long as you like. On the other hand, a cup of coffee is short and finite. If you meet someone for a cup of coffee, you can finish your coffee and leave. There's no appetizer, entree, dessert, aperitif drawn-out dinner to sit through uncomfortably if you're not enjoying your date. But if things are going well, you can always get a second cup, share a piece of cake, shop for a new espresso maker... the possibilities are endless.

What Time Should You Meet?

It's always best to meet your date during the bright light of day. Try to come up with a scenario that involves the date beginning and ending in daylight. If you meet at a coffee shop in the middle of winter, meet at 1:00 in the afternoon so that, unless you're getting along incredibly well, you're likely to end the date when it's still light out. Everything's safer in daylight.

If you do decide to have an evening date, again, keep to well-lit areas. Plan to leave for home before it gets too late so there are still people on the streets.

Transportation

You should always arrange to meet at your chosen meeting place for the first date. Remember how we told you not to give anyone your address in the electronic stages of contact? This still holds true until you've actually met her. Plan for each of you to handle your own transportation to and from the date. Even if you're the one who would be doing the picking up, being alone with someone you've never met in a car is not a good idea.

This may make it a little awkward when you first arrive at your meeting place. You may find yourself scanning the crowd to see if you're the first one there. You may find yourself uncertain of whether you're seeing your date or not, even if you've seen her picture. But if you've followed the rules, sent each other honest pictures, and described yourselves honestly, you should be able to meet up without too much effort.

Your Safety Net

Prior to your first date with your online suitor, you should pick someone in your life to be your safety net. This person will know everything about the date you're about to go on so that if anything goes wrong, she can do whatever she needs to do to make things right.

Start by e-mailing your date's online profile to your safety net before you go out. Most online dating sites have an option to e-mail a profile to someone else. Figure 19.1 shows this mechanism.

Your safety net will then have a photo and a lot of basic information about your date, including height, body type, hair and eye color—all identifying characteristics that the police might ask for… . Still not trying to scare you, bear with us. Then give her all the basic information you know about your date. Give her his phone number, his full name if he's given it, and anything else he's told you that would help identify him. The more she knows, the better prepared she'll be if something goes wrong. Next give her the details of the date. Tell her where and when you're meeting. Tell her if you're driving or taking public transportation.

And finally, arrange a couple of times to call her. If you're meeting your date at 2 P.M., tell her you'll call her at 4 P.M. This is just a check-in call. You need to let her know you're okay. The temptation might be to tell her you'll call her at the end of the date so you can tell her all about it. But it's better to set up a time not far from the beginning of the date, so if something goes

Figure 19.1
At most online dating sites, you'll see an option at the top of a profile for e-mailing the profile to someone else.

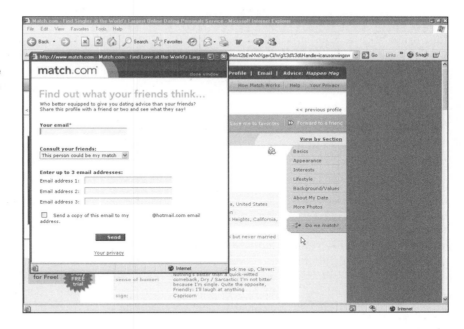

wrong, she'll know about it sooner rather than later. Just slip away for a minute, excusing yourself to the restroom works well, and call your friend. Give her a quick run-down—"Everything's fine, he's cute, he's nice, I like him, I'll tell you all about it later. I'll call you at the end of the date or at 8 P.M., whichever comes first." And *do* set up another time to call her. First impressions can tell you a lot, but things could still go bad. It's best to have an extra security step. Make sure your safety net knows to call you if you don't call her. And if she can't reach you, she should call the police. It may sound extreme, but this is your safety we're talking about here. You need to do whatever you have to do to stay safe. Just don't forget to call her when you say you will. If she calls the cops, and you're just lost in each other's eyes, you'll feel pretty stupid, and so will she. And your date might not be too happy, either.

The safety net has one final purpose, which can be less security related. She'll get you out of a bad date. You slip out to the restroom to call her, but your quick run-down is slightly different—"Oh my god, he's so dull and looks nothing like his picture and he smells really bad." Then you can arrange with her to have her call you 15 minutes later and tell you there's an emergency. Just come up with a good lie. This is one of those times when we give you permission to lie. Especially if it's more than just a bad-smelling date. If he's creepy at all or you feel you're unsafe, do whatever you have to do to get out of there. If you think the phone call won't be enough, go ahead and ask one of the perky counter staff to help you out a back door or walk you to your car. Or call the police, if you really feel you're in danger. It's more important to get out of a bad situation safely than to worry about what your date or others might think. Safety first.

During the Date–How to Be Both Flirty and Cautious

You're sitting in the coffee shop of your choosing and talking to your date. She's cute, looks just like her pictures, and she's smart and makes you laugh. The conversation is flowing. And you're starting to let your guard down. And that's a good thing. Just don't let your guard down too much.

The more you start to like your date, the more open you're going to feel you should be and want to be. And we recommend openness; this whole book is about openness. But you still need to remember our security rules while trying to have an honest and entertaining conversation with your date. Yes, we're asking you to mentally multi-task.

Go ahead and tell her about your family. You can even use their names if you like. She'll like hearing your stories and about your past. It will make her think more warmly of you, knowing you're a person with a strong family background and who has good family attachments. But when you're talking about your 10 year-old niece, don't tell her she goes to St. Anne's middle school and gets out of school at 3:15. And when you're talking about your sister, don't mention that you worry about her when she walks home from her job at Jake's Bar at 3 a.m. down dark alleys in the Haight. Is your date likely to go try to abduct your niece or send her thug brother-in-law out to mug your sister? It's not very likely. But if it's likely at all, if there's even a chance, don't say it.

Go ahead and tell her about your job. Tell her all about the fabulous people you work with. Tell her about your manager and how he keeps dumping more work on your lap. Tell her about the copy machine that broke when your buddy Chris tried to photocopy his butt. She'll think it's all interesting and funny, and she'll like knowing you have a solid, real job that you enjoy (or willingly tolerate) and that you're a stand-up guy. But don't tell her exactly how much money you make. Don't tell her your boss's name. Don't tell her exactly what time you arrive and leave each day. Don't tell her your office number. Is it likely that your date is going to try to steal your bank account information once she knows how much money you have? Is it likely that she's going to follow you to work or call your office 50 times a day, finally calling your boss to tell him you're embezzling just to get even for you telling her to leave you alone? No. It's not very likely. But again, why tempt fate until you know who you're really dealing with?

Go ahead and tell her how pretty she is. Tell her you think she's fascinating. Tell her you think she's really smart and well informed about politics and literature. Tell her you'd like to go out with her again. But don't tell her that you love her. Don't tell her she's all you ever wanted. Don't suggest you run off to Vegas to get married. Is it likely you'll get married and she'll turn into a psycho and if you'd bothered to really get to know her you never would have made such an awful mistake? Likely, no. Possible, yes. Is it likely she'll ask one of the perky counter staff to walk her to her car and suggest they might want to call the police because you're clearly nuts? Yes, it is likely.

Don't Lead Him On

You're sitting in the coffee shop of your choosing and talking to your date. He's not cute, he looks nothing like his pictures, and he's boring and makes you want to be anywhere else. The conversation is not going well. But he seems to really like you. He doesn't seem to notice that you're yawning and flirting with the guy at the next table. And you're gulping your coffee as fast as its heat will let you, wishing you'd added more cream.

He's not horrible. He's not creepy. He's not scary. He's not a liar. You just don't like him. But he was so great in his e-mails. What could have gone wrong?

Rather than sitting there and thinking it has to get better, that you couldn't have been so wrong, you just have to face the music. He's not the one for you. And unless you nip this in the bud, you could end up on a second date with this guy.

Don't lead him on. When he tells you how pretty he thinks you are, thank him but don't reciprocate with something nice about him. It seems impolite, but don't do it. When he tells you how fascinating you are, again thank him. But since he's boring you to tears, don't lie and tell him the same. And when he tells you how smart and well informed you are about politics and literature, go ahead and agree with him. And maybe add that he should start watching Jon Stewart or reading the *New York Times* because there are a lot of interesting things going on in the world right now, and he might want to be able to talk about them with his next date. Assuming you're almost done with your coffee.

Once you're done with your coffee, go ahead and give in to a little white lie, tell him it was nice, and that you'll e-mail him. Tell him you have to go meet a friend if you need to. But go ahead and leave. And don't try to tell him you're not interested. It will be much easier on both of you if you e-mail him later to let him know how you feel. If you try to tell him now, there could be arguments or tears or worse. Just wait and let him down easy from the safety and comfort of your own home.

Sending the Right Message

You've finished your date and you're safely home. You've called your safety net to let her know you're home okay and to give her a play-by-play of your date. Things went well. Or things went badly. Or you're not quite sure what you think yet. Regardless, one of you is going to call or e-mail the other one, and you need to know what to say when that happens.

I'm Interested

The easy e-mail to send is the one saying you want to meet again. You had a great time, you think she's swell, and when can you meet up again? Just don't be too eager. The same guidelines apply to online dating as with real-life dating once you've had that first date. In fact, you are real-life dating now. You've met in person. There's a solid person out there who you can talk to and touch. So what happens after a real-life date? A day or two might pass, then one of you calls the other and you talk. You make plans. You're dating. The only glitch here is that you're used to e-mailing with this person. And as a result, you may e-mail her as soon as you get home, saying what a great time you had and talking about the same sort of things you always talk about. While this may seem endearing to some, it may seem over-eager and pushy to others. The best tack to take is to e-mail or call her the next day, say what a nice time you had, and suggest another date. But keep things light, and make sure she seems to be on the same page as you are. You're moving along. Just stay within the speed limit.

I'm Not Interested

The hard e-mail to send is the one saying you're not interested. You're probably going to crush her a little bit. But it needs to be done. If you're not interested, she needs to know, and you need to move on. At least you don't have to do it on the phone or in person. E-mail has given you an easier way out. Take advantage of it. This e-mail you can send as soon as you get home, if you're sure of your feelings. Better to pull the Band-Aid off quickly than to linger. Just be kind. This is a person you e-mailed with and liked enough to want to meet in person. Just because there was something that turned you off, it doesn't mean there's anything wrong with her. (If there did turn out to be something actually wrong with her, you still probably want to be nice, as you don't want her coming after you.)

So make it short and quick and simple. Tell her you just didn't feel there was any chemistry, you think she's a nice person, and you wish her luck in her search. If you want to be friends, go ahead and tell her that. But make it clear that's all it would be. Don't pussyfoot around anything. Make it all very straightforward and honest, and leave no question in her mind what you're saying.

I'm Not Sure Yet

The "I'm not sure" e-mail is the trickiest. You've met for coffee, you spent some time together, she still seems nice, and nothing seemed overtly wrong. You just haven't quite decided yet. Maybe you're not sure if the chemistry is there. Maybe she said a couple of things that struck you as strange, but you're not sure what that means yet. Maybe she had a strange mole that kept you transfixed, and you're just not sure if you can get past it.

If your issues are conversational, you need to try to address them in your e-mail. For instance, if you had a great conversation but she said a couple of things that could have been construed as racist, you can try to address that question in your e-mail. Explain that you had a good time, but you were wondering what she meant when she said that she didn't see why it was so wrong that Thomas Jefferson kept slaves. Or that you were having such a nice talk about your time in Germany, but you were wondering what she meant when she said the Holocaust was invented by movie studios and politicians. Okay, so probably if she really said those things, you'd know whether you liked her or not. It's unlikely to be quite so obvious if you're feeling conflicted. But these are questions you can ask over e-mail without letting any judgment in, something that's harder to keep out of your voice when asking in person.

If your issues are those of chemistry or getting past a flaw, your e-mail just got easier to write. The only way to know is to have a second date. Therefore, you just need to e-mail her and ask her out again. Try to avoid being overly romantic or flattering to her without seeming dismissive. You don't know where this is going yet, so operate on the assumption that you're going to be just friends. Treat her like you would a friend, nicely but platonically for now. Then go out on that second date and see how it goes. You might be glad you gave her a second chance.

Where Do We Go from Coffee?

After having a first date that goes well, you may wonder how to proceed. What are the rules now? Can I tell him everything now?

The rules start getting a little more blurred once you've gone out on a good first date. A lot of what happens next depends on how you feel about the person you're dating—which doesn't mean you can let go of all our security suggestions, but it does mean that you can start letting them drop along the way when you feel it's appropriate.

Next Steps and Next Date

Continue to e-mail with your date. And continue to talk on the phone, if that's a more comfortable medium for you. Just because you've seen him in person, it doesn't mean you can't keep the conversation flowing when you're not face to face. Just bear in mind that, now that you've seen each other in person and have another date set up, you might start e-mailing a little less frequently. You still want to stay in contact between dates, but you don't want to tell him everything by e-mail anymore because you want to have something to talk about when you see him. This is normal.

Make your next date. Keep to public places for the next one, but go ahead and meet at night if you want to. Go ahead and eat dinner, since it seems likely you won't get tired of him before dessert. And you can even go into a dark movie theater with him, if you feel comfortable. You might still want to let your safety net know where and when you're going out with him again and to give her a call when you get home. But she shouldn't have to sit with her finger ready to hit 911 all night.

Continuing to Learn More

As you continue to talk to and see your date, you're going to want to talk more about yourself so he can get to know you better. This is good. This is dating. Go ahead and tell him some of the things you've been holding back, if you're ready to tell him.

Don't reveal anything you don't feel comfortable revealing. You're getting to know your date just like you get to know anyone else. Reveal what you want, when you're ready to reveal it. Generally speaking, it's a good idea to go out on another date with him before you let him pick you up at your house. But you can probably go ahead and give him your last name. You could let him pick you up at work if you felt okay with that. There are usually a lot of people around at an office in case something goes wrong. You probably still want to keep your social security number to yourself, but if you feel like revealing your date of birth, go ahead. Use your common sense. Do what feels right.

And go out with him again. Go out with him as often as you want to. Go forth and date!

Summary

The most important things in the world to you should be your life and your safety. And there's no reason you can't hold on to those things and still date online. As long as you're smart about dating, you can go out there and meet the potential date of your dreams. Take precautions at each stage of contact with your date. Don't reveal too much too soon. And follow the rules for meeting in person. The rules are there for a reason. You can be cautious and flirty at the same time and still end up with a successful date and the potential for more. Just remember your mantra—safety first!

GUY SAYS

When it comes to playing it safe, guys tend to rely on the fact that they are big and tough and can handle themselves. Most men don't worry about the physical aspects of first meetings. They aren't worried that the woman will pose any physical threat, such as forcing them to stay or pouncing on them.

But, men should think that through. If you meet too quickly or without the cautions recommended in this chapter, you can end up with a stalker or simply a pest. If the date doesn't go well, your date may find it in her heart to paint a warning on your front door or even start calling your office.

That said, beyond the cautions that any online dater should practice, men need to consider why women are careful. One of the things I learned is that women do want to take things slowly when it comes to meetings.

As a guy dating online, you will find it hard to get a phone number or even an actual e-mail address. Even once you get to a first meeting, you will learn that it's all separate cars, public places, and short meetings.

At first, this may seem stand-offish, but it's simply a good practice. Since you don't know that much about each other, the woman is considering the fact that you are bigger, can possibly be a physical threat, and may be a crazy stalker. It's not that you are a threat, but if you display such tendencies, she will be in a public place where she can get help.

It's smart for both people to wait a bit for riding in each others' cars, exchanging phone numbers, and visiting each others' homes. If the date goes well and you each establish trust, then all of that will happen.

When it does, it will be nice, since it is trust that you have earned. Be understanding and considerate that women need to be careful and that a smart date will wait, play it safe, and build on trust earned along the way.

—*Terry*

CHICK SAYS

I tend to be a bit of a rule-breaker myself. I never was one for listening to authority if I could help it, and I never liked doing things because someone told me I had to. I was one of those rebellious kids in high school who arrived late, passed notes, and laughed at my principal when he tried to impose discipline.

I do believe that some rules are made to be broken—but that's not true of the rules of security in online dating. Being a rebel is all very well, but not when your personal safety is on the line. I might not say it at any other time or in relation to anything else, but—you must CONFORM!

I'm a big believer in not revealing your last name or date of birth in the early stages of contact. Aside from the fact that I'm Google-able, which results in some interesting questions about whether I'm online dating for research, I just don't think it's safe. There's too much information floating around out there about everyone. Once you give a firm, identifying marker, the unscrupulous can easily find you.

I would never tell someone where I live until I was certain I could trust him. The idea of coming home and finding someone sitting outside my door waiting for me is incredibly disturbing—unless we've been dating for a few months, and he's there to cook me dinner. That's very okay with me.

Likewise, the idea of someone showing up at my office out of the blue is unpleasant. Even if the visitor is someone I know well, I much prefer some advance warning. If someone I've only spoken to in e-mails who I only know from his photo showed up at my office, I'd be calling security. It's not cute, and it's not romantic.

It goes without saying that I follow the rules when I go out to meet someone in person. These are the most important rules to follow, and they are unwavering. Luckily, I have friends who think it's fun to be my safety nets and get periodic check-in calls. And luckily the guys I've met haven't had a problem with me meeting them places instead of being picked up, and they have been perfectly fine meeting in daylight in public places.

That's the thing—if a guy has a problem with the security rules you're following, chances are there's a reason for that. If he just wants to meet you in hope of making a happy connection, he'll be understanding of your rules. In fact, he may be wanting to follow them himself, for his own safety. Just because I know I'm not a stalker or serial killer, that doesn't mean my date knows that. If he balks at any of the rules you impose for your own safety, he's got some plans in mind that will be difficult to follow through with if you're taking care to be safe. And that's someone you want to steer clear of.

Be a rebel. Be a macho, tough girl. Be yourself. But follow the rules. I know it's hard. But you'll be happy you did when you get home after a great date, safe and sound, dancing on air. I mean moshing on air with your tough girl Doc Martens. Yeah.

—Alyssa

Chapter 20
Dating Technology 101: Getting Tested for HIV and STDs

*T*echnology has changed the nature of dating. Online dating takes full advantage of personal computers and the Internet. Technology for dating also extends beyond the PC and online dating sites—it has made it easy and cheap to get tested for HIV and sexually transmitted diseases.

If you are dating, whether online or the old-fashioned way, getting tested should be a way of life, if you are planning to have any form of physical or sexual contact.

With all of the care and concern you have for the history of any potential date—their past loves and spouses are more than the standard to judge yourself against, they are also the history of infectious diseases. As the old saying goes, you aren't sleeping just with your partner; you're sleeping with everyone they have ever slept with.

Yuck.

Well, you can't change that past, but you can find out if it will come back to bite you, or even worse—kill you.

HIV infections are not slowing down. STDs such as syphilis and gonorrhea may be treatable, but they are still knocking around from lover to lover. Other diseases such as genital herpes are lifelong afflictions and hard to detect. The field of love is fraught with little bugs that love to infect.

If you treat HIV and STDs like you do every aspect of the online dating process, meaning with an honest point of view, you will be able to take the right actions to protect yourself from any infection. And when you aren't sure, you have to say, "No, let's wait."

The Testing Process

HIV and STDs are so widespread that local governments and many social service agencies have a wide array of testing and prevention programs. Many of these testing programs are free, and they are confidential.

HIV testing is most often free, and it can be done as an oral or a blood test. STD testing usually comes with a charge; these are usually blood tests for men and blood tests and vaginal testing for women. You can take all of the tests or ask just for HIV or the STD tests. It is a good idea to get fully tested when you start dating and be sure that both you and your potential partner get tested prior to any sexual contact.

FREE HIV TESTING

Getting tested often during the dating process is important. Both you and your partner should get tested before any contact. You can get free HIV testing by contacting your local county health service or searching for a free test location at www.aids.org.

To prevent the spread of HIV and AIDS, almost all local county health agencies offer some form of free or low-cost HIV screening and testing. You can find your local county health agencies by looking for "Public Health" in the Government Agencies section of your phone book, doing a quick online search using Google or Yahoo!, or finding private agencies that offer free testing for HIV at www.aids.org, as shown in Figure 20.1.

Figure 20.1
You can find free HIV testing locations at www.aids.org or your local county public health agency.

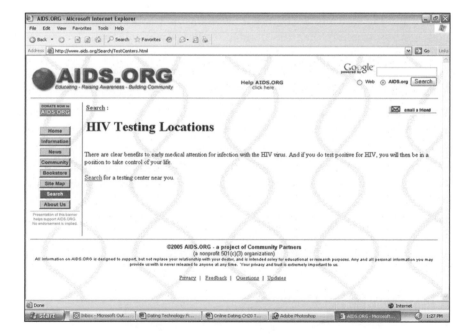

Blood tests are more accurate than oral tests, and you can elect to have one or both. The general process is that you are identified by a number and you call the health agency and use the number to get your test results. If you volunteer your phone or address, they will call or mail you the results.

Since you will want to be showing your test results to your partner, it is a good idea to get a paper copy from the agency or call the testing number with your partner so you can both hear the results.

STD testing is a bit more complicated. Although it is possible to get free testing (depending upon your income), most often there will be some charge. Prices at public health agencies run from $25 to $100 for men; this may be higher for women, since a physical exam is required to rule out all possible infections. Your insurance may cover such testing; however, it is elective, and you may have to pay the full amount yourself unless you have actual symptoms and your doctor initiates the tests. Planned Parenthood offers testing and treatment costs based on your income. You can get checked for a very reasonable rate as well as get cheap birth control and free condoms.

DON'T DONATE TO TEST
Don't attempt to donate blood to find out if you have HIV or an STD. Blood banks will warn you that you are in violation of laws if you are using the donation for such a purpose. Most blood banks will refer you to a free testing agency.

Using Home HIV Tests

There are a number of home HIV test kits you can purchase at drug stores or online. The tests are essentially the same as those you would get for free at a local county health agency. The test is either swabs that you place in your mouth to "wick" saliva from your mucous membranes, or it can even be a blood testing kit.

Figure 20.2 shows a typical home HIV testing kit, which is sold through online vendors and is available at many clinics and drug stores. You take the test at home, then mail the test kit to a laboratory where your test is processed. Using a provided telephone number, you call the service and enter your code to hear the results.

The cost of home HIV tests is usually around $50 for each test, and you can purchase multiple test packs if you plan to be tested often—or will use the test for both you and your partner.

The FDA has good information on their Web site about home testing and where to locate test kits. The address is www.fda.gov/cber/infosheets/hiv-home.htm.

Figure 20.3 shows the FDA Web site. It is a good idea to visit this page for information on getting tested for HIV and STDs.

Figure 20.2
Home HIV tests are easy
and confidential to use.

Figure 20.3
The FDA has a lot of
good information about
home HIV testing on its
Web site.

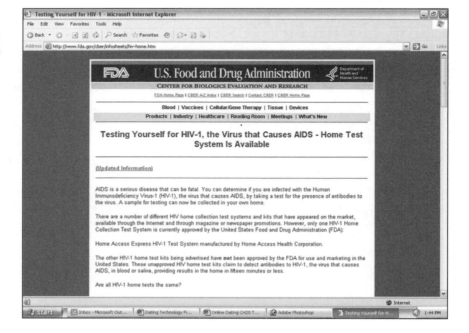

Using Home STD Tests

In addition to HIV home testing, there are home test kits for sexually transmitted diseases, including herpes virus. Although this may seem like an easy and less-embarrassing way to get tested for such conditions, they do fall short of the accuracy and reliability of HIV tests.

Not all sexually transmitted diseases can be home-tested. Since you will want to check for any and all diseases, the only solution is to go to a public or county health agency or clinic for a test.

Keeping on the Safe Side

It's a good practice to get tested before you start dating. If you are "clean" then you'll know it, and you'll have a great starting point in any relationship. When you meet someone and you are both considering physical relations, be sure to provide proof of your test and ask your new partner for the same. If your partner has not been tested, offer to be tested again.

Since HIV often takes several months to be detected, it is a good idea to get tested about three months after any relationship has ended or begun.

The following items are a guide to when to get tested.

HIV and STD Testing Schedule:

- ▶ Prior to starting any physical relationship.
- ▶ Before starting any physical contact with a new partner both you and your partner should be tested.
- ▶ If you are in a succession of physical relationships with different partners, be sure to be tested before—and after—each encounter.
- ▶ Get tested if any symptoms of HIV or STDs occur, regardless of your last tests.

Summary

When it comes to your health, and the health of your new partner, you should take every precaution to prevent HIV and STDs. Get tested for both HIV and STDs by a private doctor, at a testing site, or at a public health agency. You can use home tests for HIV, and although some STD home tests are available, you should get all STD testing at a doctor, clinic, or public health agency for the greatest accuracy.

GUY SAYS

This one's a no-brainer. Get tested, and make your partner get tested.

It's a tough life, and you just never know. Even the nicest, most wonderful person may have had a previous love who was a jerk and had a disease and didn't tell her. Testing is the only way to be sure.

Before I started dating, I wanted to get all the tests done, even though I wasn't worried in any way about my health. I figured it would be good to go through the process to know what to expect and also to find out where to go. That way when I had to get tested in the future, I would know what to do and how it all worked.

My first call was to my doctor. He explained that my insurance wouldn't cover it and that he could do it, but it would be expensive. He suggested calling the county health board for a list of places that offered free or low-cost testing.

My local county health agency offered free HIV tests and also offered STD testing on a "sliding scale" fee, based on my income. The STD test could range from $25 to $75 for men (and more for women, since there is a physical involved).

I was a bit worried about going, but it turned out to be professional, clean, and respectful. The people understood how important testing was, and they were helpful and very nice. The tests took only a few minutes, and for the results, I called a number and gave them my ID. After the good news that I was clean, I was able to face the dating world with confidence, both in my health and how to get tested when I met someone.

When I met my sweetie, I didn't rest on the past test, although I had taken it just a short time earlier. I took the tests again, and so did she. We both felt great about the testing and couldn't be happier at how easy it was.

—*Terry*

CHICK SAYS

What can I say? Get tested, get tested, get tested. What, are you stupid? Get tested. Make your partner get tested.

Would you jump into a vat of used syringes? Would you lick a toilet? Would you roll around naked in medical waste? I'm not comparing these things to having sex, but, actually, yeah, if you have unprotected sex with someone who hasn't been tested for HIV or STDs, it's pretty much the same thing. Only it feels a lot better than the syringes.

Don't be stupid. Get tested. Make your partner get tested. Use a condom. Keep using the condoms. And get tested.

—*Alyssa*

Chapter 21
Tricky Situations: Dating While Involved Elsewhere

Sometimes failed relationships or marriages take a long time to end. Separations and divorces take time, and even an old-fashioned breakup can drag on while both people deal with parting and go through the ritual "let's give it one more try" scenarios.

Part of the process is the hope of finding someone new—someone who will make you feel better than you do and represents where you're going, not where you've been. Online dating is one of the places to find such a future and to do a bit of exploration, to see if there's someone out there who understands and excites.

Just as with traditional dating, it's always tricky to meet someone while you're still married or still involved with someone, even when it's ending. The instinct is to start fresh—to suppress the fact that you're still involved with someone in some way. As this book strongly recommends, it's always best to start with the truth. As easy as it is to hide facts and paint an idealized picture of yourself online, you will learn that the online dating world is actually very accommodating to people in existing relationships who are searching, shopping, or just in transition.

Telling the Truth Is Easy

When you first create an online dating profile, you will discover that when you come to the field asking you to describe your relationship status, you can come right out and say where you are romantically. Choices generally include

- ▶ Single or Never Married
- ▶ Divorced
- ▶ Separated
- ▶ Widowed

You will also have choices to explain what you're looking for:

- ▶ Friendship
- ▶ Romance

▶ Marriage

▶ Correspondence

Figure 21.1 shows a typical profile signup page where you can enter your marital status. It's interesting that online dating services use the term "marital" status. It shows how important being married, or not married, is in the relationship cycle.

Figure 21.1
You will be able to clearly define your marital status when you create your online profile.

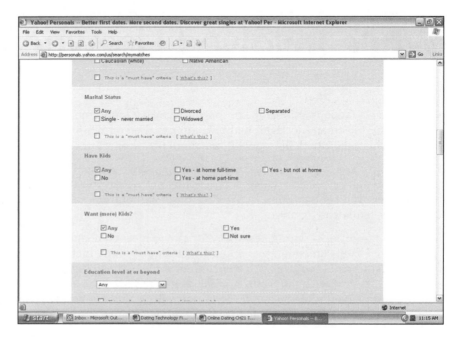

The Separated option is very important. Whether you're in the process of ending a marriage or are in the final days of a relationship that's ending, this is the best possible choice to pick. Although it may be temping to check off Single, it's much better to choose the Separated option. It allows you to be truthful and make it clear that you still have some association with a spouse or partner, although you're not still together on a regular basis.

BACKGROUND CHECKS

Chapter 14, "Background Checks: Additional Peace of Mind," shows how easy it is to do a background check on people to find out if they're married. If you've gone through a recent divorce, you may want to run a background check on yourself to make sure the records reflect your correct marital status.

Shopping

A common temptation when in an existing relationship that's going sour is "shopping." Sometimes people who haven't completely ended their marriage or relationship will take advantage of online dating sites to see what types of people are there—and if anyone may be interested in them.

Shopping is a dangerous and unfair practice, but it does take place. The person who states he's single may not be—he may just be testing the dating waters to see if there's any interest, for his information, once his relationship does end. There are usually clues that you can spot when people are shopping. Some classic telltale signs are:

- ▶ Lack of a photo or reluctance to send one to you if you correspond.
- ▶ Only willing to communicate through the service—even once you've known each other for awhile.
- ▶ Unwillingness to reveal any details of current marital status.
- ▶ Profile is on and off the service on a daily basis.
- ▶ Contacts you without having a profile publicly posted.

If someone is married and using a popular online dating service to "shop," you will find the above clues provide a good indication that she is possibly a shopper. People who are married or still in a relationship do not want their photos posted or even to have their profiles on public display. They will sign on to the service, shop profiles, and contact people without making their profiles visible. This is a form of controlling their identities, and they'll often make excuses for this, including the following:

- ▶ "I have a very public job, and I don't want my coworkers to see me online."
- ▶ "I don't know if I'm ready to post a picture yet."
- ▶ "This is a small town, and I don't want everyone knowing my business."
- ▶ "I'm a very private person."

The above excuses may indeed be true for an unattached person. But if you're spending a good deal of time communicating with someone via emails or instant messages, and she is being evasive about sending you her photo or about who she is or where she lives, she may be hiding an existing relationship. If you have a public profile and your photo posted, you should expect the same from anyone who contacts you. If she's not willing to share such personal information, this is a warning sign that needs to be heeded.

The best strategy in such a situation is to be honest and ask her about it. You can simply ask if she's still in a relationship. If she says she's not in a relationship but is still evasive and unwilling to share any real information with you, you need to reconsider whether you want to continue communicating with her. You can tell her that you're only interested in continuing your communication if she shares her picture and some basic information about herself—at least as much as you have shared with her.

If you're a victim of shoppers, you will feel used and like your time has been wasted. If you have any self-esteem, you're not online to fulfill the fantasies or aid the research of a person in an existing relationship. Ask questions, and don't spend time on someone who is hiding, evasive, or reluctant to assure you that she is single.

Hiding Your Love

Sometimes people in an existing relationship feel that the only way out of the relationship is to find someone new. Or they may not want out; they may just want something else for awhile. If you're in this situation, we don't recommend you do your searching on a mainstream site. Mainstream dating services, such as Match.com or Yahoo! Personals, are filled largely with single people looking to meet single people. There are dating services specifically for people who wish to date while married or in a committed relationship.

If you're someone who feels a need to cheat on your love, don't play games. You can do your cheating with people who are okay with it or in the same boat. Dating sites, such as Married Secrets shown in Figure 21.2, are designed to connect married people with partners who accept the situation—or who are excited by it. As upsetting as such ideas may be to most people, it's better that people in such a mindset have their own dating services rather than fooling you on a singles dating service.

Such services allow you to hide your photo and only reveal it to people you choose, providing you an extra layer of privacy. More than anything else, these sites come out and say, "Hey, I'm really married," for you so that you don't have to.

Figure 21.2
There are a number of online dating services for people who are married and want to date anyway.

SECRET SEARCHING

If you're married or in a committed relationship and are dating online, no service can protect your identity completely. The person you're chatting with or e-mailing with may be your current partner checking up on you! Or doing the same thing you're doing!

Looking for Friends Who Understand

The final situation for many people in an unhappy marriage or relationship is to go online to find a friend or someone to talk to. Sure, most people on dating services probably have been in several relationships and can sympathize, but they are there to meet people to date, not form your support group. If you're simply looking for a friend, be sure to state that you're seeking friendship and be clear that you're married or in a committed relationship.

There are a large number of message boards and support sites for married people who need to talk and make friends outside of their relationship. These are great resources for meeting people who can share your feelings and experiences. Online dating sites are about dating, so they're not good places for that type of support.

Large portals such as MSN and Yahoo! have links or active chat rooms for married people or people going through a divorce. These chatrooms and sites will provide a better solution for finding friends than online dating services.

Figure 21.3
Use large portals such as MSN to find support groups and chat rooms for married people looking for friends.

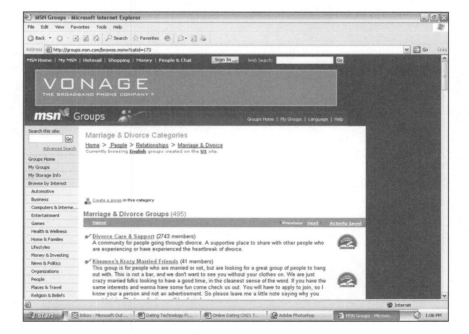

Summary

If you're in a marriage or a relationship that's ending, you may wish to get online to meet someone. Be honest about your marital status, give the other person the information he will need to understand what you're going through, and let him know that your current relationship may not be completely over. If you're looking for a single person and have an inquiry from someone who is evasive or hiding too much basic information, you may have met a "shopper" who is flirting or testing the waters while in a current relationship. There are sites specifically for married people who wish to date, and support groups and chat rooms for people who are married and looking for friends to talk to about their marriage.

GUY SAYS

When I was online, I had several women contact me who I know were married and just playing the field. I didn't like it or appreciate it, and it was upsetting.

The most amazing thing was how easy it was to spot. Each of those inquiries was from a woman who didn't post her photo and who said very little about herself. A few were from women who had their profiles hidden from public view. My reaction to each one was the same: "She's hiding something."

I responded with a letter that said that I posted my picture and profile, and that I was not comfortable with someone who wouldn't do the same, as I was worried that she may still be in a relationship and that's why she was shy with her photo or background.

In each case I was right. They were married or in relationships and were exploring a way out or just wanted to meet someone who "understood."

As Bob Dylan sang, "It ain't me, babe."

I had no prejudice against someone who said that she was separated. By the time you get online, chances are you've been in a serious relationship of some sort and that's understandable. Sometimes divorce or breakups take a lot of time. It doesn't mean you can't move on or aren't ready to, so at least I would understand that.

I was looking for a true-blue and honest person. I found that. The last thing I was looking for was someone using me as a pawn in her breakup.

It ain't me, babe.

—*Terry*

CHICK SAYS

I've flirted online with someone who was married. Yes, shocking, I know. I didn't know he was married until we'd been talking for a bit. And as soon as he told me he was married, I knew it wouldn't go beyond flirting. But I didn't really feel guilty about the conversation because I'm single—I'm not the one hanging out on online dating sites while married.

It's not a double standard. I'm single; I can do whatever I want. You're married. You should know better. And you should go spend some time with your wife instead of coming on to me. You're the one cheating. Not me.

And that's the thing—you are cheating. If you're at an online dating site, talking to other women, flirting with other women, propositioning other women... you're cheating on your wife. And that's not okay. Unless your wife is sitting next to you being turned on by it. This can happen, but it's a low percentage of what marrieds are doing online.

If you're in the process of a breakup, there's a little leeway. If you're separated, okay, you can be looking for someone new. But tell me that. Be upfront about your situation. And, yeah, a separated guy is probably not going to be my first choice when I'm searching, as there's likely to be a lot of baggage there. But if you contact me—and you're cute and interesting and smart—and you tell me you're separated and it's really true, then I'm not going to turn my back on you. I'll give you a chance to show me you're really ready to move on.

But it's not okay to tell me you're single if you're married. If I'm getting along with you really well in our communications, then I'm starting to think about dating and the future—but if you're married, there's no future for us. And to lead me on in that way is patently wrong.

Like most people at online dating sites, I'm looking for someone single who I can date and with whom I can possibly build a future. You, like a smaller but ugly percentage of people at online dating sites, are looking for someone single to have an affair with, or you're just entertaining yourself. Our goals are too divergent. You need to stay away from me and all my fellow single girls.

Online dating sites generally can't screen for married people. If you say you're single, they believe you. So it's important to be aware that marrieds are lurking out there under the guise of earnest single men. And if you're one of those marrieds, take your unavailable ass out of my single dating site, and go over to a site where they're okay with adultery.

If you want to be online dating while you're married, ultimately that's your choice and your wife's problem. Don't make it my problem. Don't lie to me. If you're married, tell me. Then I can make an informed decision about what to do with you. And if you're married and at an online dating site... maybe you should reconsider being married. It's clearly not working for you.

—*Alyssa*

Conclusion
Truth, Lies, and Online Dating

We're all looking for the same thing in this world—someone to love us for who we are. It's ingrained in us, in every pore of our beings. And we're likely to feel a little afraid that we'll never find what we're looking for. After all, in this modern world in which we're all incredibly busy and living rather insular lives, it can be just as difficult to figure out where to look for that person to love us as it is to find him or her.

Where there's a will, there's a way. The modern world recognized a need, and it gave us online dating. A safe place to look for our potential mate. A place to find that person to love us.

But the online dating world can seem intimidating and scattered with land mines. It's just not as easy as finding someone you like and asking her out. It's not like asking a friend to introduce you to the cute guy she works with. It's sifting through profiles, reading between the lines, and telling the truth while making yourself look good. We never told you it was easy. But it can be a lot safer and easier if you follow our suggestions and know all of our tricks.

Embracing the Truth

You've got to be honest in online dating. If we've taught you nothing else, we hope we've taught you that. It's the most important thing. If you're honest with yourself and about yourself, you'll find someone who is truly right for you. And we've made it easy for you to be truthful.

You can easily find the online dating site that's right for you. There are a lot of sites out there, and it would be easy to wind up on the wrong one. But knowing what you now know, you can find the perfect site for you. If you're looking for a big pool of love to choose from, the mainstream sites will be best for you. If you're looking for sex, there are sex-focused sites out there for you. And if you're looking for someone very specific, of a certain religion or a single parent, then there is a specialty site for you. You just have to do a quick search, and you'll find it. Be honest with yourself about what you're looking for, and you will find the site that fits you.

You know how to tell the truth in your profile. You know to be honest with yourself when deciding which boxes to check in the multiple choice questions. You know not to compromise on the things that are really important to you. You know how to be honest about things like body type and age, no matter how hard it can be. And we've shown you how to write a good profile essay question in which you're forthright about what you're looking for.

You know how to take an honest picture of yourself that's both flattering and realistic. You know the dangers of using old photos, deceptive photos, or photos that have been overly Photoshopped. You know the tricks of using Photoshop to make yourself look good while still looking like yourself.

We've given you all the tools you need to be honest in your own presentation and interactions with your potential dates. And we feel that we've taught you well. We hope you will go out into the online dating world with your eyes on the prize, your head held high (that'll eliminate a double chin, too).

Avoiding the Lies

The world is not necessarily an honest place. Look at the people we have running our country. Look at the people running some of the major corporations. Look at the saleslady who told you those spandex capri pants looked just fabulous on you. It's not pretty out there.

So you have to be cautious. And that especially applies to the people you meet online. It's an informal medium. Anyone can talk to anyone with just the push of a button. And it becomes very easy to lie about who you are and what you look like when the person on the other side of the screen doesn't know who you really are.

You have to be smart when you're online dating. You have to know what to look for and what tricks to use to weed out the truth from the lie, the honest from those who would pull the wool over your eyes. And we've taught you those tricks and shown you what to look for.

You know how to spot an honest picture. There are always give-away signs. A person who says he's 45 but has no wrinkles. A woman who says she has a few extra pounds but looks like a bikini model. Old-fashioned clothing worn in a picture supposedly taken last Christmas. Bad photo editing. A suspiciously odd-shaped body. If you look closely and know what to look for, you can tell the reality from the fiction.

You know to carefully match up someone's profile with her photo. You know that a happy person should post a happy photo and vice versa. The photo is representative of how the poster feels about herself. If she's been honest about how she feels about herself and what kind of person she is in her description of herself, you should see that reflected in the face looking back at you.

And on top of everything else, you know the right questions to ask to get to the truth. You know how to spot someone who's married as well as what questions to ask to find out for certain if he is. You know how to find out what he's really looking for. You know how to trust your intuition if something doesn't seem quite right.

And if everything else fails, you even know how to do a background check or credit check on your potential date. The dishonest can run, but they can't hide. And they can't date you.

Being Loved for Who You Are

Never forget these words:

If someone can't love you for exactly who you are, then you shouldn't be with him or her.

As long as you do everything right and are honest with yourself and your potential date, there's no reason you won't find the person of your dreams. And when you find him or her, you'll be glad you were honest every step along the way.

If you lie about who you are in your profile, when you talk to your potential date he'll hear the inconsistencies. If you send him a picture that's not honest of yourself, he'll see the inconsistency when he meets you. Why would you lie to someone you hope to share a future with? You wouldn't want him to lie to you.

But if you always tell him the truth, if you always show him the truth, he'll like you for who you are. And when you meet in person, he'll know exactly what to expect. And what's a better jumping off point for future bliss than showing him you're happy with who you are and having him be happy with who you are?

The Road Ahead

Once there was a time when we grew up in small towns. We ran down the shady lanes, excited to see our friends from school. We left our bikes on the lawn and lay under the stars while we contemplated the magic of the stars and the moon. As time went on, our little friends grew into teens and young adults and innocence gave way to passion. We knew who our friends were, and we shared experiences and places. Our families knew each other, and we knew who we were and who we could trust.

What would a book be without a little poetic license? As much as we all wish for those idyllic times (whether or not they ever happened in our lives), the world just isn't that sweet or simple today. It's pocket rocket cars racing down the street filled with blaring rap music with drivers hell-bent on getting to the bar to get laid, get wasted, and get laid again. You meet people, and if you aren't willing to jump into bed right away, you're a loser and worthless.

So, it's a choice. You can decide that you want something nice. You *can* meet a nice person. In the online dating world you can forgo the bar scene and the games. You can be on a tree-lined street and find a friend to run to and lie with to gaze at the stars—and into each other's eyes. It's the one place where you can escape the social circle you're in right now, the place where you live, the conventions of your past, and create the future you have dreamt of every day that you've been alone. You can find your love if you know how to look.

If you want to meet someone special, you need to be someone special. If you want to meet someone nice, be nice. If you want to meet someone who is truthful, be truthful with them.

Tell the truth. Be proud of who you are. Learn to find people who tell the truth and who are proud of who they are—enough to reveal all there is to know.

This book has been a roadmap to that small town you grew up in, even if only in your dreams. Wave to us as you run by on your way to your new love.

Terry and Alyssa

Index

Q

T

Y

Z

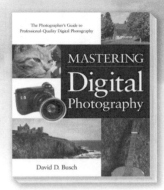